PENGUIN BOOKS

UNBALANCED ACCOUNTS

Lieberman and Lindner have spent years studying women's emotional relationship to money, investigating how and why Money-phobia begins and defining its crippling symptoms.

Annette R. Lieberman is a New York–based psychotherapist who specializes in women's issues. She has developed unique Money Awareness Groups to help women confront their problems with money.

Vicki Lindner is the author of a novel, *Outlaw Games*. She is a regular contributor to *Omni*, *Cosmopolitan*, and *New Woman*.

Unbalanced ACCOUNTS

How Women
Can Overcome Their Fear
of Money

By Annette Lieberman & Vicki Lindner

Penguin Books

PENGUIN BOOKS
Published by the Penguin Group
Viking Penguin Inc., 40 West 23rd Street,
New York, New York 10010, U.S.A.
Penguin Books Ltd, 27 Wrights Lane,
London W8 5TZ, England
Penguin Books Australia Ltd, Ringwood,
Victoria, Australia
Penguin Books Canada Ltd, 2801 John Street,
Markham, Ontario, Canada L3R 1B4
Penguin Books (N.Z.) Ltd, 182–190 Wairau Road,
Auckland 10, New Zealand

Penguin Books Ltd, Registered Offices:
Harmondsworth, Middlesex, England

First published in the United States of America by
The Atlantic Monthly Press 1987
Published in Penguin Books 1988

Excerpts from *Complete Brothers Grimm Fairy Tales*, edited by Lily Owens. Copyright ©
1981 by Crown Publishers, Inc. Used by permission of Crown Publishers, Inc.

LIBRARY OF CONGRESS CATALOGING IN PUBLICATION DATA
Lieberman, Annette.
Unbalanced accounts.
Originally published: New York: Atlantic Monthly
Press, c1987.
1. Women—Finance, Personal.   2. Money—Psychological
aspects.   3. Women—Attitudes.   I. Lindner, Vicki,
1944–   . II. Title.
[HG179.L49   1988]   332.4'01'9   87–32840
ISBN 0 14 01.0989 7

Printed in the United States of America by
R. R. Donnelley & Sons Company, Harrisonburg, Virginia
Set in Electra

To our parents
Dorothy and Irving Lieberman
and
Mary and Victor Lindner
who made it possible for us
to become the kind of women
we wanted to be

ACKNOWLEDGMENTS

We would like to thank Neil Shandalow, economist and financial adviser, who gave knowledge, inspiration, and support to this project; Atlantic Monthly Press editor Joyce Johnson, for her editorial sensitivity and acumen; literary agent Berenice Hoffman, who word-processed, negotiated, and sold with a passion; writer Jacqueline Thompson, who knew about money and steered us to much of the biographical material we used in this book; Robert Stewart, for his initial encouragement; Shearson Lehman Brothers second vice-president/financial consultant Virginia Wasser, who gave valuable information about the world of finance; and Ellen Gorman Forbes and Martha Niebanck, who organized and hosted our suburban and Massachusetts money-awareness groups, respectively. Most of all, we would like to thank the 123 women who participated in our money study, particularly those who agreed to be interviewed. Without them, this book would not exist. We are especially grateful to the women in our New York money-awareness groups, who met over a period of a year and gave themselves, body and soul, to the emotionally trying subject of money. We can only hope these generous women took away a portion of the knowledge they offered us.

CONTENTS

This is a book for women who have problems with money, and want to know why.

We are not going to tell our readers how to earn $100,000 a year. Instead, we will help them examine the personal fears and social pressures that hold them back from fulfilling their earning potential, or even from deciding how much money they want and need. We will not tell women how to plan for retirement or explain the difference between a stock and a bond. Instead, we will explore the deeply rooted reservations that have kept them away from the shelves of finance books that already exist, and the talented financial professionals who could give them important information. We will tell our readers why they spend too much, save too much, and fear becoming homeless bag ladies in their old age. We will describe the way ambitious women confuse their emotions with their self-interest when they negotiate with employers or with people in their personal lives. Most important, we will show our readers how to define and discover their true financial identities by looking at the messages about women and money that they have gotten from their culture, and the way those messages were transmitted by their families. We will reveal how the "money myths" we inherit in childhood continue to plague our intimate relationships with men, women friends, and family members, and keep us from living happy, healthy financial lives.

We believe that when women look at the reasons for their financial behavior, they take the first step toward positive change.

We are not really writing for the highly successful "corporate woman" or for the woman who seems to "have it all"—these are the figures the media so often feature on their pages and screens, making most of the rest of us feel that we have not taken advantage of modern opportunities, easily within our grasp. Even though very few women make a lot of money (only 56,000 of 12 million working women earn $75,000 or more a year), these high-earners have received a disproportionate share of attention. The attention, however, tends to focus on their personal dissatisfactions or on their highly polished "successful" images; the media seldom tell us what the high rollers do with their money or how they feel about it. Nor are we writing for the woman (often a single mother) who is clinging to the poverty line and earning a little more than half of what men do in a nonprofessional or sex-segregated job. These women, reduced to featureless statistics, do not get *enough* attention, let alone help with their difficulties. The women we are addressing are women like ourselves—college-educated, middle-class professionals who have achieved, or *want* to achieve, significant career goals, but who are struggling with personal, domestic, and work-related problems. These are the women who, like ourselves, could be doing better with money and who could use knowledge about their relationship with money to enhance their lives. Many books have been written exploring the psychological background of other problems that afflict millions of women (love relationships and overweight, for example), but no book has been written that investigates the emotional and social origins of our problems with money, or describes them in detail.

How did we come to write such a book? Annette Lieberman, a New York psychotherapist who specializes in the psychology of women, began to notice a change in the issues that preoccupied the female patients in her clinical practice. *Money* began to enter her sessions with them in ways it never had before, and she observed an increasing concern with financial issues. Patients who were earning adequate (or less-than-adequate) salaries worried that emotional blocks were preventing them from making as much as their capabilities indicated they could. Some noted money troubled their relationships. Others reported irrational or compulsive spending patterns and disturbing feelings of guilt and greed in relation to money. Money was involved in fears about the future, even for women with high earnings. A few remarked that they were becoming uneasy about their lack of expertise in managing and investing. Sometimes, Lieberman felt, the issue of money was conspicuous by its all-too-obvious absence. Women who were living alone did not seem to recognize the need to take care of themselves. Some, clearly on a precarious financial edge, refrained from exploring money issues and continued to dwell on problems with men. All seemed to lack the vocabulary to talk about these important money issues. The time, Lieberman thought, was exactly right for a new kind of book, one that would provide a major breakthrough in our understanding of the emotional relationship between women and money.

Economist John Kenneth Galbraith has said, "There is nothing about money that cannot be understood by the person of reasonable curiosity, diligence and intelligence."[1] What prevents intelligent women from understanding, or wanting to understand, money? What are the fears and confusions that beset women when they earn, negotiate, invest and manage money, and where do they come from? How do women relate to money in a new world, where for the first time, it is not only possible, but desirable for them to be financially successful? These were the questions we asked and set out to answer.

The Money Study

We began our study of the relationship between women and money with a preconceived, and as it turned out, inappropriate goal. At first, we wanted to tell women how to eliminate the emotional blocks that were standing between them and large amounts of money. We wanted to make a lot of money ourselves! We believed, like many women, that there was a kind of "magical" attitude and source of information about money-making that certain people—mainly males—were privy to. We thought we could discover this "money secret" and disseminate it. As we thought about and researched the traditional role money has played in women's lives, talked to other women, and examined our own money issues, however, we realized it was more important to uncover the real meaning of money to women than to tell them how to make "magical megabucks." We began to realize that making a lot of money was no more the answer to modern women's complicated problems than making too little to take care of their needs. We quickly changed our original plan: We wanted to tell women how they could use money to achieve balance and harmony in their lives.

We began our money study, then, with a simple hypothesis—that women had different perceptions of their relationship to money than men. We set out to elicit subjective information that would expand and define this hypothesis, and that could be interpreted from a clinical perspective. We wanted to see if we could associate women's feelings about money with some of the new theories about how female psychological development differs from the male's. We were not interested in obtaining "yes" or "no" answers to questions like, "Do you balance your checkbook?" that could be quantified to produce statistical generalizations. If it is true that three out of ten women review their finances once a week, as one recent study of women's financial behavior enthusiastically proclaimed, what about the remaining seven? Why aren't they doing simple financial acts like checkbook balancing or keeping track of their financial situation? With this in mind, we designed a study that would give us information about how women integrated money into their lives, using money to adapt to problems and changes, and how their financial behavior reflected their upbringing and the complex social and economic changes that were so rapidly altering women's roles.

First, we asked our participants to fill out a questionnaire, which we later expanded to include seventy-five questions. Although some questions asked for factual information, like the participant's marital status, job description, income, and assets, many asked for an essay-type answer. We encouraged the participant to comment on her particular problems with money, and to describe her attitudes toward earning, spending, career goals, and the way money entered into her relationships. (Some of these thought-provoking questions are included in Appendix 1.) The participants could refuse to answer any of the questions, provided that they explained why. From the clinical perspective, what they didn't say was as important as what they did.

We looked for white, American-born college-educated women who were "ambitious" (or who derived a sense of self-worth and mastery from professional achievement) to participate in the study. We did not include black women because we felt their history and culture would put them in a very different relationship to money (for example, in 1960, only a third of white women were employed, but half of black women were working), or foreign-born women, for the same reason. We sent the questionnaire to 175 women we knew, and women they recommended, who, in turn, steered us to other willing participants. We tried to get a sampling from a variety of age groups, income brackets, and occupations, and to include married, divorced, and single women. We contacted most participants personally before sending them the questionnaire, and, in some cases, "kept after them" to complete it.

One hundred and twenty-three women filled out the questionnaire. The breakdown of their age, place of residence, occupation, income bracket, and social status is as follows:

Age

Women 29 and under: 21	40–44: 28
30–34: 29	Over 45: 13
35–39: 32	

Our study focused on the thirty to forty-five age bracket because it soon became apparent that these were the women who, having settled into a life pattern, were beginning to focus on economic problems, and seemed most anxious to recognize and resolve them.

Place of Residence

New York: 72 women	Outside New York: 51 women

Most of the New York women were born and raised in other parts of the country, and relocated to "The Big Apple" to pursue their ambitions. Our sampling from outside New York included women from other states on the Eastern seaboard, as well as from Western, Southern, and Midwestern states.

Occupational Categories

Writers, reporters, editors, public relations specialists, artists and entertainers, designers and graphic artists: 18%

Social scientists and related workers, including lawyers, psychologists, and social workers: 18%

Educators, librarians, and guidance counselors: 15%

Marketing and sales personnel: 12%

Health practitioners and technicians: 11%

Administrators or managers: 9%

Administrative support personnel, computer programmers, or secretaries: 7%

Natural scientists and mathematicians: 7%

Technologists, technicians, service personnel, and construction workers: 3%

Our occupational categories are the same as those established by the United States Department of Labor. Some women combined two of these careers, as in the case of artists and entertainers, who were doing other jobs to provide basic support. We changed not only the names, but in most cases also the jobs of the women we used as case histories.

Salary Range

Below $20,000: 33	$50–$75,000: 10
$20–$29,000: 28	$75–$100,000: 6
$30–$39,000: 25	Over $100,000: 5
$40–$49,000: 16	

Social Status

Single: 40	Never married and cohabiting: 11
Married: 52	Divorced and cohabiting: 4
Divorced and living alone: 16	

Children

Childless: 80	One or more children: 43

Though the majority of women in our study did not have children, many of the thirty-four and under group and even some of the older women planned to have them, or wanted to have them. Three that we knew of had their first child while we were writing the book; one single mother was planning to adopt an infant, and one married woman was in the process of adopting her second child. The ambitious women in our study reflected the national trend to have children later, after careers have been established.

From the questionnaires we selected twenty-seven women for two-hour interviews—a combination journalistic fact-finding and clinical session. Since we knew these participants would provide much material cited in our book, we chose articulate women who had expressed a great deal of personal interest in our subject, and who were highly focused and self-aware (though not always about the role money played in their lives). These women had "voices" we thought were compelling and tended to dramatize the money issues, sometimes in unusual ways, that affected large numbers of women.

We also established four money-awareness groups. These were issue-oriented consciousness-raising groups designed to break barriers around the "taboo" topic of money, and help women open up and explore this little-discussed issue with us and with each other. The groups helped women define and compare money problems in order to find solutions by setting personal goals, and gave them a vocabulary for thinking and talking about financial behavior. (The format for the money-awareness groups is described in Appendix 6. We discuss the importance of the groups in creating a climate for change in the final chapter, "Life Without Moneyphobia.") Two of the groups were formed in New York and met monthly or bimonthly for almost a year. We formed another group in Massachusetts and one in a New York suburb. Altogether the groups provided us with thirty-six hours of tape, which we analyzed for our research. A number of the women who joined the money-awareness groups had also filled out the questionnaire and participated in the two-hour personal interview; they gave many hours of their time to investigating their relationship with money and provided a solid "cast of characters" for our book. We are deeply indebted to these intense, interesting, and hardworking women who gave so much of themselves to our project without getting paid.

The questionnaires, personal interviews, and money-awareness groups provided the core of our original research. In the course of the two years we worked on the book, however, we had hundreds of informal conversations with women on the subject of money, which we recorded, too. At parties, on buses and trains, in exercise classes—everywhere we went—all we had to do was mention the title of our book to a woman, and financial confessions and confusions, as well as vital information, would come pouring out. In fact, it was largely through this "informal" research that we sensed that by writing about women's problems with money we had taken a tiger by the tail. Men, on the other hand, tended to pooh-pooh our book. Some declared that women's problems with money were no worse than men's (possibly true; but women's problems are *different*). Others became inexplicably angry or took a patriarchal attitude. Said one of these well-meaning "father figures," who dismissed our book as "inconsequential," "If women have problems with money, they can ask a man for help."

The Money Mirror

As the strong reactions to our book indicated, money is a loaded topic. Both Sigmund Freud and Aristotle viewed a desire for unlimited wealth as unnatural, because, in itself, money doesn't fulfill any basic need, like the need for food, water, or sex. There is no inherent limitation to our need for money, as there is to our need for food and water. In our capitalist economy, moreover, money can increase without our necessarily having to do any labor to make it grow. As a result, this important tool has a "magical" feeling, and a wide variety of emotions can be projected onto it. From the psychological perspective, it is easy to form a transferential relationship to money, and to the people and institutions that are responsible for paying, saving, and handling it. For both sexes, money can become a mirror that reflects their fantasies, as well as their struggles to make them come true. Onto this magical money mirror we can project our dreams, frustrations, and fears. Whereas men see money as a reflection of their desires for power and control, women, as we shall discuss, project their traditional identities onto money, and at the same time, see in money what men have taught them to see.

As we investigated the relationship of women to money, then, we found we were also investigating a spectrum of other problems and concerns. For women, to look at money was to look at every confusing facet of their twentieth-century identities. Our subject evoked reflections on virtually every topic of interest to women and inspired a wide range of emotions. As we discussed the meaning of money to them, our participants ran the gamut from laughter to tears. Some women cried when they talked about the money messages they had received from their parents, or about their inability to achieve all they had hoped for professionally. Sometimes *we* felt like crying as we listened to the sad stories that money inspired. Although money was deeply enmeshed in other problems, when the women in our study made a conscientious effort to separate it out and look at it clearly, they saw many of the other issues that troubled them from a new perspective. Sometimes they saw solutions.

The goal of our research was not to help the women involved solve specific financial problems, but to help them establish a new way of talking and thinking about money that they could take and use as they wished, hopefully to obtain more power and freedom. Many of the women in our study did become more conscious of the role money played in their lives and thoughts, and would call to tell us about each exciting "new discovery." Most were able to define unproductive attitudes toward money that were keeping them from becoming more efficient earners and managers, or that were interfering with their personal relationships. Some were able to make concrete changes in their financial behavior. The changes were not always earthshaking: No one made a fast million after working with us. However, even small changes gave important feelings of self-esteem and control over a previously feared area of her life to the woman who made them, who now felt capable of greater financial accomplishments. Two of our participants became involved in their husband's business. Another hired an accountant to teach her how to read and organize her financial statements. Another was able to see that she had enough money to reduce her teaching hours and pursue her vocation in art. Another was able to take the first steps toward investing a large hunk of savings. Several became better negotiators. All of the women who made these changes were surprised to find financial tasks they had regarded as "formidable" easy to accomplish, once they acknowledged the need to do them and examined the emotional blocks that were standing in their way. Said one woman who learned to negotiate with her boyfriend to "straighten out who pays for what":

> Every conversation I had with him was much easier than I thought it would be. I was very anxious about ever talking money with him. And now, we're actively talking about buying a house together. It's premature, because we're both financially insecure at the moment, but we can talk about it. It feels clean, and very easy.

Our hope is that our readers, too, will learn from our book what they need to know to feel "clean and easy" about talking about money— the first step toward "balancing their accounts" and improving their financial lives.

New York City   Annette R. Lieberman
September 1986   Vicki Lindner

Unbalanced
ACCOUNTS

Why Women Are Afraid of Money

Modern women are afraid of money.

In a world where for the first time it is possible for many to earn significant amounts, they are beset with terror and confusion when they contemplate increasing their incomes, investing, saving or spending, or even discussing the financial rewards for their ambitious goals. We call the paralyzing fear so many women experience in relation to money Moneyphobia. Before we define this new feminine problem and its origins, however, let us take a brief look at four women from different generations who suffer from the symptoms.

● We first met Sally, twenty-seven, at a New York party. This dark-haired gamin, dancing wildly in a trashed sweatshirt, hardly looked like our idea of an assistant vice-president of an international bank, earning $50,000 a year—more than her adored father, a Protestant minister, had ever made. Sally spoke enthusiastically about her job, which involved representing her bank's services in European capitals, and discussed the way the image of women in banking had changed. We had, we thought, encountered one of the famous "yuppies" we had read so much about, and looked forward to interviewing Sally to discover the secret of her early success.

By the time the interview took place a year later, however, Sally had changed. She was about to quit her job and was supporting an idealistic anthropologist she had "rescued" from a politically unstable foreign country, after knowing him less than a week. The two of them were planning to marry, then head for Bolivia to interview Aymara Indians—a trip that would eat up a large chunk of her savings.

After that? Sally hadn't the faintest idea what she or her future husband would be doing for money, or how much money they would need to earn. In a suspiciously short time, she had gone from enjoying her career and the opulent lifestyle she had earned to loathing banking and dismissing the importance of money. "I began to feel my contribution was insignificant and I was selling superfluous services," she said.

Though she had trained for a career in business, she also seemed to feel her meteoric rise in the banking world had been an accident, and that her job required no particular talent or ability. "When I was traveling in Europe I had to pinch myself," she said. "I couldn't believe I was little Sally Boch from Kalispell, Montana, meeting with bank presidents of foreign countries."

Though approaching thirty, Sally is willing to return to a "more exploratory mode," live on less, and stay in touch with what's "good and beautiful." She is contemplating low-paying careers for which she has no demonstrated ability or training, like photography and writing. "It's funny," she told us, "but I've never known what I wanted to be when I grow up. When I talked about this problem with my dad he said, 'Why don't you just be five feet two?' " Sally is not only afraid of money, but also of being the kind of woman who is able to earn more than her father.

• June, thirty-five, began her career as a high school teacher, sorting out professional and personal goals with a psychoanalyst. When the male analyst opposed her risk-taking career change to theatrical production, June fired him. Today she is the artistic director of a major philanthropic institution, for which she produces theatrical benefits in San Francisco. June creates operating budgets, persuades high-powered corporation executives to fund each production, and nurtures the fragile egos of actors and directors. Clearly June is not afraid of risk. She is, however, afraid of money.

Recently she hired an assistant at a salary larger than her own. Why? "We needed him and he wouldn't work for less." When the new assistant, who took over June's budgeting responsibilities, recommended a $5,000 raise for her, June trimmed it to $2,000. Why? Her salary could be put to better use within the structure of the institution. Finally, the president of the board of directors himself persuaded her that she richly deserved the more substantial raise.

Now earning a salary of thirty-five grand—modest for a man, but one few women could claim before the present decade— June's savings total zero. She has no investments, owns no property, and hasn't the slightest idea where retirement money will come from.

Where does her money go? She shrugs her shoulders. How would she react to a six-figure raise? She replies, "I'd feel that everyone would hate me and I'd be completely alone."

• Darlene, forty-three, was divorced in 1981. She had been supported by her husband for most of their thirteen-year marriage. Though she had supplied most of the family income in the first few years and neglected her career as a graphics designer to nurture two children, she felt too guilty to contest her divorce, and as a result, was awarded less than an equitable share of her family's wealth.

A striking beauty, with warmth, vitality, and an articulate intelligence, Darlene has achieved much on her own. She has raised her two teenagers, gotten a part-time job doing layouts for a popular magazine, and earned an advanced degree in design. The magazine job pays her under $15,000 a year, however, so she is largely dependent on the maintenance and child-support payments that were awarded her by the court.

When we met Darlene, she had not checked her divorce agreement to see when the maintenance payments were scheduled to end, making her completely self-supporting, calculated the amount of money she would need to earn, or decided exactly how she would earn it, though she fantasized becoming well-known in her field. While she avoids thoughts of her future responsibility, she spends every penny she has.

She told us, "Right now I have no money, but I'm spending money. As soon as I get involved with a man, I feel that I don't have to worry about money, because he's going to take care of me, even if I know that's not true. And even though I know I don't want him to! I still want to avoid money issues. I really feel I shouldn't have to be concerned with money . . . that I should just be able to live my life and get a check in the mail for doing my best. I wish I could market who I am, instead of having to fit myself into a job that has nothing to do with me, just to make money."

• Jan, fifty, is also afraid of money, though her fears express themselves in different ways. A high-ranking editor at a major publishing company, Jan battled her way out of the typing pool in an era when few women in her field were unleashed from typewriters and file cabinets. When she won a promotion to editorial assistant, Jan took home manuscripts and read them, developed personal relationships with writers, and finally brought in a lucrative property on her own initiative. Soon after that, she was promoted over a male editorial assistant to an editor's slot, to the horror of one of the company's vice-presidents.

Now in a position of responsibility and power, her feeling of personal clout does not extend to her purse. "I've never been afraid of ambition, even at a time when women were supposed to be," she said, "but money . . . well, I've worked long enough to put a good chunk of it aside, like a squirrel hoarding nuts, but I just leave it in the bank and never do anything more creative with it." The very thought of sending money, by mail, to a commodities broker fills Jan with unreasonable apprehension, and the financial planning seminar she attended was unable to quell her terror of taking her money out of a certificate of deposit at her local bank and investing it in municipal bonds or a co-op apartment she both wants and needs as a tax shelter. Jan goes on paying taxes at premium rates and pretending to forget about her secret hoard.

These four women all suffer from Moneyphobia. Though they are psychologically sophisticated and self-aware, unrecognized anxieties, shared by many career-oriented women, cause them to mishandle money and avoid confronting their financial situations. Their fearful attitudes restrict their earning potential, jeopardize their security, and prevent them from enjoying money and using it freely to enhance their lives.

The New Female Phobia

Why have we given women's anxieties about money a clinical name? Our research revealed that many women think about and relate to money in ways that resemble a phobia. A phobia has been defined as an anxiety that attaches itself to a specific object, activity, or situation. This fear, unjustified or out of proportion to the danger involved, is irrational. The phobic person may be aware of the irrationality of his fear, but he succumbs to it anyway, going to great lengths to circumvent the disturbing thing, place, or situation and the terror it inspires. He scrupulously avoids planes and elevators, taking endless train rides or climbing flights of stairs. When he confronts the phobic situation, he may suffer a "panic attack"—frightening physiological symptoms. Some phobics deny their fear, or force themselves to deal with it, but they are still afraid. Others may rationalize, saying it is perfectly logical to be afraid of planes and elevators, citing crash and accident statistics. What the phobic fears, however, is only a *symbol* of the real source of his fear, buried in his unconscious mind. In theory, when the phobic person uncovers the hidden fear, he loses his terror of the substitute situation and his irrational anxiety melts away.

History and culture give birth to new phobic objects and situations. Before the invention of the elevator, for example, no claustrophobic would fear to ride one. Some phobias affect one sex more than another. Agoraphobia—or panic attacks triggered by being in public places—

is a female phobia; 95 percent of agoraphobics are women. As psychiatrist Robert Seidenberg has suggested, agoraphobia symbolizes the dramatic way our view of the role of women in Western culture has changed.[1] In fifth-century Athens, no respectable married woman was allowed to visit the agora, or marketplace, unless she was escorted by a slave or eunuch guard. Married women were locked up at home, under the close watch of servants and vicious dogs. In this way, the Athenian noble was ensured that the heir to his property was truly his son and not the bastard offspring of some salacious intruder. Prostitutes, the only women who earned any money, were the only women allowed to go to the agora, also a public meeting place, and participate in the rich cultural and intellectual life of the time. What was normal for the average Athenian woman is abnormal for us. In the twentieth century, women who are afraid to leave their homes and go out in public are considered ill with a crippling psychic disorder—a modern phobia—and undergo psychotherapy and drug treatment.

Money: The New Agora

Today's women find themselves in a new relationship to money, and this new relationship has bred new fears. Those of us who take money-making careers for granted, tend to forget how recently women have begun to earn. Though women have always worked, few worked for pay before the Industrial Revolution, few worked in male-dominated professions before this century, and almost no woman worked who had the option of being supported by a husband or family. Whereas a middle-class Victorian woman, schooled according to her era's best standards, undertook paid work as a desperate last resort in dire financial circumstances, working and getting paid for it is a positive experience for today's educated women. To stay home and raise children, while a man provides support—what most women did three short decades ago—is seldom seen as an enviable life plan. In fact, new statistics show that only 10 percent of American families subscribe to the traditional model in which the husband is the breadwinner and the wife is a homemaker. Fifty-three percent of married mothers of children under six are working outside the home, compared with 12 percent in 1950. A woman's sense of self now includes accomplishment, and in our society, accomplishment is symbolized by dollars. Both married and single women want to have money they have earned themselves, and this, in historical terms, is a radical desire.

Despite ongoing discrimination, this desire is being fulfilled. Janet L. Norwood, United States Commissioner of Labor Statistics, has called the increase in the number of women who work, "the most striking demographic change in the U.S. labor force in recent decades," and believes "Women clearly are doing much better than they have ever done before."[2] In 1986 the United States Labor Department reported that women now hold the majority of professional jobs—over 29,000 more jobs than men. There are more female psychologists, statisticians, editors, and reporters, and women have gained in traditionally male-dominated fields such as medicine, law, and engineering.[3] In the previously all-male banking profession, at least one-third of entry-level jobs are now filled by women, who, when experienced, may earn salaries in the $50,000 range.[4] Though women are still discriminated against, and paid less than men in almost every job and every field, the gap in pay between the sexes is narrowing in white-collar professions. Recent studies by the Bureau of Labor Statistics have shown that in some scientific fields there is no gap at all.[5] Women's optimistic attitudes toward earning reflect this good news. Of the 123 in our money study, 102 said they would like to earn more and believed it was possible.* Women value earning power, or think that they should.

Women's relationship to money, then, like their relationship to the agora, symbolizes the vast extent of cultural change. Though money is not a place, it comes from the agora, an imaginary place where money is earned, traditionally inhabited and controlled by men. In our century, women have gradually left the safe but confining boundaries of the home and integrated this marketplace. Initially they did so to help

---

* The women who did not want to earn more had either already earned or inherited a lot of money, or realized that in order to earn more they would have to sacrifice important personal time and other interests.

out at home during depressions and times of personal financial stress, or to keep the economy rolling during major wars. Educated women worked in professions that helped and nurtured others, as social workers, teachers, and nurses. In the sixties, it became acceptable for women to work for personal as well as for economic reasons—to banish the "feminine mystique" and to win self-fulfillment. The next step was the one women are taking now: to work for recognition and financial reward, as well as for necessities, and to play an equal and more powerful role in maintaining their families' standard of living. (Because of the decrease in the real value of money, some economists theorize that it now takes two salaries to purchase what our parents' generation bought with one.)

Another new social phenomenon has also changed the significance of women in the marketplace: Women who never expected to be alone are finding themselves heads of households and sole financial decision makers. Forty percent of American women are currently single[6] (more than 87 percent participate in the labor force) and according to the Women's Bureau of the Department of Labor, as of August 1986, 13.2 percent of all white families were maintained by women. In women's steady progress from home to marketplace, then, earning money for oneself, and the traditional male values money implies—independence, power, and financial reward—is the final frontier.

Most women are not emotionally or practically prepared to make this last, arduous journey. Many of those now in their early twenties were raised with an awareness of economic responsibilities and goals, but women of previous generations were not taught to define careers in financial terms and got minimal instruction in financial skills, seen as "male" (such as investing, managing, and negotiating) because their families assumed they would not need them. When women now in their late twenties, thirties, forties, and early fifties entered adulthood, the cultural messages they got about money were modified. From their colleges and universities they learned that they were intelligent and capable, and could aspire to careers not available to women when they were growing up. From the feminist movement they learned that they had the inalienable right to economic equality, and the collective strength to fight for it. Finally, from the unexpected social and economic situations in which many found themselves, they learned that they had to make a larger amount of money than they had ever thought of earning, and manage it effectively. They began to define their lives, goals, and concepts of success in very different ways than their families had taught them. Inside, however, these new concepts, traditionally male, were only partly acceptable. The result: a complex cat's cradle of confused emotions, anxieties, fantasies, and needs, often concealed by positive definitions, ambitious life plans, and impressive achievements.

What should a woman be like? What should she do to survive in a society where women's needs and values are changing dramatically? How can she preserve a network of relationships, so important to women, and succeed in a man's terms in a man's world? Can she challenge the time-honored power structure between women and men without ending up alone, and find a way to balance her emotional needs with professional priorities? Burdened by these questions, ambitious women, often called *transitional women,* struggle to integrate a traditional view of their femininity with the new view they have of themselves. Money is one of the important issues that reflect the modern career-oriented woman's uncertainties and fears.

In our society money has a specific value: As a means of exchange, it stands for the worth of goods and services, and for accumulated wealth. For a transitional woman, however, money can symbolize conflicted desires. She both wants and fears it, like a forbidden romance. When we looked closely at women's financial behavior (how they related to the money they earned, or wanted to earn), we found them using money to express mixed emotions about the place they had come from and the exciting but threatening new territory in which they had landed—the marketplace. They handled money in self-destructive or inconsistent ways. Money made them uneasy, so they circumvented it, failing to earn what their capabilities and needs told them they should. They didn't negotiate for what they deserved for their goods and services, or with people in their personal lives. They knew they had to make money and spend it, but they refused to think about it, avoiding information that would help them manage or invest effectively. Some had squeamish attitudes about "filthy lucre." Like phobics in other situations, they actually experienced "panic attacks" when forced to negotiate, invest, budget, or even spend. Many rationalized their inefficient financial habits, or denied they existed, spending compulsively, investing unwisely, or building protective fortresses with what they earned.

As we progressed in our study of modern women's financial attitudes and behavior, it became apparent that their fears fell into distinct, sometimes predictable patterns. To facilitate the difficult job of describing these patterns, we gave them names and called them *symptoms*. Let us now briefly identify the Seven Deadly Symptoms of Moneyphobia. In subsequent chapters we will describe each symptom and its particular origins in detail, and look at the women who suffer from each one closely.

The Seven Deadly Symptoms of Moneyphobia

SYMPTOM # 1: MONEYBLINDNESS

The moneyblind woman closes her eyes to money and thinks of it as vague or unreal. Because she has confused money with other emotional conflicts, she often finds it anxiety-producing to look at all aspects of her financial situation, and may not read financial statements, balance her checkbooks, or know exactly how much she earns and spends. She leaves money management tasks to men she designates as "guide dogs."

SYMPTOM # 2: MONEYSQUEAMISHNESS

Even in the moneyhungry eighties, moneysqueamish women believe wanting money is "greedy" or "corrupt," and that talking about money is "tacky." Those who persist in thinking that money is not "nice" include Financial Virgins, who associate wanting money with inappropriate visceral desires for food and sex; Weaker Vessels, who believe money will corrupt their life or work; the Genteel Poor, who keep their needs to a minimum; and Money Martyrs, who think it is "morally superior" to be victimized financially. The moneysqueamish moral attitude harks back to the Victorian concept of the way women should feel about money.

SYMPTOM #3: MONEYDENYING

Modern moneydeniers do not believe their financial responsibilities will go on forever and entertain fantasies, often unconscious, that a man will rescue them. Brought up to believe that life is a fairy tale, they may also associate financial rescue, or "living happily ever after," with the satisfaction of their emotional needs. They usually spend every penny they earn, do not take income-producing work very seriously, and think making money should be glamorous and exciting.

SYMPTOM #4: MONEYELUDING

Moneyeluders want to make megabucks, but are paralyzed by anxieties they have not defined. They do not attach a price tag to success. They also fear finding themselves in a work situation that is not a comfortable home but which represents "foreign territory," where they will be exposed to the envy of others and their own lack of perfection will be revealed. Though a sexist society is often at the root of moneyeluders' problems, they take their inability to earn personally, and may have difficulty balancing their desire to make money with other needs and goals.

SYMPTOM #5: MONEYFOLLY

Moneyfolly victims blow their money or throw it away, as they attempt to solve emotional conflicts by excessive spending. They fearfully regard budgets and savings as punishments instead of useful techniques for taking charge of their financial lives, and sacrifice their future security in exchange for immediate gratification.

SYMPTOM #6: MONEYPARANOIA

The moneyparanoid use their money to build "fortresses" that they believe will protect them from an uncertain future and from people who plan to "rip them off" or "suck them dry." They solve emotional dilemmas by maintaining financial control at any cost. They may hoard their money or use it in the wrong way to sabotage themselves and their important relationships.

SYMPTOM #7: MONEYCONFUSION

Moneyconfusion strikes the Moneyphobic when they negotiate for pay, or for financial advantages in their personal lives. These women are afraid to separate money from their emotions and do not see that negotiation is a game between adversarial forces. They try to take care of their opponents' needs or expect their opponents to take care of them. They may also personalize money and financial institutions.

Though we have identified women's fear of money as seven distinct "symptoms," few Moneyphobic victims suffer from only one of them. The symptoms are interrelated, and, in fact, one may be the cause of another. A moneysqueamish woman, for example, is almost always moneyeluding, and a moneydenier is usually a moneyfolly victim, too. Sometimes a Moneyphobic woman will express one symptom one day and another the next. A moneyparanoid may have a bout of binge-spending, then guiltily return to her money fortress. A moneydenier may become an eluder when she emerges from her fairy tale fantasy long enough to recognize the need to earn. Women may also suffer from different symptoms at different stages of their lives. A moneyblind woman who signs her husband's tax return without reading it, may become moneyconfused when she has to negotiate a divorce settlement. The symptoms may also have different meanings at different stages. A twenty-four-year-old who fantasizes that someone may rescue her has a less severe problem than a forty-year-old who cherishes this dream.

The same cause can result in a variety of symptoms. Women who were emotionally deprived in childhood can use moneyfolly to express their feelings of loss, become moneyparanoid to protect themselves or moneydeniers with a poverty mentality. The same symptom can also have different causes. Not all moneybingers, for example, are inspired to shop by the same anxiety. Some Moneyphobic women, too, suffer from only mild cases of the new phobia, whereas others are deeply afflicted with hard-to-cure versions.*

The Underlying Anxieties

Moneyphobia is not "typically female financial behavior," as some would like to suppose, or due solely to a lack of training in money-related skills and practices. Troubling conflicts are at work when women are afraid of money. Our research shows that these conflicts are inevitably related to a woman's stress-filled attempts to unify the mixed messages from her family and a changing world into a personally satisfying life plan. Moneyphobia, then, is not necessarily *negative* behavior; it is part of the way women are reacting to a changing picture of their role in society.

For women—certainly for those thirty and over—the old cultural picture was transmitted by their families. In order to separate from traditional definitions of what women are and what they do, then, these women had to separate from their families.

Separation-individuation is a term psychoanalysts use to describe the internal process by which children gradually become independent adults. Those who are loved and given proper nurturing are better able to achieve this distance, so necessary to their emotional well-being and, ultimately, to their sense of closeness with their parents. Every child "separates" from his parents to some degree, but some children remain much closer and more dependent than others, and more accurately embody parental concepts of their identity, even if such concepts are

---

* Men, of course, suffer from Moneyphobia, too, and almost every reader will be able to identify the seven symptoms in male friends and relatives. Male Moneyphobia, however, has different cultural and psychological origins, or is the exception more than the rule. For example, a female overspender may fantasize that her purchases of clothes and beauty products may attract a rescuer. A male moneyfolly victim, on the other hand, may fantasize he will soon earn millions or that he possesses the power and influence of a really high roller. A man who eludes earning possibilities may be rebelling against cultural norms, rather than acting the way he was raised to behave, as money-eluding women are. Moreover, because middle-class white men have an economic advantage to begin with, their Moneyphobia may affect them less severely.

not personally satisfying. (The unseparated child, in fact, may resent his parents.) A separation process that involves becoming a completely different kind of woman than one's parents had in mind—the kind of separation we are talking about here—is inevitably a difficult and dramatic process, fraught with anxiety and potential self-conflict.

An ideal mother is one who lets her daughter explore the world on her own, yet remains a reliable, comforting base. As the little girl separates, she internalizes this "good mother," whose soothing qualities give her confidence and protect her. During the separation process, the little girl is supposed to learn that the world is a place where she is loved and valued, and where she can fulfill her own potential, and become the person she wants to be. She should learn that her physical as well as her emotional needs are manageable and not oppressive, and that she can have satisfying, non-exploitative personal relationships.

Because so many of our mothers were deprived of meaningful social roles and real power, they could not teach these positive lessons. They passed along to their daughters their feelings of worthlessness, including depression, hopelessness, anger, and fear. The fears included symptoms of Moneyphobia—or anxieties that are expressed in relation to money. These mothers, who felt "stuck" in the safe, but confining boundaries of the home, communicated the ways a "stuck" woman lives and feels to their daughters, narrowing their horizons, too.

Many of the middle-class women we have interviewed had mothers who were depressed to varying degrees. Some were even alcoholics or hypochondriacs. A few were agoraphobic, staying inside the house and seldom emerging, except to go shopping. Many mothers were afraid to drive. Some were angry at being stuck and fought back furiously, but ineffectively. Most stopped working after marriage or worked for their husbands without getting paid. Those mothers who did work had low-paying, sex-stereotyped jobs, and if they were single parents, had a great deal of difficulty supporting their families; many required help from their parents. Though the women we interviewed spanned three generations, only a few of the youngest had mothers who worked in professional fields.

Emotionally, these mothers, whose lives were defined by domestic roles, needed their daughters to be like them. If the daughter became different, the mother would lose her sense of worth; she would feel that she no longer existed, even if her daughter was fulfilling her own secret dreams. Daughters, then, got the message that they could validate their mothers' lives by following in their footsteps.

What happens when a daughter, who wants to stay close to her mother, yet break away, because she perceives the powerlessness of her mother's situation, decides to lead a life tailored to new aspirations? She is flooded with a tidal wave of anxieties and feels:

- disloyal
- guilty
- out-of-control
- worthless, without self-esteem
- afraid her mother and other women will envy her
- trapped by traditional boundaries, as her mother has defined them, yet
- terrified of the great unknown that lies outside

Fathers, too, played a crucial role in modern women's psychological development. Unwilling to identify with their powerless mothers, daughters often identified with their more sophisticated fathers, who brought knowledge of the world into the home. Naturally curious about the world, these daughters imagined themselves learning about it by forming relationships with men like their fathers, or by going out into the world themselves, or both. The world, of course, included the marketplace—the new agora. Ironically, fathers often encouraged their daughters to be quite different from their hearthbound, noncompetitive mothers; during the postwar economic boom they were able to educate them, providing the essential base for future accomplishment. But the girl who identified with her father, and tried to emulate his experience and goals, fell prey to other confusions. How could she imitate male behavior, which involved competing with men, and have satisfying relationships? How could she relate to men, who were like her father, without becoming "stuck" like her mother? She grows up fearing loss of love, and loss of femininity and sexuality.

As they struggle to lay these troubling anxieties to rest, women maneuver to find a space in the world that feels different from their mother's space, yet feminine and comfortable. They try to relate to men and other women in satisfying ways, and acquire tools that will help them function and equip their new space, both its psychological and physical dimensions, with what they need. One of these tools is money. Yet money itself is anxiety-producing because, in our society, earning it is a symbol of male identity, and the reward for competitiveness and independence. Her relationship to money, then, reflects a woman's anxieties about her relationships to family, men, other women, and her own femininity. Her financial state is more than an easily altered pattern of earning, spending, and saving habits; it is a mirror of her psychological state in a world where women are changing.

"The Shower of Gold": An Old-Fashioned Parable for Modern Women

"The Shower of Gold," a fairy tale by The Brothers Grimm, portrays a "junior bag lady," who represents the way many ambitious modern women, conflicted between old and new definitions of their role, relate to money and to the frightening prospect of taking care of themselves. We will reproduce this brief tale here.

THE SHOWER OF GOLD[7]

Once upon a time lived a poor maiden whose father and mother were both dead, and the child was so very poor that she had no little room to live in nor even a bed to lie on. At last all her clothes were gone excepting those she wore, and she had nothing to eat but a piece of bread given to her by someone who had a kind, pitying heart. Still, she was good and pious, and although forsaken by all the world she knew that God would take care of her, and she went out into the fields and prayed to Him to help her. On the day when the kind-hearted person had given her the piece of bread, she was walking along the road when she met a poor man, who said to her, "Pray give me something to eat, for I am so hungry."

Immediately she offered him the whole of her bread and went away after he had taken it, saying: "Heaven has sent it to you."

Presently she saw a little child sitting by the roadside crying, and as she passed, the child exclaimed, "Oh, my head is so cold; do give me something to cover it."

Instantly the poor maiden took off her own cap and gave it to the child. A little farther, she met another child, who said she was freezing for want of a jacket, so she gave up her own. Another begged for her petticoat, and that she gave also. At last she entered a wood, where it was quite dark, and here she intended to sleep. But she had not gone far, before she found another little child with scarcely any clothes at all, and who appeared to be almost dying with cold. The good child thought to herself, "It is quite a dark night now, no one will see me."

So she took off all the clothes she had on, covered the poor little shivering child with them, and went away. This pious child had now nothing left in the world at all, and she was turning to go into the wood and cover herself with the fallen leaves, when all at once a golden shower fell around her from heaven. At first she thought that the stars, which look like golden money in the heavens, were falling, but when the drops reached the ground they were real golden dollars, and as she stood still under the golden shower she found herself covered from head to foot with warm and beautifully fine clothes. She gathered up the golden dollars, carried them away, and was rich instead of poor all the rest of her life.

The poor orphaned maiden, lost in the woods, symbolizes the way women feel when they go out to make their way in the world. Unprepared for the journey, they confuse traditional concepts of what women should be, and how they should behave, with the assertive action necessary to provide for their needs.

The poor little maiden suffers from almost all the symptoms of Moneyphobia: She is moneyblind because she does not calculate her needs or take stock of her limited resources. She is moneysqueamish because the "modest" girl believes it is essential to keep her own needs to a minimum. She is moneydenying, too, because she believes fate will take care of her needs provided she remains "pious," which can be defined as "having or showing duty and loyalty to friends, family, and others." Her neediness, she seems to think, will ultimately ensure her financial and emotional well-being. She is also moneyeluding because she is uncomfortable outside the home, and prefers volunteer work to creating income-producing opportunities. She suffers from moneyfolly because she generously gives away or wastes her resources. Last but not least, she is moneyconfused because when others demand what she has, she feels it is more important to take care of them than herself and does not negotiate. (She could have kept half the bread for herself.) The only symptom she does not express is moneyparanoia, which usually afflicts successful women.

The end of the fairy tale leaves us with doubts. When the poor, pious maiden is magically rewarded with a "shower of gold," it is unlikely that she will be "rich instead of poor all the rest of her life," as the fairy tale claims. Given her predilection for Moneyphobia, it seems more probable that the maiden will continue to mismanage and squander her resources. She will regard her magical megabucks as "filthy lucre" and go on being comfortably pious and poor. As we shall see, so much of the mythology about women and money, like this old-fashioned story, depicts women's financial well-being in the hands of fate, and encourages us to take care of ourselves by believing in magical forces and traditional definitions of women's role.

Developing a Healthy Financial Identity

Modern women, who have worked so hard to achieve their professional and personal identities, do not have to go on relating to money like poor, pious maidens. The healthy financial identities we both want and need, too, can be achieved. Developing a healthy relationship to money is not unlike developing a healthy relationship to one's own body. Both require changes in traditional behavior, and abandoning outdated concepts of feminine prototypes and female lifestyles.

A healthy body is strong, flexible, and efficient, and resistant to injury, stress, and disease. A healthy financial identity, too, functions more efficiently and is less vulnerable to anxiety-producing changes. To have a healthy body, women today take steps women have never taken before: They eat different kinds of foods, and practice sports and exercises previously thought to be traditionally masculine, such as running, calisthenics, and weight lifting. Most important, they know their bodies will not stay healthy without regular attention and maintenance. A healthy financial identity, too, calls for changes in the way we view and deal with money, and new financial attitudes and behavior, which were thought "for men only" before this decade. At the end of our book, we will define a healthy financial identity and offer suggestions about how the important changes necessary to develop one can be made. Before changes can occur, however, we must look in a mirror that does not lie and examine the fears that keep us from living happy and healthy financial lives.

CHAPTER 1

Moneyblindness

Moneyblind women do not see their financial lives clearly. Social and emotional forces obscure or distort their financial vision.

Of course, it is impossible to be completely oblivious to the presence of money. At the very least, everyone must handle it, and spend some every day. However, it is easy to be blind to one's total financial picture —a past, present, and future with money that includes earning goals, spending and saving patterns, and a support plan for retirement years. A thirty-five-year-old woman, without a penny in savings, may be ambitious, good at negotiations, and proudly aware of the competence that earns her a substantial salary, but unable to "see" where her money goes. A woman who earns, spends wisely, and saves may blind herself to lucrative investment opportunities. Another, who loves money and would like to earn more, fails to see that the time and energy she is willing to devote to money-making activities do not add up to the income she believes is ideal. Some women, even accountants and financial advisers, see other people's money with perfect clarity, but are afflicted with an inexplicable myopia when they look at their own. All symptoms of Moneyphobia are really variations of moneyblindness, because they represent different ways money is not seen and different methods of groping through the dark.

Different situations can produce temporary or permanent moneyblindness. Love is a great moneyblinder, and women who join their hearts (and bank accounts) to a moneyblind man's are likely to develop peripheral vision themselves. The difficulties we have in separating from our families, periods of transition, a heightened level of events or activities, deaths and births, may all result in lapses of financial vision. A woman of twenty-five whose monetary resources are appropriate for her age may become moneyblind ten years later if she has not adjusted her focus on money to match the new priorities inevitably supplied by time. The difference between moneyblindness and the other symptoms of Moneyphobia is that the moneyblind *do not know that they do not see.* It is like the old one-line joke, " 'I see,' said the blind man."

Moneyblind women often close their eyes very quickly once that they begin to glimpse their problems, because what they see makes them intolerably anxious. In fact, moneyblindness can be a rather creative tactic to avoid stress-provoking people, thoughts, and situations to which money is inextricably bound.

Detecting Moneyblindness

It is easier to detect a case of moneyblindness by what a woman does not do with money than by what she does. The moneyblind tend to avoid serious thought or conversation about money and view it, especially in large sums, as esoteric, vague, or unreal. Moneyblind women do not balance their checkbooks or learn to read financial statements. One victim we talked to threw them away.

> I like my 5 percent savings accounts and my checkbooks, but these stupid moneymarkets send you a statement—like a light bill. You don't get a bank book, you get these stupid little papers. They come in and I throw them out. I think they're junk mail. I never open them. . . . I just rip them up and throw them out.

Women afflicted with moneyblindness do not keep close watch on the money they spend or have a clear picture of their financial needs. They may not know exactly what they earn or what their husbands and boyfriends earn. When asked to name an ideal income, they cannot give a specific figure. Additional evidence of moneyblindness is the invention of elaborate systems for juggling and managing insignificant amounts of money. Moneyblind women may have a plethora of bank accounts and checkbooks, devise petty ways of robbing Peter to pay Paul (all with their own money), and attach different meanings to their different caches. As they focus on the myriad pieces of their financial puzzle, they obliterate the whole.

By contrast, the moneyblind can also remain blissfully unaware of the system that they use to allocate day-to-day resources. They unknowingly leave the cute waiter in their favorite cafe a 40 percent tip, credit card debts sneak up behind their backs, and end-of-the-month bills are an unpleasant surprise. Moneyblind women are not really able to add and subtract because their emotions have partially erased the figures.

Another distinguishing characteristic of moneyblindness is lack of interest in the topic of money. Money, as long as it is disposable cash, is "fun," but finances are "boring." Though most women are aware that nowadays an interest in financial matters is supposed to be not only savvy but chic, the moneyblind secretly roll their eyes heavenward when the talk turns to tax shelters. Even those who have been in therapy or analysis, and may be able to ferret out the nuances of other problems, discuss problems with money on a surface-scratching level. We have noticed how tempting it is for the moneyblind to change the focus of any conversation about money to a related subject. Begin delving into the deep-seated reasons for a binge-shopping syndrome and the binge-shopper starts talking about clothes—Calvin Klein versus Donna Karan and those shrimp-colored buckskin boots she is dying to buy.

The moneyblind women who filled out our lengthy questionnaire did not find it interesting. One California artist, an Ivy League graduate rescued from a bohemian hand-to-mouth lifestyle as a street vendor by her romance with a wealthy man (whom she had not yet married), termed our questionnaire "lackluster." She explained she may have found the subject unilluminating because money had never been a "priority" for her. Even women who seemed competent with money were shocked to see unexpected gaps and discrepancies in their financial picture when asked to account for income status, goals, and spending, saving and earning patterns in a comprehensive format. What they did not see, and what they saw for the first time, made many of them anxious; some said the phantom figures made them "nauseous."

Keep a day-to-day budget and note where their money goes? Call the bank and ask questions about the investment they don't understand? Withdraw money from a passbook savings account and purchase a bond with a better rate of interest? Moneyblind women agree these suggestions are good ideas, but they have difficulty carrying them out. They think financial action is a nuisance and a bore (and let's face it, for a large number of people it is exactly that, but then, doing the dishes is, too), so they postpone these uninspiring but necessary tasks. Their money, they believe, has a life of its own and will go on living it without their intervention. If you ask why they haven't kept the budget, called the bank, etc., they let you know that their lives are full of obligations far more intense and pressing.

Why Women Are Moneyblind

If the above symptoms sound distressingly familiar, it is because the family and society unwittingly conspire to make sure most women become moneyblind. Moneyblindness first develops in the family context: Children of both sexes are seldom made privy to the actual process of resource allocation—the amount of income the family receives, how it is budgeted, the process of making financial decisions. The dollars and cents of family finance are more often than not a cloak-and-dagger affair from which children are excluded (presumably because the worldly knowledge of money would sabotage their innocence). Women from working-class families often grew up with much more awareness of how money was obtained and spent than middle- and upper-middle-class women, for whom the facts about money were kept obscure. Secrecy about money and financial maneuvers breeds anxiety at an early age. Women we interviewed said that though as girls they appeared to be living in comfortable circumstances with their families, they could not help fearing this comfort was illusory and that their family's financial stability was actually precarious. Whereas resources available to the family, and the logic that determined their use, remained invisible, the parents' own neuroses about money were all too obvious. Their parents, of course, were also Moneyphobic and projected their neurotic concepts of money on to their children, who absorbed them unconsciously. Janice, for example, registered her upper-middle-class parents' guilt and confusion about money by the time she was a teenager; this parental Moneyphobia gave her an unrealistic concept of how much actual money was available and what it was worth.

> I never wanted to take money from my parents. I always felt I was taking it out of their blood. . . . If they bought something for me, I felt very badly. The way I chose my prep school was to go through the catalogue and pick the one that cost $100 less, even though I didn't like it. My mother said, "Oh, don't worry about it. We have enough money. Go to any school you want"; but I didn't feel worth it. I didn't feel I was a good investment.

The emotional conflicts Janice had already absorbed about money distorted and inflated its real value, so that she had no way of ascertaining how much $100 was worth in relation to the family's financial picture, and the sum became a negative symbol of her own worth instead. Most of the women in our study were able to describe their parents' "quirks" about money, yet were often unaware that they exhibited the same quirks themselves.

As boys get older, their fathers may teach them facts about finance, but they rarely teach girls. While the family failed to give its daughters any financial training, or an objective idea of the value of money, the schools, too, failed to include information about money in their curriculum and encouraged women to blind themselves to the area of study most related to finance—mathematics.

Though boys and girls tend to do equally well in school on an overall basis, girls have better verbal scores on college entrance exams, while boys score 34 percent higher in math. Studies have indicated that beginning in infancy boys are better at spatial perception—or the ability to visualize objects out of context—a skill related to the abstract, analytical logic required by the sciences and math. Psychologists believe that although boys are born with an edge in this area, this reasoning ability is not an innate "masculine" talent so much as a result of the way little boys are socialized to relate to the world. Mothers are usually less protective of infant sons than they are of daughters and allow them to explore more freely, giving them a more expansive and varied concept of space and objects at an early stage of their development. The schools do much to promote the boy's "natural" mathematical ability and to discourage the girl's, because teachers see numbers as masculine territory. Now that women are becoming more visible in business and in the sciences, hopefully this prejudice will soon be obsolete; however, we suspect this thirty-eight-year-old lawyer's horror story is typical of the experience many older women had with math:

> I had scored a 99 in the Geometry Regents and was put in an advanced placement class in intermediate algebra and trig. There were five girls in the class and fifteen boys, several of whom went on to MIT. The teacher, Mr. Leone, had a reputation for being strict but fair. Though I began the class full of confidence from my recent success with geometry, after about two weeks I found myself huddled in a corner with the four other girls for protection. Mr. Leone was out to prove that math was no place for a woman. And he did! He would ridicule any girl who got a right answer, making sure to tell us he would give us good grades just for being able to sit through his class. He made these five girls (all of whom graduated at the top of the class) feel like dummies, stupid and ashamed. I had to take a statistics course in college, but I never again felt confident about my ability to understand mathematical concepts.

The school's pejorative view of a girl's math ability often becomes a self-fulfilling prophecy. Many women fear financial tasks because they believe it is impossible for them to comprehend any number-related concept, and are surprised when they can. One woman, whose female algebra teacher made her "promise" not to go on to more advanced math, told us:

> I'm forty years old and I just learned that 45¾ in the stock market report means $45.75. Nobody ever bothered to tell me that all my life. I thought it was an esoteric algebraic formula.

The socially instilled belief that they are "dummies" at math and, by implication, finance, and that men are the smart ones, leads women to make men their financial "guide dogs," and abdicate control of their money to male advisers, relatives, and friends. A forty-three-year-old interior designer told us:

> When I started earning a lot of money I didn't deal with it at all. Any financial decision I could leave to my husband, I would. The myth was that he was the one who was competent to do that, and I never noticed he made a complete mess out of it. I can't see why I couldn't take control over the money when I was earning it. Could it have been the simple calculations, the math part? I never was good at math, but I'm not that terrible at it.

Socialized moneyblindness also often influences a woman's choice of career. Though most middle-class women were educated, and expected to work at least part of their lives, few took the monetary value of the career they chose into consideration. In our study women between thirty and forty-five often expressed job dissatisfaction when limited earning power was built into their chosen career; some teachers and nurses felt "burned-out" on their jobs because they saw a definite ceiling to their income level which did not reflect their talent or devotion. Most said parents and guidance counselors had pushed these "secure," role-stereotyped professions, and without support or information, they were unable to see other options. Today, some women in their twenties have gone to the opposite extreme and selected careers primarily for the high salaries they offer (which can also result in "business burnout" and job dissatisfaction).

Most women, then, enter the marketplace with a peculiarly distorted image of money. On the one hand, money seems an abstract, incomprehensible science, terrifying in what it says about their lack of ability to manage or understand it, and on the other, it is an all-too-personal symbol of parental neuroses and their own attempts to reconcile mixed messages about women and earning power. No wonder most women feel the best way to deal with money is to close their eyes to it!

Society and the media continue to reinforce our blindfolds by making it seem acceptable and feminine to be moneyblind. In the media-created myths about enviable women's lives, money is invariably a vague or invisible part of them. The message is transmitted that financial understanding is not a natural feminine concern. Consider, for example, the popular 1978 movie *An Unmarried Woman*, starring Jill Clayburgh as a gutsy divorcée who leaves her unfaithful husband and posh Upper East Side apartment to brave life on her own. The movie portrays marital separation as strictly an emotional challenge, which its latter-day heroine meets with a courageous spirit. Erica gets her own Greenwich Village apartment, a job in an art gallery, a lesbian psychotherapist, women friends, and falls in love with a new kind of man, a trendy SoHo artist. Her newfound independence, however, is never accounted for in dollars and cents. Erica's checkbook simply doesn't balance. Her village pad costs a staggering fortune, and art gallery jobs pay the minimum wage. How did she ever afford that expensive therapist, not to mention the different $90 silk blouse she wears in every frame? How did she negotiate with her husband? We never see her asking for alimony or "severance" pay, but we assume her husband gave it to her, which means her independence was a lot less painful than the movie implies. The Hollywood concept of separation leaves money out of the picture. Even in a film which purports to be so realistic that it shows its star vomiting on the sidewalk when she learns her husband is having an affair, money is *too* real to be part of the plot. In fact, we are hard put to think of many movies or television dramas in which money plays a visible or realistic role in a heroine's lifestyle.

Women themselves, even those admired for their success, perpetuate the notion that it is acceptable to be moneyblind. In her amusing autobiography *D.V.*, Diana Vreeland, the former editor of *Vogue*, confesses that she worked at *Harper's Bazaar* for twenty-eight years without getting, or apparently asking for, a raise.

I was the most economical thing that ever happened to the Hearst Corporation. Perhaps they loved me because I never knew how to get money out of them.

Diana also confesses:

> My father had the English accounts for Post and Flagg Stock-
> brokers. I never really knew what a stockbroker did; I'm not sure
> I do now.[1]

Diana appears, we hate to say it, almost proud to admit that she does
not know what her father did for a living. Would a woman whose father
was a physicist or a neurosurgeon make a point of stating in her
autobiography that she didn't understand exactly what he did? We
assume D.V. is being slightly facetious—as she is throughout—and is
counting on her readers to find this know-nothing stance about financial professions not stupid, but an additional proof of her chic brand
of charm.

The link between moneyblindness and femininity, in fact, has been
so securely forged that even women who are not moneyblind occasionally find it politic to pretend that they are. Corinne, a New Jersey
mother and teacher with a knack for real estate, took a night course
in investing at a local high school.

> My husband didn't want to know about the course, and it was
> inconvenient, but I went. I came home and said, "Don, we've got
> to get into zero coupons," and I started reading up on them and
> collecting information. So I'm the one who got us into zero cou-
> pons, and come to think about it, I'm the one who got us the
> mortgage deal on our new house. I'm the financial risk-taker! And
> do you know what I did? Last night when we were filling out the
> mortgage forms, I sat there and polished my nails instead of
> helping. Sometimes I like to act like a kept woman.

The Problem with Moneyblindness

For better or worse, it is possible to remain moneyblind and be perfectly happy—that is, as long as life does not remove the blinders by
force. The moneyblind woman's rose-colored glasses transform storms

brewing on the horizon of her financial future into romantic sunsets. The storm, however, with its disruptive winds and lightning shards may actually arrive. Sometimes it proves to be a squall that does minimal damage, and other times it is a virtual typhoon that may wipe the unprepared woman right off the map. Let us look at some examples of how moneyblindness can affect women's lives.

DORIS DAY: A TRAGIC CASE
OF BLIND FAITH

The rich and famous are by no means immune to moneyblindness. One near-fatal case is that of Doris Day, who entrusted the millions she earned as a hardworking performer to her third husband, Marty Melcher, who, in turn, entrusted them to an unscrupulous Hollywood shark, Jerry Rosenthal. Rosenthal, who was later tried for ripping off other superstars, "invested" the Day money in mythical oil wells and other bogus or ill-fated properties. From the beginning Doris had doubts, not about the character of either of these fellows but about their choice of investments, and wanted to buy art. She felt she had "no business in high-risk ventures." Whenever she protested her husband told her it would take too long to explain complex contracts to her, defended Rosenthal, and asked a crucial question, "Don't you trust me?" Although many of Doris's friends and fellow actors did not trust Melcher, who earned no money of his own, Doris did trust him.

Although I didn't like being in oil wells and hotels, there was no question that I did trust Marty.

When she didn't understand the investments Melcher made, she did not consult outside sources to obtain this vital information.

I did arrange a couple of confrontations with Rosenthal to protest his investments, but his explanation of what he was doing, and how it would benefit me as a tax shelter was too technical for my comprehension . . . (When people mention tax shelter to me I

always have a mental image of a little lean-to somewhere where
you run to hide when the tax collector comes).

After Melcher died, Doris discovered she was all but broke and that
the investments she had instinctively distrusted were meaningless
pieces of paper. To make matters worse, Melcher had signed her up
to do a television series she did not want to do to pay off his debts, and
had borrowed against her future salary. Doris, grief-stricken over her
husband's death, now had penury to contend with.

Who was Marty Melcher? That was the question that constantly
thrust itself at me. How could I have lived with a man for seventeen years and not known who he was?

How indeed? How had such a bright, talented woman, who had been
so farsighted in developing her career, become so nearsighted, not only
about men, but about money? Though Doris blames her lack of interest
in money and Melcher's foolishness for the destruction of her financial
empire, like many of us, she had compelling emotional reasons to put
blind faith in a man.

When she was young her father, a remote musician who never paid
much attention to Doris, proved untrustworthy; he abandoned Doris,
her mother, and brother because he was having an affair with a family
friend. Throughout her childhood Doris dreamed her father would
return, and the family harmony she so desired would be restored.
Sometimes we use the power of our imagination to manufacture our
dreams—in Doris's case, a loving, protective, trustworthy man, and
family harmony—and close our eyes to the glaring difference between
reality and myth. Unfortunately for Doris, money got mixed up with
her unresolved emotions.

Doris Day and Marty Melcher provide an interesting example of the
blind leading the blind. Though Melcher was no more moneysighted
than his wife, he was moneyblind for typically *masculine* reasons: He
saw money as a source of power and prestige, and getting rich as a way
of maintaining his superiority in a marriage to a woman who was far
more talented and successful than he was. Doris, however, like most

women, was moneyblind for more feminine, emotional reasons—because, despite her nationwide fame and her millions, she was still a lonely little girl, yearning for a daddy she could trust.[2]

GETTING ROBBED BLIND

Many moneyblind women, unlike Doris Day, are married to trustworthy men who have their best interests at heart. However, if these women consistently close their eyes to family finances, moneyblindness can cause disasters in their later years. Virginia Wasser, a second vice-president of Shearson Lehman Brothers Inc., a large financial firm, has many women clients who arrived at her doorstep after their husbands died. Grief-stricken and alone, their inner turbulence is increased when they are faced with a complicated portfolio of investments that they do not understand. Their financial as well as emotional stability is suddenly precarious. These widows, according to Virginia, often fall to the mercy of male bankers, accountants, and advisers who, preying on their sense of loss and desire for a surrogate husband, "rob them blind."

One of these potential sacrificial lambs was Virginia's own aunt, whose husband died unexpectedly without apprising his wife, also ill, of the details of his electrical supply house business. So preoccupied was this good and loving man with his wife's illness that he let his business go to pot and spared her his problems. Virginia said, "My aunt didn't know the difference between receivables and payables, and was in terrible physical and emotional shape." Virginia came to the rescue, and called a meeting of her uncle's attorney and accountant and the company's major stockholders.

It took me four minutes to ascertain that the lawyer and the accountant were suffering from tavern burnout. The lawyer walked in with liquor on his breath and minus a briefcase. He hadn't done any of the paperwork, or brought the will or legal papers. We had to remind him to take notes, and give him a pad and a pencil. He advised liquidation of the company. I advised my aunt that if she liquidated she'd get 10 cents on every dollar of what the company was worth, and I suspected the lawyer had his network of good old boys lined up to buy. He gave my aunt no alternatives as to what to do with the business. I fired the attorney and the accountant, and hired others, and am now getting the company in shape to sell, collecting my uncle's debts, and putting the workers on an incentive-based salary plan. Imagine the nightmare that could have occurred had I not been available to take charge.

Needless to say, few widows are fortunate enough to have VPs of financial conglomerates in their families, and may become victims of those who, through evil intentions or innocent incompetence, rob them of their assets.

Women who suffer from moneyblindness, however, are thoroughly capable of robbing themselves. A participant in our New York money group agreed to learn to read her monthly statement from a large financial firm as a "personal goal." Carolyn, though a cautious binge-spender, had managed to accumulate some savings, the bulk of which she had invested in Ginnie Mae units, or the Government National Mortgage Association, a safe investment that pays a high rate of interest. Carolyn had been advised by her father and male financial planner to put her money in Ginnie Maes, but had never understood the basic concept involved. Essentially, she had loaned money to the government, which, in turn, loaned it to people who needed mortgages to buy homes. Every month the borrowers paid the government back, and the government divided up the sum it received and paid back the investors, along with a monthly rate of interest. Carolyn, however, did not realize the monthly checks she had requested and automatically received from her financial firm included the repayment of her principal plus the interest. She believed both were pure profit, and blithely spent the money, usually on clothes, regarding it as "mad money." About the time Carolyn decided to enlighten herself, her male adviser retired. A new female financial adviser set her straight.

She told me that I'd already spent $4,000 of my principal, and if I kept it up, I'd soon have Ginnie Mae units without any money in them. Since I am a freelancer without a pension or unemployment benefits, it is important for me to keep these savings intact. When I really looked at the statement, I couldn't understand how I'd gotten so confused. Right there in black and white it said *principal*, and on the line beneath it said *interest*. Every month the total sum of my assets was decreasing on the statement, and I never noticed that either. Boy, did I feel dumb! I called my father and accused him of not explaining the Ginnie Maes to me, and he accused me of not being interested, just like my mother, who always protests that she's cooking dinner or folding the laundry when he tries to explain their finances to her. He said women were "congenitally uninterested in finance." I had to admit he was right. I was the one who never asked questions. I wonder why not?

Roget's Thesaurus lists *blindness* as a synonym for "ignorance." But, as Carolyn intuited, there are hidden reasons why intelligent, sophisticated, professionally competent women are moneyblind.

THE CASE OF THE MONEYBLIND PHOTOGRAPHER

Beth is an unusually self-aware New York photographer, with a talent for analyzing her own inner landscape and the world outside with a perceptive eye. This vibrant, intense, thirty-four-year-old woman seemed to be leading an enviable life, doing exactly what she wanted to do, and doing it well. After a difficult divorce, she was living happily with a supportive man she truly loved and with whom she shared all basic expenses. Her years of persistence were paying off and she was beginning to show her black-and-white portraits in prominent galleries, supplementing her basic income photographing weddings with sales to collectors. Though money was not "growing on trees" it did not appear to be an immediate problem; Beth had enough and expected her work would soon produce more. Why, then, was she so anxious about money? When we met Beth and asked her to participate in our study, she was intrigued but very scared.

I feel nervous; really nervous. I just feel very nervous and anxious about this subject. I don't know why. I don't even really want to know why. Money, to me, is like a bottomless lake. I know there are slippery fish down there. I don't know what kind of troglodytes and eels we'll find . . . but, yes, I want to talk about it.

Despite her clear vision about her self and her goals, Beth was moneyblind. She didn't balance her checkbook, or have the slightest idea how much she spent in a month, or earned in a year, until her accountant did her taxes. She didn't know how much the man she lived with earned either, and didn't want to know; they never discussed money, and both considered their income a "private affair."

Though Beth's moneyblindness seemed harmless enough, when we probed a bit deeper we saw other symptoms of Moneyphobia lurking beneath the surface. Her self-imposed blindfold had resulted in some destructive financial attitudes and actions. A combination moneybinger and moneyholder, she described herself as "penny wise and pound foolish." A victim of moneyconfusion, she had supported her former husband for many years, yet when they separated, she had let him take half the worth of their house, which she had paid for. Her moneyconfusion also made it difficult for her to price her work, which she often felt she had sold for less than its value. Moneysqueamishness had prevented her from applying for grants and awards in her field because she thought other artists were more deserving of the money than she because they "struggled." Moneyparanoid, too, she refused to tell us or *anyone* exactly how much money she had at her disposal, pleading inexact knowledge of the amount. These problems, as well as her anxiety and guilt about the money issue, tipped us off that there were indeed "slippery fish" in Beth's lake. She was, however, willing to dredge them up from the bottom.

Beth had a money secret. She confessed that the income she earned by teaching and selling her prints was supplemented by "family money"—interest on a trust fund left to her by her paternal grandfather. Though this stipend was small, she was worried that friends and colleagues might find out about it and view her negatively.

I feel guilty about the free money I get—money I don't earn. I don't want people to know I have the backing of powerful money. It's really easy for people to feel resentful and jealous, and make you into someone who has an easier life than they do. It would negate the fact I work so hard and take my career so seriously for them. I want to escape blame. I want to be in the spotlight, but not the hot seat.

We wondered about Beth's use of the term *powerful money*. She told us that she associated money with masculine strength; she felt earning power might make her feel less feminine, and change the balance of power between herself and her boyfriend.

I want fame more than money. I think of my ambition, which is so fierce, as being very male, and not naturally female. And to want to make money, too, in addition to being recognized for my talent, is, at the moment, more than I can handle. I don't want to be thought of in that powerful way. Being helpless is fake . . . everyone knows that . . . but it's a game that I play.

Beth had admittedly absorbed society's message that money is synonymous with male power, but, as we soon learned, her own unique background had reinforced that message in a significant way. Beth had another money secret. Her father, she told us, had suffered from episodes of severe manic depression in her childhood and had occasionally been hospitalized. Though he was not always mentally stable, he had been a powerful family figure who had garnered most of the attention. And one of his major sources of power was his talent for finance. He had quadrupled the family inheritance by making astute investments, even when his psychological problems were most apparent. Though he, too, felt guilty about the family money, calling it a "curse," he maintained total control over it, spending it, even giving it away, as he saw fit.

He got his identity from showing he was available to give money away in the town that we lived in, and he put people through hoops for it.

While he used money as an instrument of power and manipulated others with it, Beth's father instructed only her brother about the complex art of finance, and kept Beth and her mother in the dark.

It was his domain, and he kept it his prerogative.

No wonder money made Beth nervous! Unenlightened about the financial skills that created money, she was able to see money only as a symbol of guilt and a manipulative male omnipotence, threatening and out-of-control. Though she was aware of the ambivalent emotions she had about her father, she was not aware of the way she had confused money with her feelings about him, or the way that confusion had scrambled her financial vision.

There is a connection in my mind between money and mental illness. Maybe I fear that line of succession. I have this inherited money, my father inherited money . . . maybe, therefore, I am like my father. I do identify with him in so many ways.

Beth's moneyblindness, then, was a way of avoiding the anxieties and fears that money symbolized in her personal world, which, as it happens, was a reflection of the way money appears in the larger world mirror—as a symbol of male power. Though few moneyblind women have fathers with severe psychological problems, or an inheritance to inspire guilt and confusion, most close their eyes to money for exactly the same reasons—because money conjures up alarming images of psychic "troglodytes." Sometimes, however, moneyblindness proves to be an ingenious way of adapting to anxiety-producing changes.

HOW ANN-MARIE SURVIVED CHANGE AND LOSS

Ann-Marie, a Connecticut social worker, had been a self-supporting single woman for fifteen of her thirty-seven years. She had carefully budgeted her $18,532 salary to include courses toward a master's degree and foreign travel. Then her aging mother fell and broke her hip, and Ann-Marie rediscovered an old high school pal—her mother's orthopedic surgeon. They fell in love and soon were married. Though this may sound like a fairy tale with a happy ending, Ann-Marie's new lifestyle involved some difficult adjustments.

In five years she had moved from her tiny "bachelor" apartment in the community where she had always lived into a luxurious suburban home, given birth to a daughter after a difficult late-life pregnancy, and lost her mother, father, and a favorite uncle, all of whom had died after lengthy illnesses. Between coping with a young child, who suffered from constant earaches, the medical problems of her relatives, a bad back of her own, and the responsibility of managing a large house with little help from her doctor husband, who was at the hospital until late at night and often on weekends, Ann-Marie found it impossible to continue working. After a stressful year of trying to be a "Supermom," she quit her job.

> I just canceled my subscription to a magazine that really sells this Supermom idea. It's not realistic; something has to give. Our society is saying, "Yes, you can have it all," and I was saying, "How can I have it all? I have all this stuff going on here."

Ann-Marie had been raised to believe she should be financially self-sufficient, work, and take care of herself; when she found herself thirty-seven and still single, she had not really expected to marry. Suddenly her identity had changed. She was no longer a hardworking social worker, but a wife and mother.

> I am not one of those people who go around saying motherhood is wonderful, because, oh God, it was a shock to my nervous system on top of everything else. It has its rewards, but when my daughter was tiny, it was very boring. I was going nonstop before she was born, and then here I was at home with this baby that didn't do anything except spit food at me and sleep. When she got to be a year old, I realized how much work it all was, and then I really started going crazy.

Ann-Marie's economic identity had also changed. She had crossed the boundaries of the working-class family and community into which she (and her husband) had been born and moved into upper-middle-class territory. How much money did her husband make? Ann-Marie didn't know, and didn't want to know.

> He's making it, and in my mind, it's his money. He puts it all in these moneymarket things, and he has this corporation, and it pays him a salary and buys a car. . . . I don't understand, even though I'm secretary of the corporation.

She worried that people she had known all her life as well as new acquaintances would see her as a *nouveau riche* doctor's wife, with all the economic advantages that title implied, and feel "distant" from her. She was determined to raise her little girl in a way that reflected her own childhood values.

> I see her as being able to get along with everyone. There are people who define themselves by how much money they have, how many expensive possessions they have, what kind of house they live in. . . . I don't want her ever to define herself or other people in those terms.

Ann-Marie had found a very creative way to adapt to these difficult transitions and losses: She became moneyblind. She began to run her financial life in an ingeniously complicated fashion, which first involved closing her eyes to her husband's enormous income. Instead of regarding what he made as hers, too, she asked him to pay her the same salary for managing the house as she had earned as a social worker and deposited it in a checking account in her own name. Every year she called her former boss to ask him how much she would be making and charged her husband the same "annual salary," which he paid her on the fifteenth and the thirtieth of the month. The income she got for working at home validated the worth of this new job in objective terms and made her feel less supported.

I had this real thing about being supported. I've never been supported in my life. I just couldn't sit around in the lap of luxury.

Though Ann-Marie's husband would never have denied her anything she wanted, she felt that earning an actual salary for homemaking and childraising activities gave her the right to do exactly what she liked with money she thought of as her own.

I went to Macy's and had the Elizabeth Arden treatment to the tune of two hundred bucks. It's on my charge and it's going to be paid for with my money. I could never present the bill to Dick and say, "Here, I just ran up two hundred dollars at Elizabeth Arden." It's not how I see myself.

The barrier Ann-Marie constructed between herself and her total financial picture was elaborate. She also maintained a second checking account, in which she deposited the money she got from renting her deceased father's house.

I said, "Look, honey, I don't have enough to pay the guy who paved the driveway," but he forgot to leave the check, so I had to go into my other checking account—the one with the money in it I get from renting my father's house. I have all these checkbooks that I'm fritzing around with and it's probably loony. It's really small sums that I'm dealing with. It gets confusing, but I won't take money from my father's estate and deposit it in my personal checkbook.

Ann-Marie's financial management techniques appeared, as she suggests, a trifle "loony," but there was a definite method to her madness. By getting paid an actual salary for her job at home, she validated its worth and sustained the sense of financial independence she had had as a self-supporting social worker. By blinding herself to her entry into a higher economic class, she preserved the more comfortable boundaries—and values—of the old one. Finally, by separating the money from her father's estate from her husband's money and her salary, she maintained her emotional link with the family she had lost. Her check-books represented boundary lines that kept the borders between her old self and her new one from blending into a disorienting confusion; they kept Ann-Marie intact in her changing world.

There were, however, inevitable problems with Ann-Marie's moneyblindness. First of all, since she was using an elaborate financial system to mask the real cause of her stress, money was making her feel very anxious. She told us the very thought of money made her "physically sick." Second, though her financial nearsightedness made her present more emotionally comfortable, it was making her future more risky. By closing her eyes to her husband's money, she was ulti-mately hoodwinking herself. By not becoming actively involved in his corporation, she was setting herself up to play the tragic role of moneyblind widow in the event that he should die. By refusing to look at her family's financial picture, and insisting on maintaining the illusion of self-supporting independence, she had unwittingly donated money to the IRS.

> Before I quit my job, people were telling me to put my money in these tax-deferred annuities and things like that, but I was still operating with the idea of cash in hand. If my paycheck had gone down to $500 because I was putting my money in cash-deferred annuities, then it wouldn't have been cash in hand. It made sense, but I needed the cash, and I liked fritzing around with these checkbooks. When my husband told me how much we'd paid to the IRS that year, it was more than I'd ever dreamed of making.

Instead of opening her eyes, however, this experience provided Ann-Marie with a villainous scapegoat: She could now blame other money-blind actions on the IRS. She sold her father's house to a rather distant cousin for much less than it was worth on the open market, justifying this action by saying, "Why not? After all, the IRS is only going to steal the profit." Moneysightedness would have enabled her to do her finan-cial homework, and learn that (1) she could have kept the house and depreciated it as a tax shelter or (2) that, in reality, the capital gains tax actually worked in her favor, and she would have given only 20 percent of the profit on the house to the IRS at the time that she sold it.

On the other hand, we respected Ann-Marie's desire to preserve her all-important sense of personal and community relations by keeping her father's house in the family; we believed, however, that it would have been more personally satisfying for her to do so with her eyes wide open. The IRS also became the evil spectre that kept Ann-Marie from seeing the truth about another important decision: Where would she put her talent and prodigious energy once her daughter started school? She had no intention of remaining a salaried housewife, but she protested that she didn't want to return to her previous job because the IRS would "whack her income to bits." Yet, given the importance she had always placed on getting paid for what she did, she felt uncomfortable volunteering.

> Volunteering would be fun, but you can never take it seriously; at least I never have. But I'm not going to work for the IRS either. To hell with them!

Beneath this conundrum lay an important truth, which was difficult for Ann-Marie to acknowledge. She was slowly admitting to herself that she did not really like her career.

> My father wanted me to be a social worker. I don't really feel I was suited for that, but at that point in time, what else did you do—teaching, nursing, social work. I needed something secure so I could support myself. I went ahead and did that, and I wasn't really sure I liked it. It got worse.

We hoped that as time and increased self-awareness allowed Ann-Marie to adjust to the changes in her life, she would be able to view her husband's large income as a resource she could use to develop new skills (which would eventually produce the paycheck she personally needed to validate her sense of self-worth and independence), instead of continuing to blindly maintain the illusion that she was still a single woman from the working class, struggling to support herself.

Becoming Moneysighted

As Beth and Ann-Marie participated in our money study, both began to open their eyes. Beth was relieved to find she was not judged harshly for her small family stipend, either by us or by members of the money-awareness group she had joined. She said talking about money had helped her determine when she wanted to stay moneyblind and when she did not. With this new perception she was able to invest money she received from her ex-husband—payment for her share of the house they had owned—in a condominium, which she intended to rent. She enlisted her father's advice, and learned what questions to ask the financial adviser and the lawyer who assisted with the purchase. She decided that she did not want to invest the time and energy necessary to master the art of finance herself, but she wanted to know enough so that she could choose competent, trustworthy professionals in the financial field.

While we were working with Ann-Marie she began to help her aunt, a moneyblind widow, cope with her large estate. She discovered that financial matters were not impossible to understand, once one was willing to look at them.

> Once I got myself through the technical jargon on the forms I saw I could do it. The technical jargon made me nervous all summer. I had to figure it out. Lawyers who charge three or four thousand dollars to set up an estate are ripping old people off in a way. It's not that simple, and it's a lot of work, but all you have to do is figure out how much tax you have to pay and pay it.

Her experience with her aunt's estate, and her willingness to examine her own money problems, made Ann-Marie decide to learn what was happening in her husband's corporation.

> Hell! I'd better get up there and not let those fellows keep bamboozling me . . . the lawyer and the insurance guy. . . . Next time they have a meeting I'm going to have questions to ask them.

Also important, Ann-Marie got involved in community restoration, a longtime passion she had been unable to indulge in the days when she had to be self-supporting, by organizing a volunteer group of concerned citizens herself.

Both Beth and Ann-Marie, then, were able to begin the slow, often painful process of becoming moneysighted, because they were conscious of their anxiety about money and were willing to tolerate this unpleasant sensation long enough to investigate its cause. In other words, both had taken an important step toward moneysightedness before we met them, because they had begun to *feel* that money was a problem in their otherwise successful lives.

Unfortunately, our culture does not train women to tolerate separation anxiety. From the time they are in the cradle, little girls learn that others will soothe their tears with caresses and smiles. Little boys, on the other hand, who, for neurological reasons, are less responsive to soothing gestures, are allowed to cry and eventually learn how to soothe themselves. Most women, then, grow up feeling unable to withstand this anxiety for very long and are all too ready to trust others to make them feel better. When they confront the new, bewildering anxiety that arises when they look at money—what it means to women in the twentieth century and the role money plays in their personal lives— they are tempted to throw their hands over their eyes.

CHAPTER 2

Moneysqueamishness

Moneysqueamishness is one of the cultural attitudes that close our eyes to the meaning of money. Women with this symptom think money is dirty or corrupt. They believe that to want a lot of it is selfish or greedy, like an out-of-control urge for food or wanton sex. Discussing money in too much detail is "tacky," "indelicate," or "crass." Though openly or secretly they may lust after money, and the aura of power and comfortable lifestyle it creates, the moneysqueamish maintain to themselves and others that a desire to be well-off isn't a "pure" or "proper" value. To them, money is not "moral" or "appropriate." This holier-than-thou attitude toward money, and those who seem to devote their lives to getting and spending it, may appear politically rebellious in the modern gold-rush climate, but it is actually a throwback to Victorian times. Moneysqueamish women, as we shall show, are subscribing to age-old ideas about how women should relate (or *not* relate) to money and the marketplace. These rigid cultural definitions, buried in the self-concepts of too many women, can prevent them from taking care of their needs.

Because moneysqueamishness is not a modern viewpoint, most women have banished it from their awareness and may find this attitude hard to detect in themselves. Yet, our study revealed that traces of the feeling that money is not "nice" negatively affect the way ambitious women earn, negotiate, and spend.

The Origins of Moneysqueamishness

Moneysqueamish ideas and practices were introduced into our culture by the Puritans, whose fervent ethic placed no bounds on the amount of property an individual could acquire, but tempered the ways money could be made and spent.

Though the clergy saw no conflict between wealth and religion (in fact, some of the upstanding members of the congregation were merchants and tradesmen), they opposed frivolity, ostentation, and corruption. A Puritan's fortune was proof that God had elected him for salvation, but he was forbidden to make it dishonestly, squander it, or devote his life solely to the acquisition of wealth. A rich man who was also godly did not indulge in luxurious living, but used his money for the public good.

Books could be written speculating why the Puritan money message survived our social melting pot, and how it has changed. Suffice it to say that remnants of puritanical attitudes still color the way both sexes think and talk about money today. Like the Puritans, we believe that people who have made money through hard work and intelligence are privy to a special, almost mysterious wisdom, and are morally superior to those who got it some other way. The wealthy are still expected to be charitable. Though we may envy ostentatious spending, we do not really admire it. We also practice puritanical discretionary policies in our money talk, and believe the total amount we have and how we spend it—particularly large sums—is private information. Sigmund Freud once said, "Money matters will be treated by cultured people in the same manner as sexual matters, with the same inconsistency, prudishness, and hypocrisy."[1] Yet a century after Freud made that statement, most of us would feel more comfortable asking for, or confiding, the intimate details of a sexual relationship than the figures of bank accounts.

Moneysqueamishness is explained by our psychoanalytical as well as our historical tradition. Freud, the first analyst to look at the meaning

of money, theorized that it was linked to sex and filth in the unconscious mind, and interpreted money as a sanitized symbol of an infant's
feces. He said that the significance of money for each individual is
based on the way he was toilet trained, and the emotional responses this
training induced.

The slang we use for money and getting rich seems to bear out the
Freudian idea, indicating we think of money as "dirty." We talk about
"making a pile" or "rolling or wallowing in money." Those who make
money illegally have to "launder it," and the financially powerful are
sometimes described as "filthy rich."

Why Women Are More Moneysqueamish Than Men

Women are more likely to be moneysqueamish than men because
moneysqueamishness is part of our society's traditional definition of
middle-class femininity.

As far back as fifth-century Greece, a paragon of true womanhood
was "frugal, chaste, and silent." It was in Victorian times, however,
that a "lady," in the American sense, was defined by the distance
between herself and the marketplace. Before the Industrial Revolution,
Colonial women worked side by side with their husbands to run household economies; the labor of one sex was not valued more than that
of the other. When men began working outside the home in the
nineteenth century, what women did was no longer perceived as an
invaluable financial activity because it did not bring in money. Paradox-
ically, it was from this worthless "idleness" (often not idleness at all,
but an endless round of unpaid household chores), that women derived
a new sense of status and class. Middle-class women, dependent on
their husbands, were elevated to "ladies" and considered superior to
poor women who worked.[2]

The church conspired with economic history by praising women who
stayed at home as upholders of society's moral virtue. Since the seven-
teenth century women had been viewed by the Anglican church as

"weaker vessels," or morally delicate creatures, whose pure and fragile souls were likely to fall. In America, Protestant ministers expanded this concept to include the idea that contact with commerce and government made men "base." Women, naturally more modest and benevolent, could preserve their own morality, and mold the characters of their husbands and children, by remaining untainted by worldly pursuits. Money-making was seen by the church as a "contagion" from which women were free. Even important spokeswomen like Sarah Hale, an impoverished widow who had supported her children by founding the popular *Ladies' Magazine,* urged her readers to stay at home and devote themselves to "the chaste disinterested circle of the fireside."[3]

The nineteenth-century lady's attitude toward sex was the same as her attitude toward worldly pursuits—disinterested. Encased in organ-crunching corsets and stays, she was not supposed to exercise or have sexual needs. Restricted by her virtue and class to the fireside, what did the middle-class Victorian lady do with her intelligence and time? She gave birth, instructed her children, managed her household if she had help, and did her own chores if she did not. She joined literary discussion groups and formed intense friendships with other women—the basis for later pro-suffrage organizations. She also got sick!* Even early feminist pioneers like Jane Addams, the founder of Hull House, and Charlotte Perkins Gilman, who campaigned for women's rights, languished with undefined nervous ailments before they had the courage to move away from the fireside and out into the world. Gilman continued to have nervous problems. Later, when the Weaker Vessels did leave the hearth, it was not to try to make a place for themselves in an economy that almost totally excluded middle-class women, but to expand their virtuous influence and help the needy victims of the marketplace—the poor. As a result, the tradition of women in volunteer work was born. As late as 1965, one economist put the monetary value of women's philanthropic activities at $14.2 billion.

Less than a century later, most of us regard the Victorian lady not

---

* The nineteenth-century feminine ideal was a pale and ethereal woman—all spirit and no body.

as our antecedent, but as an apocryphal ghost from the past, with no relationship to modern women. Few of us would be able to recognize in ourselves a conscious desire to be frugal or chaste (let alone silent) by the hearth. Most of us want to work outside the home for as high a rate of pay as possible (philanthropic organizations are having increasing difficulty recruiting women on a volunteer basis) and believe sexual pleasure is one of our birthrights. Yet, the power of the Victorian lady—and the persistent forces that keep her alive— cannot be dismissed or underestimated. Her small voice inside our historical unconscious still sabotages even the most modern of us by whispering that our desires for worldly power, money, and sex are not ladylike.

Detecting Moneysqueamishness

There are four types of moneysqueamish women.

THE FINANCIAL VIRGINS

Financial Virgins view financial acts the way the Victorians viewed sex —as dirty or forbidden—and the desire for money not unlike an uncontrollable sexual urge. They may see spending as "giving in" to seductive forces and saving as "holding out." Said one:

> If you have money in the bank you are always all right. It's virtuous. It's like virginity. You are saving yourself.

Unlike the moneyblind, who are bored by financial discussions, the moneysqueamish do not like to talk about money matters because they feel they are "personal," or "private," like sexual behavior. One Financial Virgin was titillated by the topic when she discussed money with her boyfriend for the first time.

> Actually it was sort of fun. I realized that this was taboo . . . something you didn't talk about. There was this shiver of delight —the same feeling as when you talk about sex. It was so delicate,

so loaded in terms of identity and ego. The interesting thing was that we both understood that each of us respected the other's privacy.

Because the Financial Virgin associates spending or making money with dangerously greedy visceral desires, likely to compromise her feminine attractiveness, she may describe financial feelings in terms of food, as well as sex. A California woman who made more than six figures in a mail-order business marketing erotic products, was still money-squeamish: She said she would be "orgasmic" twenty-four hours a day if she made $500,000, but worried that her unquenchable greed for money could get "out of control." Another Financial Virgin, a law student with ambitious goals, confided that she felt uneasy after our interview. She thought she had sounded "piggy" or "money hungry," and that talking about money was like "talking about oral sex—not really appropriate." She told us that she thinks of a diet as a budget, and vice versa.

I like the structure of budgeting calories. When I buy a candy bar I ask, "Is this a good way to spend forty-five cents?"

Financial Virgins who think of money as a visceral "temptation" may find even the look and feel of it distasteful. Naomi, a Boston physical therapist, dislikes handling cash, a moneysqueamish symptom she inherited from her mother, who would follow a monthly trip to the diet doctor with a shopping binge for clothes on sale.

She'd buy tons of stuff, bags of it—all cheap shit—and she'd use plastic to pay for it. I can't see my mother's hands with cash in them.

As an adult, Naomi, who also has a weight problem, avoids cash, too, and pays for purchases with credit cards and checks. Whereas her mother used "plastic" to rebel against dietary restrictions by binging in stores, Naomi uses it to make money less "real," and to move it out of the range of spending impulses she fears are uncontrollable.

With cash, there's a sense that I could succumb to impulsive spending. Dealing with plastic takes it a step above.

Financial Virgins like Naomi are suffering from social restrictions they harbor within. They are no more comfortable with their needs to earn and spend their own money than they are with their bodily needs for food and sex. Ladylike women, some part of them believes, should not have these "wayward desires." The modern, independent side of a Financial Virgin, however, rebels against the prohibiting voices within herself by overindulging, then pays with guilt and self-denial. The law student who thought talking about money was like talking about oral sex, also compared spending freely on herself with usurping the role of a male seducer:

> Some people have sex when they are depressed. I spend money, and like with sex, I sometimes feel guilty afterwards. But if I go out and spend it, just to give something to myself, it's like it's for me alone. It's like fucking somebody instead of waiting to be seduced . . . having perfect control over the situation, getting off, and not worrying about him.

For Financial Virgins, money becomes a symbol of inner conflict, instead of a source of pleasure and fulfillment.

THE WEAKER VESSELS

Seventeenth-century Anglican clergymen termed women weaker vessels because their naturally pure souls were susceptible to corruption. Twentieth-century Weaker Vessels still profess that the purity of their lives or work could be spoiled by money. Though these moneysqueamish women may have commendable ideals and come from religious backgrounds, they live in a cultural climate which makes it hard for them to go on believing that money is the root of all evil. In fact, the Weaker Vessel's protestation that money and the people who have it are corrupt, is often a rationalization for her own failure to earn, fear of success, or career confusion.

Weaker Vessels are prevalent among women who have chosen low-paying social service professions, or financially capricious vocations that promise glory, like one of the arts. Artists believe, often with validity, that the establishment bestows its financial rewards on artistic products that are not the best. They say that they have not earned much money for their work because, by contrast, it is "good" or "pure." A California artist who supported herself on a poverty level while she painted, wrote:

> I felt, from age 22 to 35, at least, that making money would be too powerful a goal for a fledgling artist—that I was *not* making commodities, and wanting money might pollute my art-making process.

Age and necessity often urge the Weaker Vessel to revise her squeamish attitudes. Sue, a single Maryland social worker, began to modify her belief that money is not "pure" when she turned forty and realized that if she did not take care of her old age, no one else would. She told us that she still wanted a "socially useful job," but one that "pays a lot more."

> I always felt, until now, that if I earned a lot of money it would inhibit my spiritual development. I never wanted to be dominated by money, and was always proud that I never needed much. I also realize that it's not a sin to be worth it; it's a sin to take it from someone without earning it.

Originally Sue subscribed to the Victorian definition of a lady by keeping her needs to a minimum, then graduated to the Puritan idea that it was acceptable to earn, provided that you did so honestly. Why did she believe that money would "dominate" her? For Financial Virgins, money threatens loss of self-control; Weaker Vessels, on the other hand, believe that money would control them by subjecting them to changing forces.

Andrea, in our New York money group, also feared the controlling powers of money. She had broken away from a Southern Catholic working-class background, put herself through college, and was working as a reporter for a metropolitan daily. She told the group that she had recently discussed the possibility of ghostwriting a celebrity biography with a male friend, an editor for a major publishing firm. Andrea rejected the idea when she learned she would not have "total control" over the editorial content.

> He said, "There's half a million dollars there, Andy. Come on! You wouldn't do it for that kind of money?" And I said, "No, I made that mistake once, and it wasn't even for that kind of money."

A member of the group questioned Andrea about her moneysqueamishness:

> But Andy, that kind of money would let you buy your apartment when it goes co-op, and travel, and take time off to write a book, like you told us you wanted to do, and the job would be over with in a few months. Your name wouldn't even be on the book!

Andrea replied:

> Famous last words! Maybe that's my Catholic upbringing. I would love to make a lot of money, but I want to make it in a pure way.

Though there might be good reasons for Andy to turn down a half-a-million-dollar opportunity, we did not think loss of purity was a convincing one, given her ambitious financial goals. Andrea's "purity," even as she defined it in professional terms, preserved her relationship with her religious, working-class family. Half a million dollars, however, represented a potentially terrifying unknown—a new world with unpredictable boundaries, light-years away from her family's world. Andrea had wanted to get away from her family, but not *that* far away. It was not editorial "control" she feared but the irreversible changes, and the lonely feeling of total separation, she imagined money would impose.

THE GENTEEL POOR

The moneysqueamish women in this category believe there is a righteous nobility to being poor or non–income producing. Often well educated, they regard scrambling after money as a sign of ill-breeding and pride themselves on keeping their needs to a minimum. They achieve taste and style on a shoestring and think it worthwhile to try to be happy poor. Being happy poor does not exclude middle-class comforts, however, and the Genteel Poor are rarely found living in slums or shacks. They will resort to exploitation, if necessary, to survive in the style to which they are accustomed.

Among the Genteel Poor are houseguests who do not contribute for groceries and women who will not pick up their share of a check on a date. They also resent "dirtying their hands" or taking jobs they consider beneath them; they may refuse to carry their financial weight in a marriage, even when their husbands are unhappy about supplying total support. Beneath their facade of virtuous abstention from income-producing tasks, these women may actually doubt their ability to achieve financially.

THE MONEY MARTYRS

Money Martyrs think it is "morally superior" to ignore their financial needs and often become victims. They believe those who rip them off, or hustle to get the material advantages they would secretly like to have, are lower on the moral hierarchy. The supposedly guilty conscience of those who exploit them is adequate compensation for the Money Martyrs, who prefer to remain passive and pure in relation to money. Doris Day, who was also moneyblind, was unable to focus on her financial picture partly because she was a Money Martyr. Throughout her life, as we have seen, she was exploited both personally and professionally. Even the manager of the first band she sang with pocketed half her pay. Doris explains her failure to demand justice in moral terms:

> I suppose from the very beginning I was just too naive and trusting in a business that attracts predators. But it is my nature to be trusting—I wouldn't have it any other way. . . . Those who have abused it—well, I pity them, for I am none the worse, really, for their abuses, but they are.[4]

Money Martyrs have trouble negotiating for raises, or finding high-paying jobs because they believe their talent and hard work should be rewarded automatically. Like the Genteel Poor, they think that those who fend for their own economic interests are "crass." Edith, a Washington lawyer who works as a fundraiser for political candidates, did not ask for raises (though she often worked grueling sixty-hour weeks) or use her highly placed connections to steer her to lucrative and challenging jobs.

> The people I know who've made it have been single-minded about it. They've done it by shoving other people around, backbiting, demanding money, and making a lot of noise and fuss. It's clear to me that people get money, not for what they're worth, but because they know people and promote themselves. I don't want to degrade myself. I just want to be paid what I'm worth.

Like many Money Martyrs, Edith gets vicarious satisfaction from being slighted professionally, because she remains confident that she has conducted herself in a ladylike manner and done high-quality work. She vents her frustration at not getting what she is worth by criticizing those who have for their inappropriate behavior. Meanwhile, her virtue does not pay her rent.

The Problem with Moneysqueamishness

Because moneysqueamishness is a rigid attitude, and those who hold it are convinced it is correct, it is hard to get moneysqueamish women to see that their financial ideals may be working against their best interests. We do not mean to imply that moneysqueamishness is always inappropriate. We would not encourage women to model themselves after unscrupulous robber barons, or Mafia godfathers, or to sell out their true interests or the people close to them in order to become "filthy rich." Women, we believe, have to create a financial identity that expresses their modern feminine values; otherwise they risk imitating the traditional life formulas of men, which have not always been satisfying to them either. However, moneysqueamishness can be a passive or escapist attitude that functions as a shield between a woman and other symptoms of Moneyphobia—spending, earning, or negotiating problems. If a woman believes it is immoral, greedy, or selfish to act in her own behalf in the marketplace, she may never be able to examine the fears that stand between her and financial success. If she views talking about money as "tacky" she may deprive herself of useful information, which will help her price her work and make profitable investments. Moneysqueamishness in her personal life may lead to uncomfortable feelings of exploitation. To place oneself "above" financial needs and problems is a way to deny they exist; it is not a constructive approach to seeing or solving them.*

WHO KEEPS MONEYSQUEAMISHNESS ALIVE?

Women can inherit moneysqueamishness from one or both parents. Unsuccessful fathers, who condemned earning power in others and professed to believe that job satisfaction is more important than high pay, may pass on the attitude. Mothers who stopped working after

---

* No better example of the perils of moneysqueamishness could be found than in the financial tragedy of American nuns. The nation's 115,000 aging Catholic sisters, most of whom worked for subsistence wages as teachers, have no money for their retirement years. According to a study by the National Catholic Council of Bishops, there is presently a gap of $2 billion between available retirement money and what it will take to meet the nuns' financial and medical needs. Until recently, the money-squeamish nuns did not even discuss their financial problems, because they felt that to talk about their personal travails would go against their basic mission of devoting their lives to the needs of others—long-range planning was "somehow in conflict with the providence of God" (John J. Fialka, "Sisters in Need," The Wall Street Journal, May 19, 1986).

marriage and did volunteer work in the community may also transmit moneysqueamishness. Some mothers proclaimed that their homemaking jobs were a "sacrifice" they made for their children, and that staying home was more important than working. They tried to instill the same values in their daughters, who absorbed some of their moneysqueamish ideas without wanting to emulate their lives.

The moneysqueamishness we learn from parents is reinforced by men who believe that women should earn less than they do. The business world employs subtle restrictions to indicate its belief that it is "inappropriate" for women to earn as much money as men in the same kinds of ways. Though women in business are still expected to imitate the appearance of men with body-concealing suits, they risk criticism or worse when they imitate their behavior—getting involved with professional contacts or drinking too much at lunch.

Ambitious women may get moneysqueamish messages from husbands and boyfriends, particularly if they are earning less than they would like to be. Gabrielle, for example, an assertive New York woman with her own direct-mail advertising company, said her ex-husband accused her of "moneygrubbing" even before her fledgling business operated in the black.

> His career was on the rocks, yet he gave me long-winded speeches about my superficial values. Though he accused me of being a moneygrubber, if there was ever a man who liked to go to fancy restaurants and have beautiful things, it was my husband. I didn't care so much about all that. Every once in a while he would talk about how he really felt he owed me a fur coat. Mind you, I never said *boo* about fur coats.

Grub is a word with Germanic roots which means "to dig in the ground." By calling her a "moneygrubber," Gabrielle's husband reduced her talents and goals to a low form of menial labor, and yearned to restore her traditional femininity (and his male ego) by giving her a symbol of a high-class kept woman—a fur. Yet if Gabrielle had married a richer husband in order to get a fur she might have been accused of groveling in the dirt for something else—or "gold-digging."

Though many women would have been crushed by a husband's disapproval of their financial drive, Gabrielle, who had been raised to believe she was responsible for her own support, was not. She saw her husband's attack for what it was—an expression of his own feelings of financial impotence.

> I thought it was a big joke, because I could turn on him and say, "At least I'm making some, what about you?" After he started to do a little bit better, he shut up about my being a moneygrubber.

THE STORY OF "J": THE RISE AND FALL OF A FINANCIAL VIRGIN

Who wouldn't want to make a fast million writing a best-selling book? Many of the women who filled out our questionnaire named this as their financial fantasy. However, as one author who went from rags to riches discovered, hell hath no wrath greater than Victorian reactionary forces, which can seem mythical until a woman makes a pile by saying something in print that is not considered "nice." Terry Garrity's problem was that the book she wrote under the pseudonym "J," *The Sensuous Woman*, told women how to manipulate men by enjoying sex. When the book became a blockbusting success, Terry was so overwhelmed by the social furor that ensued, and the repercussions in her personal life, that she found it easier to go back to rags than to go on being "unladylike." Let's look at how moneysqueamishness destroyed Terry Garrity.

A product of the conservative fifties, Terry grew up in a Minneapolis Catholic family where one of the lessons she learned was that men didn't marry girls who were not virgins. In the sixties, star-struck Terry came to New York to pursue an acting career and worked as a hatcheck girl, secretary, and publicist for the publisher Lyle Stuart. Later, Stuart, who knew that Terry was struggling to start her own publicity agency, offered her the opportunity to write a publishing first—"a sex book by a woman for women"—for a meager $1,500 advance.

Terry agreed. As she explains in her autobiography, *The Story of "J,"* she was an excellent candidate for this novel assignment. Though she had experimented with a number of sexual partners in the freewheeling sixties, she had never succeeded in enjoying sex and had always faked orgasms. Doctors and psychiatrists advised her that, like many women, she suffered from a low sex drive. One day, while shopping, it dawned on Terry that having an orgasm was an art to be learned—like unearthing a pair of expensive shoes from the bargain table at Gimbels, which she was in the process of doing. She proceeded to teach herself to have transporting climaxes by masturbating, and then in bed with a man by "learning a higher degree of selfishness" and "focusing on her own sensations."

Terry saw the Lyle Stuart contract not as an opportunity to make a quick buck, but as a worthwhile campaign to initiate other frigid women into the joys of sex. She did, however, insist on a pseudonym: "I felt squeamish about being identified as a sex book author," she said. Stuart agreed, and Terry churned out *The Sensuous Woman* in record time. It was published in 1969.

Compared to more radical and graphic sex manuals that followed, *The Sensuous Woman* contained little that was shocking. Basically, it advised women how to get and keep a man by resorting to time-honored feminine ploys, such as wearing slinky lingerie and changing the bedroom decor to keep sex exciting. However, it also described masturbation and fellatio techniques, such as "The Butterfly Flick" and "The Silken Swirl" and anal intercourse. Though it was these details that ostensibly shocked sixties Puritans, we think what really shocked them was the more radical political message that Terry had unwittingly preached between the lines. In essence, *The Sensuous Woman* declared that a woman could manipulate and control a man by demanding—and achieving—her own sexual pleasure. And that had been, since time immemorial, a *male* prerogative. Ugly women, according to Terry, could wield power over rich and handsome men by brushing up on their sexual stimulation skills. Women with straying husbands could recapture them by making sex an "adventure." The Sensuous Woman could even obtain material wealth—"great loot like diamond necklaces, ruby bracelets and mink coats"—merely for the sexual satisfaction she was experiencing herself.

This is scarcely a feminist message: Terry was telling the ladylike women of her generation to engage in what amounts to a domestic form of prostitution. Unlike the prostitute, who is using her body only to make money, however, Terry's Sensuous Woman gets personal pleasure from her manipulative act. Terry had strayed quite far from her Catholic girlhood in Minneapolis, but since she had done so in disguise, she at first took the outraged reaction to her book in stride.

> People wrote "J" and quoted Biblical injunctions that seemed to prohibit all sexual contact between humans, up to and including handshakes. They connected masturbation with venereal disease and madness. . . . My more progressive critics conceded that performing these sexual acts might be acceptable, but *describing* them was not. . . . Radical women's libbers . . . blasted me for perpetuating the image of women as "mere" (their word not mine) sex objects.

When the paperback rights to the book sold for $100,000, however, Terry had something else to worry about—money—which she, like other moneysqueamish women, feared might control or change her life.

> This money was exciting, but it made me nervous too. I didn't want my life to change radically.

As she embarked on the first of many compulsive spending sprees, Stuart broke his promise and revealed "J"'s true identity to *Time* magazine. Terry's greatest fear was now realized: Her mother, to whom she was very close, would, along with the rest of the world, find out that the author of *The Sensuous Woman* was Terry Garrity, a girl who had prided herself on being as "wholesome as apple pie."

> Mother had never discussed sex with me. She was a very cosmopolitan, sophisticated woman in most matters, but she had a Victorian moral outlook . . . everybody respected the fact that she was a "lady," and that certain matters had to be treated delicately.

Terry decided to confess before the *Time* article appeared:

I was right to have dreaded that moment. She was shaken. Confused. It seemed completely unreal to her. For years I had hidden a side of my nature from Mother, knowing she would disapprove. I had told myself—in fact, I told everyone—that I was not ashamed of *The Sensuous Woman*. But with Mother? I felt *shame*. I had associated myself with something that was dirty in her eyes.

Though Terry's parents were divorced and she apparently had little contact with her father, she also feared his reaction:

And Daddy? How would he feel when he heard that his little girl had written a steamy sex manual?

Terry, then, had taken giant steps away from the Victorian world of her mother and her sexual squeamishness. In the end, however, her orgasms had not transported her very far; she had not really separated from her family and society's message about women's roles. Now personally connected to the "steamy sex manual" that she had written, Terry was caught in the most dramatic possible confrontation between her need to forge a workable twentieth-century identity for herself (which included making money and satisfying her sexual needs), and old-fashioned, restrictive definitions of "ladylike" behavior. To make matters worse, Terry's mother (who, it ought to be said, took the news of her daughter's fall from grace with a stiff upper lip) developed terminal cancer and died shortly thereafter. Though her mother had been ill before, perhaps Terry thought *The Sensuous Woman* had dealt the mortal blow.

A miserable nervous wreck, and suffering from gynecological problems (which resulted in her being unable to have children), Terry nevertheless began stumping bravely for her book, appearing on television and radio talk shows throughout the country. But she no longer felt in touch with herself. The fifties Victorian virgin and The Sensuous Woman were now split in two:

"J" signed aerosol cans of whipped cream that male fans thrust at her at bookstore appearances; Terry would have blushed and

fled . . . [Terry] bought beautiful clothes and objets d'art with the
money "J" was making hand over fist.

It was probably the more modern "J" who discovered that Lyle Stuart
was not paying the royalties he owed on the book and instituted a
lawsuit, but Victorian Terry justified the suit in moral terms—it would
vindicate other authors who had been ripped off by their publishers but
could not afford to sue.

Terry's squeamish feelings about having written a sex book extended
to its profits, and she began to use her money to restore herself to a
more ladylike status. She became Lady Bountiful, buying extravagant
gifts for her family and friends. She shopped compulsively. She became
the "caretaker" of the important men in her life, legally dividing her
earnings on *The Sensuous Man,* the next book Stuart commissioned
her to write, with her brother and boyfriend. Keeping her needs minimal, as a good Financial Virgin should, she accepted a piddling advance
for this project. She signed 10 percent of her earnings on *The Sensuous
Woman* over to her boyfriend, whom she named as "agent"; he, in
turn, promised to use the cash to take the two of them on luxurious
vacations. By getting rid of the most concrete evidence of her unladylike success—the "filthy lucre"—Terry tried to atone.

But she still had additional "wages of sin" to pay. Her boyfriend
never used the money he made on *The Sensuous Woman* to take her
on trips; instead they split up. Terry began to suffer from mental
confusion, health problems, and professional paralysis; she found it
almost impossible to produce a new book on love that Simon &
Schuster had paid her a whopping $200,000 to write. Living in isolation
in a Palm Beach apartment, Terry spent most of her time binge-
shopping and binge-eating. Soon she was surrounded by a virtual fortress of shopping bags containing "fire engine red moiré gowns,
Baccarat millefiori paperweights, and four pairs of shoes, all exactly
alike." Sometimes she could not remember paying for these purchases
and thought she might have succumbed to kleptomania during her
"blackouts." To pay her department store bills, her financial adviser
began to sell the stocks and bonds he had bought to provide for her
future security. Terry was using her riches to buy rags. Sex had fled from
her life, and the woman who had earned a million by becoming The

Sensuous Woman now slept alone. The lawsuit against Stuart, which was resolved in her favor, was a dubious moral victory. By the time legal fees were paid, it netted her only $30,000 and additional humiliation. During the trial a vicious article Lyle Stuart had written for *Screw* magazine was introduced as evidence. Stuart said:

> Terry Garrity is suing me as a woman scorned . . . I asked her to write a book that would make cocksucking respectable in America, and we published *The Sensuous Woman*. I've paid her more than $700,000 . . . but the sudden riches seem to have frightened away all the fellows she used to blow, and now she's hysterical because with nothing but bananas and overcooked frankfurters to suck on, her buck teeth are threatening to fall out.

If Terry had not already been convinced that she had defied all notions of common decency by writing a sex book, she might have survived this vindictive attack and judged it for what it was—an enraged sexist's predictable response to being asked to pay her more money than he thought any woman had a right to earn. Instead, she saw it as another Scarlet A branded on her forehead.

> I felt nauseous and tears were welling up in my eyes. I felt that I was a party to some uncontrollable ugliness, and that I was mired in muck and would never be clean again.[5]

Terry eventually succumbed and was treated by a psychiatrist for mental illness—a mood disorder called bipolar cyclical depression, caused by a chemical imbalance and aggravated by stress. She now attributes all of her problems to this disease. Though Terry was indeed depressed, and may have always suffered from her illness, as she claims, it never got the best of her until she defied social mores by making a lot of money writing about sex. We think Terry was a casualty in a brave new world where women were just beginning to demand the right to fulfill both their sexual and financial needs, and tended to see both as "forbidden." Because in Terry's case, an unlikely chain of events united her desire for money and sex in the public eye, she paid a heavier price than most of us, who asked for, and got, similar freedoms. In order to "repent" for her transgressions, Terry became a modern counterpart of the Victorian woman—nonproductive, confined to the hearth, dependent, with no money of her own, and sick. Like Jane Addams, whose doctors attempted to cure her nervous disorder by isolating her in a dark, quiet room, Terry Garrity "cured" herself by closing herself up in her soundproof Palm Beach apartment and letting her brother and male psychiatrist take care of her.

> I now settled into being sick. The weight of responsibility seemed lifted off me.

And so, in this way, one terrorized Sensuous Woman fled back to the safe but restrictive nineteenth century. Terry's story, hardly ancient history, has a lesson to teach about the perils of unacknowledged moneysqueamishness. Those who would dismiss her as "weak" or "crazy" should ask themselves how they would feel if their mothers found out they had written a best-selling sex book.

Overcoming Moneysqueamishness: Candace's Battle with the Curse of Genteel Poverty

When we first met Candace we thought she was struggling with a world-class midlife crisis. The school of English as a foreign language where she taught had folded, and at thirty-six she was collecting unemployment insurance and was unable to decide what she wanted to do next or, as she put it, "What I am capable of doing."

When we interviewed her, however, it became apparent that Candace's career confusion had not begun in midlife. Though she had worked since college graduation, she had yet to dedicate herself to a career or earn a high salary. A few of her many jobs had been equal to her intelligence and education—working as an assistant producer for a television news show—and others had not—selling encyclopedias door to door. Now, her husband, a hardworking, intellectual electrician, who wanted more time to make pottery and "read Plato in bed," was demanding that Candace bring in her share of income.

I think he understands my inclination to be supported, and this he does not want. The minute the news came in that the school had folded, Richard said, "Well, get to work on your résumé." And I put on the facade of looking for a job to make him happy, but I'm not really looking for a job just yet. We don't have a totally honest relationship.

While Candace "pretended to look for a job" and debated what to do with her life, she helped Richard do the bookkeeping and cost price jobs for his small business. When we asked why this vital contribution was not considered income-producing and why she didn't ask her husband to pay her a salary, we stumbled on the reason behind Candace's pattern of moneyeluding: She was moneysqueamish. For her, pay would *devalue* her contribution.

I don't want to be someone you can pay off and forget about. When people say to him, "What does Candace do for you?" that's what I do. If I got paid it wouldn't be the same at all. I wouldn't be valued for doing it personally. It reminds me of when I was a kid and did the dishes at a dinner party. The guests said to my mother, "Oh, Candace is doing the dishes! Isn't that nice!" My mother, a bit embarrassed by this, said, "Well, I'm going to give Candace a dollar!" And I started to cry.

Like other moneysqueamish women, Candace did not want to "dirty her hands" unless she got the vicarious moral satisfaction of working for free. She felt guilty that she did not earn and tried to compensate for her lack of income by keeping her needs to a minimum.

Richard struggles so hard working in filthy basements and driving his wretched old truck around. But his expenses haven't gone up radically since we got married. I don't eat much. It's a question of whether I contribute. I do feel guilty . . . I should be doing more for Richard.

In fact, doing something for her husband was the only good reason Candace could think of to earn a salary. She admitted to a personal "disdain for money" and thought sacrifice was required to "launder" it.

> I think I could go out and earn money if I had a couple of dependent children. If you go out and work and make a lot of money for yourself, I think people are really saying, "Greedy! Tacky! Insensitive! Low values!" But if you go out and support your children, they say, "Isn't she terrific? We know Candace isn't the type to make $150,000 a year, but she's doing it for her children . . . !"

We laughed at Candace's ironic humor, but we knew that beneath her wit she was also sincere. We learned that her moneysqueamishness went back two generations. Her current lifestyle in a modest Boulder, Colorado, house, and her marriage to a philosophical electrician—even her struggle with money issues—were very different than the atmosphere of genteel poverty in which she had been raised. Candace's story provides a dramatic illustration of the way moneysqueamish messages are passed from parents to daughters, and how difficult this inheritance is to shake.

Candace was a Montgomery. Her old Virginia family traced its origins back to the early colonists, and lived in a crumbling estate that had once belonged to Thomas Jefferson. Neither of her parents worked for money. Her mother, a biochemist, was the first woman to earn a doctorate in her field from an Ivy League university, but she claimed that staying at home was a sacrifice that she made for her children.

> She was a great victim of the fifties. She said she couldn't bear missing us take our first steps, and so on, but she was always out doing errands and volunteering—the ladies' this and the women's that. And she was always bad-tempered and angry. She talked endlessly about how she'd sacrificed her own career to be a good mother. "My children are the most important thing in the world to me, and I don't care if they hate me, I'm going to bring them up right," she'd say. "Love is a four-letter word: W-O-R-K." Work-

ing hard! She was always working away, but I think her feelings of inferiority were overwhelming.

Candace's father was an art historian who had never fulfilled the promise of a luminous career. He had been working for years to finish an authoritative book on Giotto while curating the collection of the state museum, for which he received more of an honorary stipend than a living wage.

Every now and then Daddy would say, "I think I'll take a half year off and work on my book," and we all knew not to follow up on that. Nobody ever mentioned the book, and he never got anywhere as far as we knew. Nevertheless, we all thought my father was more gloriously smart than the critics who actually wrote all those books. Perhaps he wasn't as famous, but then, he didn't do the crass thing. Achievement was thought of as a little tacky. You had to be on the inside circle. He was a wonderful curator, and everyone respected him all the same.

How did Candace's family survive? On inherited money that her great-grandfather on her father's side had made in business. The succeeding generations, however, despised the family's source of income. Her grandfather had continued to operate the factory, but for "charitable" reasons—to keep local people employed during the Depression.

By the time he died there was so much money that it liberated his sons. My father didn't have to do anything for money, and he felt guilty about it.

With a guilty, underachieving father and an angry, economically powerless mother, Candace and her siblings got a confusing negative message about the value of money and how it should be earned and spent. Her parents professed that money signified "low values" and lived in a deceptive state of genteel poverty, which Candace wittily described like this:

My parents are quite upper class in terms of squalor. They never
fix anything. The place crumbles away and is filled with old trash.
They let their couch go for twenty years, and the cats scratch it
to bits, but they still think it's a grand old couch. It was very
oppressive to me.

Because money and material things were disdained as "worldly" or
"tacky," Candace was not encouraged to value them.

They didn't want us to think money was important to have. They
were small allowance givers, and I was always very badly dressed
in hand-me-downs. I was dying for a horse my whole life, and
when I finally got one, it was twenty-one years old and horribly
swaybacked. A year later, some colonel who had originally owned
it came and took it back. Why didn't they buy me a horse? They
could have afforded it! I didn't understand that they were trying
to keep my values intact, and instead took all this to mean that
I wasn't worth much. My father, however, never hesitated to
spend money on himself.

In order to keep her from acquiring another "worldly" value—a
sense of competence, known in the Montgomery mythology as "a
swelled head"—Candace was seldom praised for her achievements.
Because money, "like toilet training and sex was not an item you
discussed," her financial life plan was never mentioned.

We just assumed that life would take its happy course, whatever
that would be. They never pushed me into anything, or made any
suggestions. I took this to mean that they didn't really think I
could do anything. How they thought I was going to get by in the
world I'll never know, because by the time the family money
comes to me, they will already have spent it.

Growing up with a sense of worthlessness and impotence, throughout her childhood Candace was terrified that her parents might discover that she secretly held values of which they would not approve.

I always felt my needs were unworthy. For one thing, I liked boys. I felt I should have been reading Dante, but instead I was reading *Double Date.* My parents insisted on this upper level, and I grew up thinking my feelings were wrong, and hiding them. I worked very hard at presenting myself as a "correct Montgomery," but I was a pretend person.

No wonder Candace was bogged down in career confusion! She had grown up feeling like a "pretend person," but actually she had been part of a "pretend world," where an inability to work or make money had been reinterpreted to be a superior moral value. In the Montgomery family myth, fathers could be brilliant and respected without succeeding financially, and a mother, however impressive her education, could stay home from the marketplace and be worth more than if she had earnings.

Candace now criticizes her parents' values and jokes about her painful upbringing. However, the Montgomery myth was instilled in her at an early age. Though she can dismiss it intellectually, she has trouble separating from its powerful emotional influence. Because she inherited the family moneysquamishness without inheriting its money, she still struggles to realize that she needs to earn and feels her precarious financial state conceals invisible wealth.

I feel there is always something between me and the streets . . . that I am most fortunate in my wealth, and all I lack is the money. Work, for me, is just a little exercise to find out how real people live.

When we met Candace, she appeared to be floundering, but our interview revealed that she had achieved a great deal. She had managed to sever the tight strings of her childhood, and battling great psychological odds, had moved away from her family's inherited moneysquamishness. As she put it:

I've become a real person. I've been able to live in a reasonable, normal way, and by being fairly sound and sensible, I've gotten by.

To ensure her future as a "real person," Candace had married a "regular guy" who insisted that she earn, however reluctantly. Through him, she was learning to value her financial contribution and was proudly discovering that she was "good at business"—a low-class calling by Montgomery standards.

> I told the two guys who work for Richard that the place was under new management. From now on they report to me. I'm going to cost out the jobs and find out why Richard isn't making more money.

Later, Candace wrote to say that she was now charging her husband for her work in his office, which she found "enormously satisfying." She had applied for actual jobs, instead of pretending to apply, and had been delighted to be selected from hundreds of applicants for a personal interview for a good position editing educational textbooks. Candace was traveling further away from her family's imaginary world, where, unlike the world of our Puritan forefathers, hard-earned money was despised.

CHAPTER 3

Moneydenying

A moneydenier regards the need to earn money as a strictly temporary state of affairs, an imposition she must graciously bear until a generous man comes along and rescues her. The man may be a father (or another relative) who will leave her his fortune, or a fantasy employer, who will reward her talents with a glamorous, highly paid job. Most likely, however, the rescuer is a "handsome prince" from a modern fairy tale, who will marry her and happily absorb her financial burdens—or at least half of them.

Few moneydeniers will recognize themselves in this description because they imagine any woman who entertains such old-fashioned fantasies must be passive, uneducated, or uninterested in a career. The modern moneydenier, we have found, can be quite different than her description implies—an ambitious, dynamic, or fiercely independent woman who is not wholly aware that "rescue" is her financial plan. In fact, she fears being rescued because history, and perhaps her personal experience, have taught her that *rescue* spells *control*. Fifty-five percent of women who filled out the questionnaire for our money study answered "no" to the question, "Do you like the idea of being supported by someone else?" Thirty-one percent were ambivalent. They said that although they would enjoy not having to work for a living, they were afraid that support would come with "strings attached"—loss of independence, as well as the ability to make vital decisions.

Despite protestations to the contrary, a great many women are moneydeniers. Nothing about the way they plan their careers and manage their money indicates that they expect their financial responsibilities to go on forever. Though their personal, even their career identities, may be securely forged, their financial identities are still undefined. Their rescue fantasies are so deeply rooted in their psychosocial histories that they can live their financial lives as if these fantasies were going to come true, while remaining unaware of them. Sometimes the "handsome prince," inheritance, or magical career opportunity sneaks into a daydream, but most moneydeniers would be embarrassed to admit they were there. In fact, many moneydeniers remain blissfully unconscious that they lack a lifetime financial plan until their fantasies are challenged by dramatic changes in their life situation, or expectations that do not get fulfilled. At this point, they may become resentful and angry, not only at the circumstances that have pricked the bubble and brought about the painful new awareness, but also at the social forces that have duped them by not preparing them adequately for life. They may also feel furious with themselves for collaborating with a myth that is the basis for the economic lives of middle-class women— that if they remain needy and ladylike, someone will take care of them.

Most women enter the marketplace under the shroud of this myth. A conflicted personal and cultural history has prepared them to be career-oriented moneydeniers (a contradiction in terms) instead of the assertive wage earners with a realistic financial blueprint that they need to be. As we shall see, women who were not taught to develop their financial identities (the vast majority) often confuse emotional needs with financial ones, and are afraid that if they abandon their rescue fantasy, they will also abandon the possibility of love. This fear is often at the root of other symptoms of Moneyphobia.

The Two Kinds of Moneydeniers

There are two categories of women who deny the need to provide for themselves. The first, the *classic moneydenier*, expects a man to take care of her financially and sets out to find one who is willing to do so. These are the Southern Belles, Jewish Princesses, and Cinderellas, who have been unaltered by changing times. Though many exist, few classic moneydeniers strayed into our study, which was directed toward ambitious working women. One who did, a Massachusetts housewife, told us:

> I love being a "kept woman"! I was raised to believe that was the way it was. Man supported woman!

"Kept women" like this one may fall on hard times if their husbands divorce them or die and leave them impoverished. Like Scarlett O'Hara, they may find themselves digging for turnips in a frozen field. They have an important psychological advantage, however: They are clear about their needs and the way to meet them. We will not say more about the classic moneydenier because we doubt very many of them are reading this book!

The second type of moneydenier is more complex and less easy to detect. She is usually working, supporting herself, or carrying at least part of her weight in a marriage; but her financial behavior indicates she does not expect to be doing so for long. We call her a *postmodern moneydenier* because, like most of us, she is caught in a cross-cultural tide that is pulling her in two different directions—toward the future of women (a promising but frightening new territory) and back to the past. How can a postmodern moneydenier be identified?

Her main characteristic is that her financial biography is written entirely in the present tense. She may work very hard, dream of success, and even make money, but she lives hand-to-mouth. Generally, she is moneyblind and does not calculate the amount of money she needs or spends. Why should she? Her financial responsibilities, after all, are only temporary. She is also likely to be moneysqueamish in that she believes acting assertively to realize financial goals is tacky. But money itself? She loves it and would like to have a lot. While she waits for The Shower of Gold, she earns enough to meet her present needs and seldom feels anxious about money.

Many moneydeniers are ambivalent about career goals and may practice elaborate methods of moneyeluding. Some place boundaries on the amount they feel they can safely earn without jeopardizing the possibility of rescue. One self-aware instructional designer voiced her fears of earning "too much."

I am moderately successful financially, but if I let myself become very successful, then the mythical, wonderful man—the absent father—would never save me. I'd have to give up my fantasy.

Unlike non-Moneyphobic women, who see earning as an enjoyable, as well as necessary part of their lives, the moneydenier takes a rather grim view of supporting herself or her children. She regards income-producing as an unjust obligation she must endure for a limited time. For her, the strain of making money gets in the way of life.

Moneydeniers feel making money should be glamorous and exciting. A number of those we interviewed had two careers—one that supported them and another "dream" career, which they thought of as "real"—usually in the arts or an entertainment field. They saw their money-making career as tediously demeaning, and the dream career as fascinating and prestigious. In some cases, they had done little to actualize the "dream career," and in others, they had done quite a lot. Alice, for example, was a postmodern moneydenier, age thirty-four, who showed no savings or assets on her questionnaire. She had invested all of her hopes, extra time, and cash in a singing career that, after a number of years, had produced some moments of glory, but no living wage. Meanwhile, Alice worked at a "boring" job for a record company. Though she was respected by her employer and saw opportunities to advance, she preferred to ignore them, fantasizing that eventually she would earn $200,000 a year as a recording star, which she said she would give away and spend on clothes. She took great liberties with sick days and lunch hours to pursue her "real" career, secretly hoping the record company would fire her so she could collect unemployment insurance. When a new management took over the company and asked Alice to do a job she did not like, she quit, scraped together a few hundred dollars, and flew to Hawaii. What would she do when she came home? Alice shrugged, "Get another job, I suppose." If Alice did not imagine she would one day be rescued from the onus of self-support, she might have taken both her singing career and the job that produced income *equally* seriously. She would have seen that both were important, and both were real.

A moneydenier can also be detected by her spending habits. Since she believes her future finances will be taken care of by someone else, she binges, blows, and throws money away. No one is less likely to save, buy real estate, or invest than a moneydenier. She thinks IRA stands for "Irish Republican Army" and does not plan for retirement, because to do so would constitute an admission that she might end up alone, still self-supporting, in her (not so) golden years. When asked how she intends to take care of herself in the future, she answers that she will work until she dies—a noble, but possibly unrealistic aspiration. Meanwhile, she gathers her rosebuds while she may. Though she may suffer a financial crunch when she loses a job or overspends, deprivation does not inspire her to review her money *modus operandi.* In fact, moneydeniers like to seem a little needy; their need, after all, might prove to be bait for a wealthy Prince Charming.

Because the moneydenier hopes to be rescued (usually by a man), she can be overly concerned with her weight and appearance. No woman is as likely to subscribe unquestioningly to cultural prescriptions for ideal beauty and fashion as she. The moneydenier spends most of her discretionary income on clothes, makeup, and hairstyles, regarding these expenditures as necessary "investments." One moneydenying woman in our study called to say she thought our interview had helped her, and that we would be glad to hear she had decided to earn and save. The reason: She had realized that she would want to have at least one facelift when she got older and needed money in the bank to pay for it.

Though afflicted with a traditional definition of women's role, the moneydenier often appears rebellious and may lead her life in unorthodox ways. People view her as a "free spirit" because they do not see the traditional side that she scrupulously hides, even from herself. Because she both wants to be saved and fears the pound of flesh her rescuer may extract in return, she defends herself against her fantasy by doing everything in her power to make sure it does not come true. Ironically, no one fears rescue as much as these victims of conflict. Because of her fear, the moneydenier specializes in "inappropriate" non-rescuing men—dashing, handsome, neurotic "princes" who provide charm, intellectual stimulation, even thrilling sex, but who are either essentially unavailable for long-term relationships or who suffer from male versions of Moneyphobia and are poor themselves. Instead of seeing these love objects for what they are, and enjoying what they have to offer, however, the moneydenier tries to extract from them what they cannot give and feels furious or humiliated when she fails to get it. The more involved she becomes in these immediate emotions, the less she is able to examine the economic fantasy that underlies them and her conflict about the fantasy. And as she fails to get from men what she both wants and fears, her dream of a utopian form of rescue, which will not compromise her freedom, remains unchallenged. As we shall see, there are many reasons why a postmodern moneydenier would rather fantasize about rescue than actually get "saved."

Moneydeniers are often single or divorced, but they can be married, too. If a moneydenier chooses a mate who does not fulfill her rescue fantasies (a prince who is charming, but not ambitious or successful), she may feel betrayed by the myth. She becomes jealous of other women for whom the fairy tale came true, and angry at her husband. One of the married moneydeniers in our study worked until she started a family, as she was raised to believe a woman should do. Now that her children are of school age, she resents her husband, a dental technician, for not making as much money as her friends' husbands, and feels victimized because she has to take up the slack in the family budget with a part-time bookkeeping job.

My husband would rather live on less than take a chance in order to have more. Most of our friends have a great deal more money than we do. Their husbands are more ambitious (a trait I never learned to recognize until I was in my thirties). Our major money problem is lack of it. We simply don't have enough, and I feel he is waiting for me to bring in the extra money we need. I resent feeling that vacations and financial security are luxuries. I never thought my life would be this way.

This moneydenier blames her husband for waiting for her to take financial initiative. Actually, it is she who is waiting—for her husband to change from a frog to a prince—and her anger will not alter her financial situation.

Married moneydeniers (even those who work) can still dream of rescue if the family income is inadequate. They imagine that someone else—grandparents or the government—will pay for their children's college educations, or that an inheritance will bestow a country house and retirement funds.

In the course of our money study, we learned that a moneydenier makes herself known by her psychological resistance to the idea that she may be waiting for someone else to provide. Though women can easily recognize moneydenial in others, acknowledging the same symptoms in themselves is difficult and painful, because to do so is to admit that they are not as independent and modern as they seem. One of our New York money groups, psychologically sophisticated and intelligent women, became angry and confused when we presented them with the symptoms of moneydenial, and asked if they could relate them to their own life experience. At one point in our long description of moneydeniers, we had used the term *old-fashioned*. The women immediately picked this up and took violent exception: How could we use such a derogatory word? They hoped we wouldn't put it in our book! Without revealing why they found *old-fashioned* so personally threatening, they then proceeded to analyze the financial habits of their moneydenying friends and the difficult plight of modern women. Our discussion had obviously strayed on to dangerous ground, and our group members found it safer to generalize. After forty-five minutes of beating around the bush, these usually highly focused, self-aware women were finally able to approach the topic of rescue, although not from a financial viewpoint. Ann, divorced for five years, described the time the pipes had broken in her country home, and her feeling that she had been victimized by her husband when it fell to her to cope with the disaster because he was away.

> Though it was in no way his fault the pipes broke, I could never forgive my husband for that . . . for making me deal with the plumber! I felt it important that he take care of certain things and that they never fall on me . . . for what reason, I can't tell you.

Rebecca, who had left her husband, saw a dead cat she found under the porch the first weekend she was alone in her house as a symbol of all the new trials that faced her.

> I thought, What do I do with this dead cat? It seemed like an omen of my life alone. I went out and got a shovel, but when I so much as looked under the deck, I felt sick, as if I was going to faint. I pulled myself together and said, "This is a test of my life! I have to do this! How am I going to live alone if I can't?" Then I thought, How would Bob have taken care of this? and the answer was, He'd pay someone to do it. That's one of the things I've had to learn since I've been on my own . . . that you can pay someone to do something. I've always thought either I have to do it or someone else has to do it for me. I'd still rather have a guy who does it because he likes me.

Financial responsibilities (like the responsibility of fixing broken pipes and disposing of dead cats) are problems women look at from a different perspective once they begin to disabuse themselves of the rescue myth.

Taking charge of one's own financial future is the basis of any modern, independent life. Since women are not emotionally or practically trained for this job, they find it terrifying and intimidating. If they deny that their rescue fantasies exist, or let them lie unexplored, they can conduct their financial lives as they have in the past, without the stress of difficult changes. *The financial behavior the rescue fantasy inspires can also become a comfortable habit, which perpetuates itself even after the fantasy itself has been exposed to the light of reality and faded.*

How Women Become Moneydeniers

Some women do manage to escape the rescue fantasy and its paralyzing conflicts. But for most of us, our culture and personal backgrounds ensure that we begin our adult financial lives in the thrall of an outmoded myth, which promises us not only security, but happiness, for taking care of a man's emotional and domestic needs.

The rescue myth, in its purest form, is found in fairy tales, which still in various modern versions make their profound impressions on little girls today. The heroines of the most popular tales are all rescued by handsome princes and have special qualities that enable them to get saved.

First and foremost, the fairy tale heroine must be beautiful. Her beauty is often symbolized by one exceptional feature, which identifies her as having "royal blood," or entitlement. Snow White has remarkable coloring: She is as "white as snow, as red as blood and as black as ebony." Rapunzel's wealth lies in her tower-length hair, as "fine as spun gold," and Cinderella has tiny feet.

Though these selfless heroines are usually unaware of their beauty, it makes them the target of mixed emotions—love, hatred, envy, and possessiveness—and vulnerable to attack. Their beauty, it seems, is the outward manifestation of their only other salient quality—virtue, which is defined as total passivity. These heroines submit to whatever injustices their beauty foists upon them without complaint. In the original Grimm version of the story, at her sadistic stepmother's bidding, Cinderella obligingly picks bowls of lentils out of the ashes. Snow White, rescued from the forest by seven dwarfs, does their housework happily, despite her royal birth. These beauties have no inner life and few emotions, even for the handsome prince who rescues them. When Rapunzel lets down her golden hair and draws up a prince instead of the wicked old witch, she thinks only, "He will love me better than old Mother Gothel." Sleeping Beauty, awakened by her rescuer, is hardly inflamed by passion: She "looks lovingly at him." It is the princes who brave hardship to win their loves and feel all the emotions as part of the prize.

Before she is rescued, the fairy tale heroine's beauty and passive virtue condemn her to persecution and isolation. Sleeping Beauty pricks her finger on a needle, and because of an angry fairy's curse, falls into a deep sleep as a briar hedge covers her castle, closing her off from the world. Rapunzel is lonely in her tower, but when her wicked guardian discovers her lover, she is transported to an even more isolated spot—the wilderness. Snow White ends up in a glass coffin, where, even dead, she is good enough for her admiring prince, who sees no problem with her lifeless state.

Their obedient passivity and enchanted sleep immunize the virtuous beauties against the furious emotions and violence in the fairy tale's "real world." Sleeping Beauty's would-be rescuers are pierced to death by the briars that surround her castle; Rapunzel's lover is blinded by the jealous witch, and in the original "Cinderella," the wicked stepsisters slice off their toes and heels in order to cram their oversized feet into the tiny golden slipper, leaving "blood on the track."

Rescue, then, saves the innocent heroines from a deathlike state, which itself protects them from passions so dangerous to other people. What happens to these beauties after they have been rescued? We know only that they live "happily ever after," and that happiness seems to mean adoration and wealth.

HOW THE FAIRY TALE GETS INTO OUR LIVES

Several of the women we interviewed for this book referred to themselves as fairy tale heroines, or saw similarities between their lives and the lives of the mythical beauties. These stories could not have been etched so deeply in so many girls' minds had their prescription for the future—rescue by a man—not been advocated by the family and culture. Many daughters were raised to be rescued and taught that real life would begin once they were "saved."

Because beauty is an essential qualification for rescue, the parents of moneydeniers placed much importance on their daughters' appearance, giving them nice clothes, dancing lessons to improve posture and grace, music lessons, and even plastic surgery. Though, in this sense, they were often "spoiled," support for their intellectual abilities, assertiveness, and any talent not seen as typically feminine was simultaneously withheld. No moneydenier was ever told a man would love her because she was brilliant or successful. Instead, her family tried to shape her personality into the fairy tale mold, making her a "good girl," or passive, obedient, sweet, and attentive to others' needs.

Unlike the fairy tale princesses, however, modern daughters often rebelled, some more, some less. They either withdrew, secluding themselves in their rooms with a book, or practiced secret anarchy—drinking, taking drugs, and having sex with men who were scarcely princely by their parents' standards. One of the non-moneydenying women in our study, raised to be a classic Jewish Princess, found a unique way to rebel: She made money during summer vacations, even though her father offered to pay her not to work. Some girls got a heavier dose of the fairy tale treatment than others, but few completely escaped it.

The fairy tale vision of life was also incorporated into career plans. College was seen as a portal to a classier form of rescue than Mother's —a stomping ground for real princes, like lawyers and doctors. A career was not a pursuit thought essential to happiness and a woman's well-being but something to "fall back on." The best careers, then, were those that required a minimum of long-range planning, apprenticeship, or competition; they waited for the girl to "fall" with open arms in the event the rescue mechanism failed. One such "fallback" career was teaching. Teaching would not interfere with the prince's timetable or the family's domestic needs in the event the princess had to work after marriage. As the girl grew up, the popular culture—movies, soap operas, romance novels, popular songs ("Someone to Watch Over Me") —echoed the fairy tale theme. Adolescent social life made getting rescued a competitive sport with trophies like fraternity pins and engagement rings. And society, which then, more than now, excluded women from highly paid jobs, or erected unapproachable barriers between women and male-dominated careers, indicated that rescue was an economic necessity.

THE DARK SIDE OF THE FAIRY TALE

Most girls growing up in the forties, fifties, and early sixties, then, were spoonfed the rescue myth and some, who became classic moneydeniers, believed it, even lived it, until life opened their eyes to other possibilities. The conflicted postmodern moneydenier, however, was able to perceive the fairy tale's dark side, simply by observing her rescued mother. Middle-class mothers of previous generations were rescued by their husbands, and given the lack of opportunity available to women then, most had little choice. (Those who worked did not have jobs with salaries sufficiently adequate to support a family, which is also true of many working women today.)

In the fairy tale, the princess heroine is often sabotaged by a wicked stepmother, or witch—an angry, envious, frustrated female—distinguished from her real mother, who loves her and is concerned with her welfare, but who is dead, absent, or dozing in an enchanted sleep. *What the postmodern moneydenier saw when she looked at her mother was a woman who embodied the characteristics of both the wicked stepmother and the passive real mother.* These rescued mothers were not the emotionally satisfied queens, adored by their husbands, and living happily ever after, that the fairy tale described, but were frustrated, bored, and irritable, even envious of their daughters' opportunities. The least satisfied were depressed, in self-induced stupors, or isolated with tedious chores, like the fairy tale heroines *before* they were rescued. Listen to the women in one of our New York money groups, all the daughters of "rescued" women, describe the way they saw their mothers' lives:

Sarah: When I was a teenager I tried to figure out what she did all day. I couldn't. Our small apartment was cleaned by the time we left for school. How long can you food shop and prepare supper? The house was never spotlessly clean, but she was cleaning it all the time. There was a sense that she was helping my father in his business for a while, but I couldn't figure out what she was doing, because she didn't know how to do anything. She couldn't even handle a phone call.

Jane: My mother was depressed, and expressed suicidal tendencies since the age of eighteen. I don't know how she would have fared if she'd grown up in this era—if she could have held down a job. She's an alcoholic.

Myra: My mother is on medication for depression and also drinks. I think she drinks because she doesn't work. She's always incompetent until there's a crisis, and then my father falls apart and she handles everything. She really needs something to focus on. When she doesn't have it, she can't get out of bed.

Jane: My mother was like that, too!

Yet, it was depressed and powerless mothers like these, with their limited view of other options and their legitimate concern for their daughters' economic security, who proselytized the myth: Women who were supported by men, especially rich men, lived happily ever after. Some of these mothers gave their daughters mixed messages, urging them to fulfill their own frustrated fantasies of adventure and freedom before they got "saved." *Though the postmodern moneydenier rejected the lifestyle of her rescued mother, she was unable to discard the myth's less obvious, economic theme.* As a result, working women who have managed to design modern, independent lives, can still harbor the deep-seated belief that real happiness includes financial support, and if they have not been rescued, something has gone wrong.

Sarah, whose mother was the compulsive housecleaner, has been self-supporting since age twenty-two. Now, at thirty-nine, she still feels the power of the rescue myth when she talks to her mother:

> Before Mom hangs up she says in this very sad voice, "I pray that this will be a better year for you, and that you'll meet somebody and won't have to work so hard!" I say, "What? Am I dying? What's going on here?" Her assumption is that I can't be happy if I'm by myself and have to work every day, and it makes me sick to my stomach. And yet, there's a part of me that connects to what she's saying, because that's my fantasy, too.

THE WITHHOLDING FATHER-PRINCE

Postmodern moneydeniers tended to be "spoiled." Some moneydeniers, however, were deprived by parents whose inconsistent material support symbolized inconsistent affection. The fathers of these women were unable to give to their daughters because they suffered from unresolved emotional conflicts. Women who have been deprived in this way, in the course of their personal development, may come to see money as a symbol of the love they were denied. They may become enmeshed in a psychological Catch-22 that makes it impossible for them to take care of their needs (or to find someone who will) because they continue to want them to be taken care of by their fathers. These victims of early deprivation often have what other writers have called "a poverty mentality." Ironically, the more withholding the father-prince, the more terrifying and difficult it is for the daughter to separate from him. Said one very low-earner whose wealthy, sadistic father refused to give her even a birthday present:

> Whenever I think of not seeing my father anymore, or even of not thinking about him much, I get a physical reaction . . . I shake!

Millions of women in our culture had fathers who were emotionally withholding or rescued mothers who proselytized the myth, or both. For them, financial and emotional needs have gotten confused. Financial rescue has come to represent love and emotional support, and vice versa. The moneydenier believes that she can not have one without the other. In her mind, the potential rescuer *also* associates financial support with love. (And it is true that many men have not been taught how to give to women in any other way.) She believes that if she takes care of her financial needs herself, she will no longer appear to need love any more than she needs money. She imagines that economic success will frighten potential rescuers away. As a result, a lifetime of earning her own money can signify Rapunzel's isolated wilderness, the glass coffin of a lifeless Snow White, or the thankless toil of a Cinderella, forced to pick lentils out of the hearth.

The Perils of Rescue

Historically, rescue has not been synonymous with "living happily ever after," as the fairy tale claims. Under English common law, introduced to this country in Colonial times, women lost both legal and property rights as soon as they married. Once she was wed, a woman became a piece of property herself, a legal ward of her husband, called a *femme couverte*. Under law, a married couple was regarded as one person—the husband. Though a single woman could own property and money, bring suit, make contracts, and secure deeds, a married woman could not. If she worked, her wages could be garnisheed by her husband, even if they were no longer living together, and she could not buy or sell anything without his permission. Her clothes, household goods, even her children, were legally his, as were her dowry and inheritance, which he was within his rights to gamble or squander. When a husband died, his property passed to his heirs, and although his widow could make use of a third of his estate as long as she lived, she could not will it to anyone else. The Colonial wife did command the right to be supported, but as she was a legal non-person, she had no redress if her husband failed her. The law also declined to specify a reasonable amount of support and never questioned the husband's judgment.

Equity laws provided exceptions to these generally harsh rules, allowing married women to own and control property in extenuating circumstances, such as when the husband abandoned his family and ran up debts. Wealthy fathers could insist on premarital contracts that protected their daughters' inheritance from debt-ridden husbands, and equitable trusts provided married women with untouchable family gifts. These agreements, however, were mainly available to wealthy women, and they had to be made before, not after the husband had wasted his wife's fortune. No wonder early feminists like Susan B. Anthony made property rights the first issue of their spirited campaigns!

A woman lost more than property rights with marriage. Legally she could not choose her own home, was obligated to perform domestic services and to accept her husband's sexual advances. (He, in return, was forbidden to beat her, though if he did, she had no legal means of stopping him.) Marriage, under law, was a patriarchy: The husband had the authority and power, and his wife was commanded to obey. Both were bound to each other until death did them part; in the event that they separated, divorce was not allowed and neither could remarry. Though then, as now, married couples may have had personal agreements that were more equitable than the law, they never would have held up in court. By the beginning of the nineteenth century, women's property acts had been enacted, but the patriarchal legal view of marital property had not changed substantially. Even today, disputes over a divorcing couple's property are usually resolved in favor of the husband, and women have difficulty forcing estranged partners to pay child support.

THE EMOTIONAL COMPLICATIONS

For modern women, however, the emotional complications of rescue can prove to be the fairy tale's unhappy ending. As many discover, economic and emotional power are inextricably combined. Philip Blumstein and Pepper Schwartz, authors of *American Couples: Money, Work, Sex*, found that in three out of four of the 12,000 relationships they studied, the partner who earned more had the most influence in any decision-making process. This was true of married couples, cohabiting couples, and male homosexual couples. (Only lesbian couples shared power equitably, regardless of who earned the most.)

The women in our money study learned that economic dependency deprived them not only of decision-making power but also of valued autonomy and a sense of self. Some reported that a husband's support had made them feel worthless or incompetent, and diminished their ability to make economic decisions that created a feeling of mastery and well-being. As they lost economic bargaining power, they lost control over their lives. Even for happily married women, dependency jeopardized their emotional stability if their sense of self-worth had been based on career achievement.

A husband's support rang the death knell for one troubled marriage. Ann, who had supported her husband in their early years together, found herself unable to pursue her career when he got a high-salary job in a suburban area. When he was finally in a position to rescue her, as a fairy tale husband should, difficulties that had plagued their marriage became insupportable to her, and she left him.

I didn't realize all those years that he was a very controlling person. I could never enjoy being supported. There was too big a price on it for me. Whenever I asked him for something specific that would make life in the suburbs work for me, like a full-time housekeeper, so that I wouldn't have to make complicated arrangements every time I wanted to go to the city to do something, he'd say, "Absolutely not. Out of the question!"

Rebecca, a forty-three-year-old college instructor, left her husband when he refused to spend money to relieve her depression:

Whenever someone asks, "Why did you leave?" this is why. I had just learned my father was terminally ill, when I found myself pregnant with my second child. My husband was clear about wanting this baby and said he would do everything to help me take care of it. I was ambivalent, but I had the child, and when he was a few months old, I felt I really couldn't cope. I had one young child and an infant. My father had died. My husband was doing his workaholic thing and wasn't there. I felt really abandoned. One night we were sitting at the kitchen table, and suddenly I put my head down. I said, "I can't deal with this anymore. I don't know what to do. . . . Maybe I should go into therapy, or we could get someone to take care of the baby." And do you know what he did? He got out his calculator. That year he was making $140,000 —the most he'd ever made. He said, "My business is doing well this year, but I don't know how it will do next year, so we have to live as if I was making only $40,000 and save the rest." I was so blown away. I think that was the one time I'd ever asked him for help; we both thought I was the strong one emotionally. I said to myself, "All's fair now. I don't owe this man anything." I also felt that I never wanted to be in that position again—asking a man to take care of my basic needs.

The Moneydenier's Shrinking World

Rescue, then, can threaten an achievement-minded woman's emotional stability; but moneydeniers, who do not get rescued, face different kinds of emotional trials. Those who persist in living their financial lives in the present may find, as the years progress, that lack of money becomes as controlling a taskmaster as a Colonial husband. As Maggie the Cat in Tennessee Williams's play *Cat on a Hot Tin Roof* put it, "You can be young without money, but you can't be old without it."

The millions of older women (one out of five) who live in poverty testify to the apparent uncertainty of rescue and the need for women to recognize their financial responsibilities and provide for themselves. When women imagine a poverty-stricken old age, they tend to focus on the dramatic image of the bag lady, with her cardboard house on the freezing street and her diet of garbage. However, there are relative degrees of poverty, and not all women who fail to take care of their financial futures end up without homes. A moneydenier whose rescuer does not arrive may have enough to eat and a roof over her head, but she may lack freedom of movement and an expanding lifestyle. The options that would make her later years fulfilling—like enjoyable vacations and country homes—are constricted without money. A career that has not been planned with financial growth in mind, too, can become stultifying with time, because in this economy, financial growth tends to reflect new professional challenges and peer respect. The postmodern moneydenier, who believes that freedom and achievement are essential ingredients of happiness, and who would like to live imaginatively as well as securely, will find her shrinking world especially demoralizing.

JEAN RHYS'S HEROINES: THE SAD FATE OF A CLASSIC MONEYDENIER

Nowhere is the plight of a moneydenier who doesn't change better illustrated than in the novels of Jean Rhys, a contemporary British writer who enjoyed critical acclaim and financial reward only in her later years. Rhys's *Voyage in the Dark*, *Quartet*, *After Leaving Mr. Mackenzie*, and *Good Morning, Midnight* can be read together as a modern morality play, showing the progress of a classic moneydenier from youth to old age. They are based on the author's own life, which was troubled by poverty when husbands died and lovers abandoned her.

In each of the four novels, the main character is a woman with no particular ambition or life plan (unlike Rhys herself, who became a writer, though more by accident than intention). Rhys's heroine sometimes has a job but places no value on it, or resists the attempts of well-meaning friends to interest her in employment. What is important to each of Rhys's women is a man who marries her, or involves her in a traumatic love affair, gives her some money, then leaves her flat. The character then finds herself living in a seedy hotel, where she gets sick or sleeps a lot, leaving only to get drunk in dismal cafes. She thinks bitter thoughts about her victimization, yet longs for the man who has deserted her.

Money plays a big role in all of Rhys's novels by its conspicuous and much-felt absence in the characters' lives. Her heroines are always flat broke, and when they do get a little cash, it is because it has been given to them by a man who ultimately degrades them. They rapidly spend it on clothes or other creature comforts, and are penniless again. When she is presented with eight pounds by the married man who eventually seduces her, the homesick young girl in *Voyage in the Dark* describes the lure, the power, and the evanescence of money for the moneydenier, who feels financial security is out of her hands:

> I took the money from under my pillow and put it in my handbag.
> I was accustomed to it already. It was as if I had always had it.
> Money ought to be everybody's. It ought to be like water. You can
> tell that because you get accustomed to it so quickly. . . . "Will
> you lay a fire in my room please?" I said. My voice sounded round
> and full instead of small and thin. "That's because of the money,"
> I thought.[1]

In each Rhys novel, the moneydenying women get older, and as they do, their poverty, lack of vitality, dreary living conditions, and negative emotional states become more depressing to the reader as well as to themselves. Young or old, they always seem to feel hopeless, and whatever hope they cherish lies outside themselves, in the hands of men. When the aging woman in *Good Morning, Midnight* is finally rescued by a minimal inheritance, the security she has longed for does not make her feel happy, but even more confined, because she has never developed a real identity.

> Well, that was the end of me, the real end. Two pound ten every
> Tuesday and a room off the Gray's Inn Road. Saved, rescued and
> with my place to hide in—what more did I want? I crept in and
> hid. The lid of the coffin shut.[2]

Isolated and disillusioned, her one pleasure is compulsive shopping, which, when combined with alcohol, produces a narcotic oblivion.

> Tomorrow I'll go to the Galeries Lafayette, choose a dress, go along to the Printemps, buy gloves, buy scent, buy lipstick, buy things costing fcs. 6.25 and fcs. 19.50, buy anything cheap. Just the sensation of spending, that's the point. . . . And when I have had a couple of drinks I shan't know whether it's yesterday, today, or tomorrow.[3]

Most of us bear little external resemblance to these wretched but honest anti-heroines; yet Rhys's novels make painful reading because, inwardly, we cannot help identifying with them. Every modern woman has, at some time, been overwhelmed by feelings of passivity, dependency, hopelessness, and isolation (given our collective history, it could not be otherwise), only to emerge from her "Voyage in the Dark" with a stronger sense of self. Too many strong, self-realized women, however, have not developed a financial identity, and like Jean Rhys's classic moneydeniers, hold fate responsible for their economic futures.

Overcoming the Paralysis of Conflict

The postmodern moneydenier, unlike the classic version, has equipped herself with the skills to earn a living, but nothing in her psychological or cultural history has equipped her to imagine taking care of herself for the rest of her life. Neither rescued nor freed from her rescue fantasy, she can become financially paralyzed. Although her relationship with money has not worked out as planned, she is unable to take decisive steps to change it. Often she becomes moneyblind in order to sidestep the fears that thoughts of her financial future inspire, and concentrates her energies on finding love. She may make bold life decisions, without taking their financial consequences into account, and end up feeling cheated.

Sylvia, a clinical psychologist, decided to have a child alone in her middle thirties. She describes the feeling of power this radical decision gave her.

I thought, I can really do this on my own. No one can stop me from having a baby, even if the man doesn't want to be involved. I saw it as an act coming out of my increasing strength, and I felt very powerful, and different about myself in a lot of ways.

Sylvia gave birth to a baby boy and used the money she had saved to do postgraduate work in her field to pay a baby-sitter when she returned to her job. When her son was a toddler, however, she suddenly realized that she had never counted on bearing the financial responsibility of childraising alone.

I started feeling that, in some way, I had been had. I had experienced my freedom, and I was glad that I did, because I have my son. But the other side of the coin is that it was a very masochistic thing to do. Nobody told me that I was going to be totally exhausted and feel like I'd aged fifteen years in three. What's this empty pocketbook here? I realized my fantasy was that I would do this on my own for a couple of years, and, at some point, I would be meeting somebody . . . that this was not going to be a forever kind of thing, and it would be easier once there were two salaries. I thought it would be temporary. Part of the disappointment has been that it has not been that easy to connect to somebody in that kind of way, and though I feel optimistic that it will happen, I realize that it might be that I'll go through the rest of my life unmarried, or living alone.

As Sylvia questioned her rescue fantasy, her financial future seemed terrifying:

The idea that I'll always be as strapped as I am now is scary. I don't have any savings, stocks, or bonds—only a pension. Virtually nothing! This is part of my anxiety. I never thought I'd be forty-one and still living for the time when it's going to get better. Because this is when it *should* be better. *How* is it going to get better? I need more and more money for the kid at this point because he needs different kinds of things than he did when he was a baby.

I can't afford to send him to private school. What am I going to do about college? It's unbearable for me to deprive him in any way.

Sylvia's anxiety is painful, but not as negative as it feels. Acknowledging, then questioning her rescue fantasy, is the first step out of the moneydenier's shrinking world. She can now become moneysighted, calculate her needs, and attach a price tag to them. She is in the psychological position to create a realistic, future-oriented financial plan and look at possibilities for expanding her own income. As a moneydenier she watched and waited, at the mercy of a psychic red light; as she becomes more moneyaffirming, she can give herself permission to move ahead.

As women give up their rescue fantasies, they may at first feel angry, frightened, and hopeless, as Sylvia did. However, once they face their financial reality and act accordingly, their lives can change in positive ways. Women who become moneyaffirming find that their feelings about both love and work are different than before. When income-producing is no longer seen as a temporary enslavement, women look for ways to introduce new challenges into their careers. Even if their jobs cannot become "glamorous" or "exciting," they accept their limitations and may develop intriguing outside interests. When the sense of injustice at "having to work" is eliminated, job stress can lessen, leaving more vital energy for other aspects of life. If a woman has two careers—one that produces income and another that reflects her true vocation—she may find that she resents the salaried job less and regards both careers as "real."

When the moneydenier develops a financial identity, she begins to see her financial and emotional needs as separate problems, requiring separate solutions. Once she accepts the responsibility of rescuing herself, she can acknowledge a different kind of man than those who formerly attracted her. Barbara Walters, the successful television interviewer who recently married for the second time after thirteen years of single life, theorized:

I think when you have an independent life and can support yourself, your reason for marriage becomes different. You really want to be with this person, and you don't get married for security or position. You just want to be with that person.

A man whom it is possible to *be* with eliminates two kinds: (1) the inappropriate rescuer, who wants to control the lives of autonomy-loving women; and (2) the unavailable handsome prince. Moneydeniers, who express rescue conflicts by trying to extract from these transient charmers what they cannot give, may find that such men lose their magnetic appeal once they become more moneyaffirming themselves.

A MINI MONEYAFFIRMING ROMANCE: HOW CLAIRE CONQUERED THE MYTH OF THE HANDSOME PRINCE

We chose Claire as our case history for this chapter because she had the modern equivalent of a handsome prince in her life, who made it easier for her to recognize and question her rescue fantasy. "Jorge," a world-famous Brazilian soccer player, was not only tall, dark, handsome, and famous, but also exceedingly rich. His father, known in Brazil as the "Sheik of Alcohol," had made a fortune processing sugarcane into ethanol, a petroleum substitute widely used in Brazilian cars.

Though the handsome prince was real, his role in Claire's life was strictly fairy tale. She had been dating Jorge for five years, but only when he visited New York, once or twice a year. The rest of the time the prince was kicking soccer balls around the world or relaxing in one of his father's fabulous mansions in Cannes, London, Bahia, or Martinique. When Jorge jet-setted into town, however, their affair was the stuff romance novels are made of. He squired her to three-star restaurants, to the opera, theater, and glamorous parties, where Claire met other celebrities. Not only was their romance full of excitement, but tenderness, intimacy, and deep communication heightened their passionate hours in bed. No wonder Claire was head over heels! But the intimate passion, as well as the fun, was as fleeting as one of Sleeping Beauty's dreams. The peripatetic prince flew off again, and Claire seldom heard from him until he returned, months later. He never invited her to join him in Rio or Cannes (though money for a ticket would have been no object), bought her gifts, or suggested that they spend more time together. Yet Claire fantasized that the prince was merely afraid of "commitment," and once he trusted her, would be "capable of giving." She hoped to marry Jorge eventually.

> It's not so much a fantasy of him taking care of me, but to live with him and have his baby. It's a romantic fantasy more than a financial one.

As we pointed out to Claire, a romantic fantasy about the son of one of the richest men in Western civilization is, by definition, a financial fantasy.

In between Jorge's visits, Claire lived the typical life of a moneydenier. Though she was extremely bright and a talented set designer, this tall, shapely brunette boasted only modest professional achievements and did not have a penny in the bank. She lived hand-to-mouth, charging luxuries on credit cards. On her questionnaire she told us she thought of herself as a "survivor, who lived on the edge," and did not plan for retirement because she was certain that "the world will be destroyed by a nuclear bomb" before she was sixty-five.

> I'm not somebody who thinks about the future much. I live in the here and now.

Since most of her original set designs had been done for off-off Broadway productions, her vocation had not produced a living wage. Claire felt she had the ability, but lacked the motivation to develop her concepts and the necessary confidence to approach uptown producers. For money, she had a Cinderella-like job: office work for a philanthropic organization, which paid her enough to "survive." The simpleminded tasks she did there, she told us, did not interfere with either her real or fantasy life, and she could daydream while she worked, take time off to "run around the streets," and write in her journal.

> My big boss told someone I was writing a pornographic novel.

Her present-oriented life was enjoyably carefree, but like many moneydeniers, Claire, now thirty-three, was beginning to feel paralyzed and deprived. She questioned her lack of career motivation and her lack of love. Although men pursued her, she rarely dated anyone but her fly-by-night prince.

> In April I said, man, my life is zero, it's totally unsatisfying, and I have to find fulfillment, because I am not happy. I think a big part of my problem has been not allowing myself to want anything but meager stuff. I'm starting to feel more worthy of material things, and other things too.

She had also begun to envy women friends who were more successful than she was, and had trouble relating to them:

> I think, Now where did I miss the fucking boat? What is wrong with me? Here's this woman, no brighter than I am, and not better looking. . . . What's my problem? How come I can't push? How come I can't hustle? How come I can't get out there and sell myself? What's wrong with me?

To learn where Claire had missed the boat, we went back to her early years and looked at the way her family had transmitted the moneydenying message. Claire is the daughter of first-generation, middle-class Jewish parents. Her father, not particularly ambitious, had dropped out of college and taken over his father's plumbing supply business in Brooklyn. Claire's mother worked as a secretary before marriage, and occasionally after her children were grown; she now helped her husband in his office without getting paid. As a child, Claire was spoiled, though her parents were far from wealthy. Like the fairy tale heroine, she was rewarded for *being* rather than for *doing*.

> I got an allowance just for being cute. Just for living. Just for being their daughter. If I did something extra, I'd get paid for it. I could always get money from them.

Cash came easily to Claire, but she got no information about family finances.

> Everything about money was a big secret in my family. I used to embarrass the shit out of my mother by making announcements at family gatherings like, "I haven't filed a tax return in four years." Afterwards, she would say, "Why do you have to tell everyone your business?"

Claire's mother, a rescued woman, taught her that she could expect to be rescued as well. A career was "just in case."

> I have this vivid recollection of being on the bus, coming back from shopping. When we'd pass Brooklyn College, my mother would always say, "There's Brooklyn College! You're going to go there and become a teacher so you'll have something to fall back on." I knew the message was that I was going to get married, preferably to someone who could support me. The career was just in case. God forbid! You should live and be vell, dahlink! I did go to Brooklyn College, but I majored in drama and art and never took a single education course.

Like many modern women, Claire rejected what her mother stood for, and began waging a full-scale rebellion in her teenaged years.

> I see my mother as someone who has to keep total control over her environment. The byword was caution. Don't take risks! Keep everything pure and safe! And be careful! She praised and rewarded me when I conformed to her notion of how I should behave. But when I did something I wanted to do, even something small—like wearing an outfit that expressed my personality—she came down on me with incredibly harsh criticism. I realize now she never showed any confidence in my ability to achieve anything —however modest the goal.

Claire thought her "survival" depended on her escape from this restrictive environment:

> The overpowering thing I felt was, I have to get away from *this!* Because *this* is a bore! If I have only one life to live, I don't want it to resemble *this*. I rejected the unsatisfying and oppressive world I came from and survived in a place I defined as my freedom.

The unsatisfying *this* that Claire rejected, we believe, was not only her childhood world, but her mother's life. Mothers tend to see their daughters as extensions of themselves, and pressure them to reflect their lifestyles and embody their dreams as well as their fears. The daughter, attached to her mother, finds it hard to resist these pressures or to see them for what they are. Unbeknownst to Claire, her security-conscious mother had fantasies of a freer, more exciting life than her own conservative upbringing had allowed her to enjoy. As a result, she gave her daughter a double message: While she emphasized safety and caution, restricting her in the family context, she also gave her the freedom to move away. When Claire believed she was rebelling, she was actually living out her mother's secret fantasies. When she was seventeen, Claire worked as a waitress at a resort.

> I was one of the only waitresses at the resort who was Jewish. My mother didn't love it, she hated it, in fact, and if she'd known the details she really would have hated it. It was a wild scene, and it was the first time I'd been unsupervised away from home. I was nuts . . . crazy . . . cavorting!

We thought it odd that a repressive mother like Claire's would allow her rebellious teenaged daughter, still living at home, to do things other Jewish mothers would not let their daughters do.

> Funny, as crazy and cautious as she is, she was cool about it. I guess I had to ask her permission, and she gave it to me. There was some story about her bumping into a friend of mine's mother, who asked, "How could you let Claire go off to the mountains? It's wild

up there!" And my mother said, "I trust my daughter!" Which
gave me no end of amusement, lunatic that I was.

The next summer, Claire used the money she had made as a waitress
to travel to Europe, which her mother also "allowed." In her twenties,
living a bohemian life in New York's East Village, she continued to
receive mixed messages from home.

When I got a job working for the City they were thrilled to death.
Security! They bought me a TV, they were so happy I had a
normal job. . . . They thought at last I was going to buckle down
and fly right. My mother, a big Hadassah lady, had wanted me to
go to Israel earlier on. Later, I got tired of doing nothing on the
Lower East Side, and I'd heard there were cute guys on the
kibbutz, so I decided to go. She said, "No, you shouldn't go. You
have a good job now, and security." I said, "Well, if you don't give
me the money to go to Israel, I'm going to live on a commune in
Colorado." So of course she gave me the money, and I went.

Today, the messages from home still contradict themselves. Claire's
mother enjoys hearing about her romance with the prince, but would
really like her to marry a doctor. She expresses little interest in her
daughter's set-designing career, yet advises her to become a female
executive.

After a whole childhood of saying, "Be a teacher," this year she
said, "You're so smart. You look so good. You're so capable. Why
don't you become an executive and earn fifty thousand dollars a
year?" and I said, "Right!" At this point she would love to see me
having visibility in the world and earning lots of money, but I'm
more interested in being a character in the underground limelight.
In being who I am.

This mother's unrealistic career advice to her daughter seems to express
the content of her own fantasy life—her unrealized desires for recognition and visibility.

As Claire struggled to integrate the messages she got from her mother with her own definition of a satisfying life, she became confused, partly because the messages were confusing. She became a "character": She was "wild"; she refused to become a teacher or marry a man who would support her. Claire believes she is still rebelling by "living on the edge" financially, instead of developing a secure, future-oriented career and opening a bank account. In fact, she is not. Financially, her "underground limelight" is merely an extension of her mother's world, not because it is "secure," but because it is restrictive and stultifying. For Claire, "living on the edge" is another way of "playing it safe." Let us listen carefully as she describes the limitations of her financial life:

> I realize that I have no bank account and no security, but *within that framework* I can stay in the position of *not really having to change my life too much.* I can maintain my *little status quo* and enjoy myself. I do realize that I can't piss away a paycheck, and that I have to keep up with my bills. *Basically I'm not going to live beyond my means.* But when I'm with friends who have more, I always have this feeling, *Oh, God, I'm a little person without any money.*

Claire's profile of her financial identity emphasizes her smallness and her inability to move freely. She stays within a "limited framework," which does not allow her to change. She does not "live beyond her means" or expand. In effect, she has put herself in a kind of prison. Financially she accepts the very restrictions and limitations she has spent her life rejecting in other ways. How does her fantasy of marriage to the handsome prince fit in?

Claire still hopes for the rescue she was raised to expect:

> I've never been taken care of by a man after my daddy, never, so I can't imagine it happening, and yet I know it is my fantasy.

She feels conflicted about her rescue fantasy, however, because for her, being taken care of symbolizes her mother's powerless existence. She expresses this conflict by being in love with an unavailable rescuer— a prince who both promises and withholds a concept of rescue, more glorious than her mother's wildest dreams, with no financial or social limitations. Meanwhile, the real rescuer is still her family, from whom she has not yet separated. We asked Claire what would happen if she got sick, had no money in the bank, and could not work.

> I'd probably have to ask my parents for a loan. I mean, they're not rich, and I'd hate to have to ask them . . . but they wouldn't let me get thrown out of my apartment.

Claire could begin to sever the tie that still bound her to her mother's world, then, by examining her rescue fantasy.

When we interviewed her, the emotional confinement she was beginning to feel was making her question her financial behavior. New events were also helping to stir up the winds of change. The philanthropic organization was cutting back, due to lack of funding, and Claire was about to look for another job. This prospect made her extremely anxious. Anxiety was positive, however, because it stimulated her to act, create solutions, and develop new skills. She decided to train for a position as a makeup artist for a large cosmetics company. Since the new job would pay commissions on sales, it would enable her to make more money than before, while giving her time to pursue her set-designing career. Freeing herself from her paralysis, however, involved questioning the fantasy that had inspired it.

> I thought, Makeup artist! Me! Claire Marion Eckstein! I'm destined for bigger things! It's okay that I was sitting there in that pigsty of an office, doing nothing half the time—that was okay, because it wasn't real. I mean, it wasn't any kind of commitment. But to actually go and learn this new skill . . . it seemed like I was going to become just another automaton, and it was like acknowledging all my fantasies—and they were fantasies—of something fabulous happening in my life would be negated by my learning to be a makeup artist.

The "something fabulous" that would be negated by making a serious commitment to earn more money was a glamorous rescue by the handsome prince.

Unlike many deniers who cherish vague or unacknowledged rescue dreams, Claire had a real prince to put to the test. About this time, Jorge conveniently blew into town. Instead of accepting the "little status quo" and imagining that Jorge would one day offer more, Claire was assertive. She decided she had to "make something happen, or get out of it, and not be in love anymore." She expressed her dissatisfaction with their present relationship and asked Jorge directly if he had ever considered having a child with her. The prince said he was not ready, and answered, "Maybe in five or ten years." Though Jorge's answer was not encouraging, once she had actually asked him if he planned to rescue her, rescue seemed more of a real possibility, and Claire became aware of her conflict. Was marriage to a jet-setting soccer star and motherhood really what she wanted? She wondered what her day-to-day life would be like when she was living "happily ever after."

He would be doing what he does, but I haven't figured out what I would be doing. I would be someone's wife; what would be expected of me? It became a concern. I mean, it didn't really make sense, or jive with anything I feel right about to be taken care of by a man, although I do think I could easily adjust to having lots of money. I caught myself thinking that maybe I could be a makeup artist in Rio or Cannes! If I became a mother, I suppose there would be a governess; but what if he didn't want a governess? I'd suddenly be saddled with a child!

Months after our interview, we checked in with Claire. She was working hard as a makeup artist, earning good money, and planning her first vacation in years. Jorge, who had apparently become uncomfortable with the more assertive Claire (or with her fantasy), had changed from a prince into Peter Pan and vanished.

Claire still had a long way to go to develop a future-oriented financial identity: She had yet to balance her new income-producing job with the set-designing career that gave her a sense of self-worth and satisfaction. She had not saved any money. We felt she still did not see the necessity to support herself as a permanent obligation. She had not yet become interested in the kind of man with whom she might share her financial future. She had, however, taken the first important step away from the passive fantasyland of a moneydenier. She told us:

> I've always thought something wonderful would happen to me automatically, without my doing anything, and I would be rich and lead a wonderful life. Jorge was not really the cause of that fantasy, but only part of it. Now I know that if good things happen, it will be because I worked to get them.

CHAPTER 4

Moneyeluding

The moneyblind, the moneysqueamish, and the moneydenying have defense systems that protect them from worrying much about money. When a woman emerges from these self-deceiving states she becomes anxious, and her anxieties focus on her present financial situation and lack of earning power. Why isn't she making more money? Other women, no more intelligent or competent, are earning megabucks. Why can't she extract herself from her dead-end job and look for a high-salary position? Once anxious, she is likely to become paralyzed. When she takes a step in the dollar-producing direction, she feels overwhelmed by confusion and self-doubts and does nothing instead. She may see herself as "lazy" or "undisciplined" and encourage others to view her that way, too. She fritters away potential earning time with social activities, volunteer work, or compulsive shopping, when she needs more income and values professional achievement. She may get bogged down for months, even years, by agonizing choices: Should she get an MBA or have a baby? What kind of job would be right for her? To the casual observer, she seems to be awaiting Divine Inspiration. Every job has disadvantages, or might be perfect under different circumstances, at another time, or in a better place. At this point, she becomes what we call a moneyeluder. She rationalizes her "laziness" or confusion in sophisticated ways that make sense to her, but not to a more objective listener. On the job, she may have trouble performing to her own or her employer's satisfaction. If her anxieties become overwhelming, the nervous moneyeluder will retreat back to being more comfortably moneyblind, moneysqueamish, and moneydenying.

Often the moneyeluder's anxieties do not focus on money but on herself. She may attribute her inability to earn to a general complaint —low self-esteem—and invoke pop psychology formulas to explain her failures: Like many women, she is afraid of "risk" or "success." Once she has found a convenient explanation, however, she tends to dismiss the problem. Even if she appears successful to others, the moneyeluder may not be successful enough to please herself. What is holding her back from becoming a high roller? She is conscious that she has placed boundaries on the amount of money she feels she can earn, but she does not know when and how they got erected, or how to tear them down.

Moneyeluders view all financial problems as earning problems and avoid investigating other reasons for personal economic difficulties, such as undeveloped money management or investment skills. We have found that women with this symptom of Moneyphobia seldom attach a specific price tag to their financial fantasies; they may simply want to earn "more" without having defined exactly how much "more" is, or even why they want to earn it. Some told us that $50,000 represented a "respectable" salary in the moneyhungry eighties. The moneyeluder also tends to blame herself for all her earning problems, without taking the hostility of the marketplace into account. She may bemoan the low-paying nature of her profession and call it "unfair," without considering that almost all professions (except some of the newer ones, like the computer sciences) pay women less than they do men.

So far, we have avoided a charged term like *sexism*, because we did not want to introduce a buzzword that would give our readers preconceived notions of what our book is about, or a way to dismiss what we are saying, because they would associate our ideas with ideas they had rejected for other reasons. In a discussion about women's earning problems, however, *sexism* is an unavoidable word. Women are still victims of institutionalized discrimination, earning between 60 and 65 cents for every dollar earned by a man—a figure that has not changed in thirty years, despite the influx of women into the work force and into male-dominated professions. Women born between 1946 and 1964—

the baby boom generation that spawned the "yuppie" we read so much about—represent a less prosperous group than market research indicates: The majority, 63.7 percent, earn less than $10,000 a year and only 0.3 percent earn $50,000 a year and over.[1] True, women are earning more money than they ever have. In 1984 more than 5.5 million had incomes of $25,000 and over; in 1970 the figure was 719,000. How does this compare to the money made by men? Almost 24 million had incomes over $25,000 in 1984.

Despite these revealing statistics, middle-class women in our study did not see their earning problems as part of a social pattern with an underlying political cause. They took them personally. When we asked the members of our New York money group why they thought they were solely responsible for their inability to earn larger incomes, one perceptively replied:

> When I think about the aspects of life that are out of my control —the nature of the market and social pressure—it makes me too angry. It's so enraging! And the reason women turn it inward, I think, is that it's too big to handle. It's just a little bit more comfortable to walk around thinking that it's all your fault. If it is your fault, you maintain the idea that you can control it.

Women are not responsible for their lack of earning power. The fears that block their money-making potential—fear of success, fear of failure, fear of risk-taking, and fear of loss of feminine identity—are not individual neuroses, but problems that almost all women bring to the marketplace, because they are the inevitable result of a sexist social process. Though a woman must examine her own unique history and financial behavior in order to overcome these fears, the history of women will help her understand why she suffers from them in the first place and remove a misplaced burden of guilt from her shoulders. With this in mind, let us look at the contradictory messages the twentieth century has given us about when and how we are supposed to make money, and how much money we can safely earn without risking our inherent virtues and values.

The Twentieth Century's Mixed Messages

In the twentieth century, the message about women and work has been packed with contradictions. According to society, the female's natural habitat is the home. Home is the place where her God-given talents are best employed and her moral influence is most effective. In response to its own needs and our own, society has gradually modified this message, but never without specifying how far we can stray from the hearth, and under what circumstances, before we lose the qualities for which we are loved and admired. Middle-class women who put career interests first, ignoring their option to stay at home, have been stigmatized in different ways and in different language for the past eight decades.

In the first quarter of the century, colleges and universities opened their doors to women. Education and work experience, however, were viewed as character-building endeavors that better equipped graduates for their ultimate roles as wives and mothers. Though many educated women worked before marriage, few worked afterward, unless the family economy was jeopardized. (Seventy-five percent of the first generation of women college graduates in 1900 had premarital careers, but only 9.8 percent stayed in them after marriage.) Married women who worked because they enjoyed working, were judged selfish and neglectful of their husbands and children. Those determined to pursue careers simply did not marry. Single working women lived at home or with other women in relationships called "Boston marriages," and were regarded as "exceptional," which translated as "unnatural." Legal restrictions on birth-control devices until the 1930's, however, made it difficult or impossible for a woman to remain childless if she also had sex, or to limit the size of her family. A houseful of children and constant pregnancies, needless to say, were not conducive to a dual role of career woman and wife. Issues that we think of as "modern" plagued educated women in the twenties, too. Why, they asked, should a man have an inalienable right to a family and a career while a woman is forced to choose between them?

Despite these difficulties, women advanced. Between 1890 and 1920 their presence increased in paid professions by 226 percent. The professions open to women, however, were then (and continued to be) extensions of their housekeeping role—teaching, nursing, library science, and social services. Those trained to be lawyers and doctors were often barred from practicing in these fields. A few women disguised themselves as men in order to get jobs in their chosen profession.

The depression years are often thought of as the "Dark Ages" for women. In the thirties, a woman who worked was not merely selfish and "unnatural"; she was considered a thief who was "stealing" a job from its rightful male owner. This stigma was particularly applied to married women. During the depression twenty-six states had laws prohibiting their employment. Public utilities, schools, and many department stores refused to hire wives, and the federal government forbade more than one member of a family from working in civil service—a law that effectively discriminated against women. Men applied in droves for female-stereotyped jobs, like teaching, and female college graduates were discouraged by their deans from pursuing careers.[2] The 1936 Gallup poll asked if wives should work if their husbands had jobs. When 82 percent of Americans said no, Gallup declared he had discovered an issue on which voters were as solidly united as on any imaginable subject, including sin and hay fever.[3] Even Eleanor Roosevelt, who saw no reason why a woman's "first duty to her home" should preclude her from pursuing another occupation, conceded that the pressure on women to stay home in the thirties was "perhaps necessary during an emergency."[4]

Though women were told not to work, statistics show that many of them did; the number of women in the work force increased slightly between 1930 and 1939. In male-dominated professions, however, the increase of women was negligible; the number of women doctors actually decreased.

World War II revoked the stigma against women working. In the thirties, women were warned not to "steal" jobs; in the forties, they entered the work force in record numbers. Women were told they could serve society's interests by getting jobs as quickly as possible. With the men at war, 6 million women filled the vacant slots they left in heavy industry as well as in offices. Women did jobs they had never done before—they riveted, ran cranes and bulldozers, and manufactured ammunition and aircraft. Though society encouraged women to work during the war, then, as now, it did not provide the government-sponsored childcare that would have made it easier for them to do so.

Most women had intended to quit their jobs when the men came home, but when the war was over, 80 percent wanted to continue working because their families needed the extra income. Nevertheless, by the end of 1946, millions had been fired. Jobs that were not too heavy for women when there were no men to do them became too heavy when there were, and we were sent back to the fireside to resume our more "natural" ladylike occupations.

In the conservative fifties, then, society did another about-face and rescinded the message of the forties. Women who were black and poor continued to work as they had previously in a marketplace that discriminated against them, paid them badly, and cast them in sex-stereotyped jobs. Those who could afford to stay at home, however, increased in number as male fortunes prospered. Society touted homemaking and motherhood as complex, satisfying, full-time occupations, and even educated women subscribed to the new propaganda.

It soon became apparent that the homemakers of the fifties were not the smiling madonnas they were supposed to be. In 1963, Betty Friedan published her now-classic manifesto, *The Feminine Mystique*, which describes the anxieties of unhappy housewives. Friedan addresses middle-class educated women, supported by their husbands, who suffered from a pervasive, unnamed dissatisfaction. Its physical symptoms—headache, or an unspecified malaise, sometimes brought on by overdoses of alcohol or tranquilizers—resembled the neurasthenic ailments of the idle Victorian woman. The victims of the "Feminine Mystique," Friedan said, felt that what they did was unimportant; yet the message from the media led them to believe that they were perverse exceptions, that other housewives were satisfied with their lives.

What kind of woman was she if she did not feel this mysterious fulfillment, waxing the kitchen floor?[5]

Friedan explained how the male establishment conspired to deter women from achieving self-fulfillment, and urged them to establish a sense of their own identity through meaningful work.

Writing at a time when economic conditions provided a climate for many middle-class women to be idle, Friedan spoke of work in terms of inner satisfaction. She cautioned women against taking jobs "not equal to their actual capacity," or only in order to "help out at home." Fulfillment, she said, calls for "lifetime interests and goals," and getting paid is a valuable asset because it implies "definite commitment."

> If a job is to be the way out of the trap for a woman, it must be a job that she can take seriously as part of a life plan, work in which she can grow as part of society.[6]

Friedan's book sold 300,000 copies in the first year of publication; reading it must have mobilized many women who were reevaluating their lives to change them.

The feminist movement provided those who sought self-fulfillment with a structure—consciousness-raising groups—where they could talk to one another and define the political origins of their personal problems. Thanks to the feminists, women not only won extensive legal rights and employment opportunities in the sixties and seventies, but were also able to give themselves permission to move out of the home. Men accepted the new pilgrimage toward the marketplace, provided women continued to perform household tasks. Current statistics show that few husbands of working wives do an equal share of housework or primary childcare activities.

But it was not *The Feminine Mystique,* or even the feminist movement, that caused so many middle-class women to enter the marketplace or changed the emphasis of their participation there from self-fulfillment to earning power. An economic recession and a surfeit of women in the population altered what women wanted from their jobs. Many who expected to be married were divorced or still single and responsible for their own financial futures. Those who were married needed a second income in order to meet the rising costs of the American dream. Most men's paychecks were no longer sufficient to send children to college, buy suburban homes, or maintain a middle-class urban lifestyle.

Women who went to college or began their professional lives in this new, more demanding economic and social climate, planned careers that were money-oriented. In the 1950's and 60's, college students studied liberal arts, teaching, and social work; now they prepare themselves for careers in law, science, medicine, and business. (Forty percent of all bachelor's degrees in business are awarded to women.)[7] Those of us who graduated from college in the fifties, sixties, and even early seventies, however, can be hard-put to transform our interests and training into the ideal income of the eighties. The feminist who attracted the media spotlight for her marching and bra-burning, has not been magically reincarnated as the high-earning businesswoman who has been chosen to grace the eighties' media stage. Though she may have achieved much in her field, a woman educated in a less money-oriented era can feel like a financial has-been, and suffer from pressures to earn more and Moneyphobic feelings.

The media emphasis on the corporate woman, so often the subject of books, magazine articles, and television talk shows, distracts attention from the fact that most women in the marketplace are still underpaid for doing the same jobs as men. The way the high-earner is portrayed, moreover, confuses other women about their needs and goals, because, on the one hand, she is held up as an example of what we all could achieve and, on the other, demasked as a personal failure, or stigmatized. The executive featured in popular women's magazines appears as well-adjusted as she is well-dressed; she has a man in her life, or a loving family, a job she adores, a high income (usually not specified), and her "busy schedule" is made to sound like fun. Social scientists' studies of the corporate woman offer a less optimistic picture. Books like *The Managerial Woman,* by Margaret Hennig and Anne Jardim, tell us how women had to adapt their personalities to succeed in a male-dominated business world, and put their personal lives on hold in order to demonstrate the career devotion necessary to overcome corporate discrimination. Some psychologists have testified that corporate women are dissatisfied and disillusioned, not only with their jobs, which have given them cases of "business burnout," but with their lives, lacking in meaningful personal attachments or family ties.

The male-oriented or male-run media subtly express society's ongoing disapproval of women who leave the home to compete with men in the marketplace. Let's look at three notable examples:

● A *New York Times Magazine* article, "Against the Odds: A Woman's Ascent on Wall Street," by Jane Gross, is a portrait of thirty-eight-year-old Karen Valenstein, the first female vice-president of E. F. Hutton & Company, who earns a quarter of a million dollars a year. The article describes Karen's "killer instinct," an ability to out-man the men in a thoroughly man's world, and an almost superhuman capacity for work. Her grueling schedule, including disco dancing with clients, shopping binges, family activities and volunteer work, while she put together a multimillion-dollar bond deal, is minutely detailed. Her young children, the article tells us, are cared for by her husband, "a sensitive man" who brings home a mere $75,000 (as well as inherited money) and places more value on family activities and childraising than his egocentric wife, "who loves to be on stage and slug it out." Jane Gross offers us a supposedly objective portrait, allowing the descriptions of Karen to come from those close to her, but gives away her bias with passages like:

> Mr. Valenstein says that his wife is "usually very good about her obligations to her children, but there are times when she just can't do it." He pauses for several seconds before adding, "I can't measure if I totally fill the gap, so to speak, and I probably can't because I'm not their mother."[8]

Mr. Valenstein's "long pause" is a detail selected with care by the writer; more than his words, it makes us suspect that he may be dissatisfied with the quality of his wife's mothering. The media are giving this female high-earner "special" treatment by raising the issue at all. The fathering abilities of male tycoons are never questioned.

What does Karen do with all her money? Again the details reflect the writer's bias. She is portrayed as a tightwad with a tendency to binge and blow, who finds cheap transportation to her country house for her family, while she drops thousands on new outfits for herself. The message is not that Karen is an unusual woman from whom we might learn something, even if we do not want to go to Wall Street ourselves, but a hard, selfish ballbuster with no inner life, nothing like other women, and therefore, impossible to emulate. Sixty years ago "exceptional" women, or those who pursued *any* career, were portrayed as "unnatural." Things have not changed. We submit that in 1985 *The New York Times Magazine* portrays a woman who succeeds in a male-dominated profession in exactly the same way.

• In June 1984, *Esquire* published a portrait of twenty-eight-year-old Lisa Wolfson, a bond trader for Odyssey Partners, "The $100,000 a Year Woman." As a preface to the piece, the writer, Peter Wolfe, included his correspondence with the editor, which divulges that *Esquire* was not looking for just any $100,000 a year woman, but a single high-earner who could not find a man. A number of Wolfe's choices were rejected by the editor, who wrote:

> The trouble is, two of them have already found their men and are as good as married, while the third, from what you've told me, feels no particular urgency. . . . Keep going.[9]

In the end, Wolfe narrowed the candidates to two, eliminating Allison Byrnes, who had chosen her high-powered job in New York over her marriage in Austin, Texas, with no regrets when she could no longer endure the unrewarding commute. Instead, he selected Lisa, who blushed and blamed the failure of her marriage on her self-absorption and selfish devotion to career objectives. While the record of this correspondence allows us to learn that some women who make huge salaries do have ongoing relationships, while others are at least able to reject a difficult dual role, the article itself links Lisa's ferocious career drive with her masochistic and lonely personal life. She is photographed in the shower at 6:30 a.m., as well as in her business suit, and segments from her personal diary are included. (In her desire to reveal herself as a "sensitive" person, Lisa unwittingly played into a preconceived negative stereotype.) Again, the portrait tells us nothing useful about what the $100,000 a year woman does with her money, or how she feels about it, except to note, predictably, the trouble it creates between herself and less successful men. The article neglects to take into account that millions of low-earners are lonely and masochistic, too. No magazine, moreover, would ever portray a successful male bond trader with the emphasis on the problems in his personal life.

• A 1984 *Playboy* pictorial, "$ucce$$ $torie$: In which three bold, bright, beautiful entrepreneurs show how to succeed in business with out-and-out trying," is perhaps at the same time the most and the least objectionable of the three articles. Instead of pretending to be a coolly appraising or sympathetic report, *Playboy* slaps the cards down on the table. The article informs us:

> Through wit and strength of will they [The $ucce$$ $torie$] have jumped to the top of professions in which men normally do all the climbing. And if living well is the best revenge, they've been taking their vengeance for some time now. . . . There are many shapes of success. Here are three of the best.[10]

We then turn the page to find the three $ucce$$ $torie$ posing for crotch shots. Though the article accuses these young high-earners of vindictiveness for flaunting their wealth at the men they have outclimbed on the financial ladder, it is actually *Playboy* that is taking revenge by showing us that even successful women will stoop to personal compromise in order to please men, and equating unconventional earning power with prostitution.

Though women have changed substantially in the course of this century, then, the messages society transmits about women and work have not kept pace. Let us briefly summarize the messages and their changes:

- Your rightful place is in the home, first with your parents, and later with your husband and children.

- You may work to support yourself or to help your family or society when they need you. The work you do is most acceptable to us when it is not work a man would want, because it represents an extension of a woman's "natural" role in the home. If you are very beautiful or talented, however, we will allow you to entertain us.

- You can work if it makes you happy, provided you continue to fulfill your natural role in the home, preferably with the same quality of devotion you have shown for centuries. Change the way you act in the marketplace, but not in the home! We love you and admire you for your traditional role, because it helps us perform our important functions, but we will not pay you for it, or give it a specific economic value. Furthermore, we do not really think it is our place to help you do it, but in the last twenty years, some of us (who risked being designated as "wimps") were convinced to join your cause and come to your aid.

- You can make the money you need, but it is absolutely forbidden to make more than you need, or to see money the way we see it—as a symbol of power—or to compete with us for significant amounts of it. If you are able to turn a profit for us, we will allow some of you to infiltrate our highest echelons and pay you well, but not without extracting a price. Once in our corporations and offices, we will ask you to act and dress like men, and then stigmatize you for "unfeminine" behavior.

Unfortunately, most of us have internalized these confusing messages. "Society" is not an outside force, as we have identified it here; we are socialized according to these contradictions, and as a result, we harbor the enemy within. Few ambitious women, then, begin their adult lives with the emotional perspective necessary to sort out the contradictions, and decide which parts of the message they can and should incorporate into their lives, and which parts they want to discard or defy. How can they succeed in the marketplace and the domestic sphere—two very different places—at the same time? Some of the bravest attempt to resolve the contradictions by denying they exist; they set out for the marketplace to earn more money than women ever have before, and at the same time, try to fulfill their traditional role in the home. (The exhausted victims of this courageous, but self-destructive life plan recently formed a self-help group called Superwomen Anonymous in San Francisco.) Since success in the marketplace demands different personality traits than success at partnering and childraising, those determined to be superwomen may feel schizophrenically split off from themselves. Less ambitious women may adopt one part of the message to the exclusion of the other, and then feel incomplete, trapped in the home, or condemned to a career that does not satisfy their emotional needs. Some younger women may plan to temporarily sacrifice part of the ideal, while they devote themselves to the other, and, in the end, have it all in sequence. This approach is not always successful. Biology dictates how long one can wait before starting a family (as some who wait too long ruefully discover, biology is not always predictable), and the marketplace often turns away or limits the accomplishments of those who "stop out" at home.

Since society (and our socialization) provide no guidelines or traditions telling us how we are supposed to integrate our different needs and goals, we are left to resolve the contradictions ourselves through trial and error. Some women are more successful at this difficult integration job than others. They have been able to distance themselves from the problems long enough to see them objectively, and identify their needs in relation to the difficulty they will have in achieving them. Those who seem to "have it all" on closer inspection have actually sacrificed some part of it: a traditional homemaking role, a traditional marriage, motherhood, the amount of time and energy they devote to a career, the amount of money they cannot live without, or, in some cases, something less tangible, and yet, more valuable to many women

—unstructured time for themselves. In addition, some temperaments are better equipped to handle more of "it all" than others.

The most severely wounded casualties of this no-win battle are women who start battling themselves. They cannot separate their own needs from what they perceive as an "ideal." They become guilty, confused, and paralyzed. They see the contradictions not as conflicts, but prescriptions for failure. Castigating themselves for their inability to achieve all they believe a "modern woman" is expected to achieve, they feel they have disappointed the world and themselves. *These anxiety-ridden women are prime candidates to become moneyeluders.* Unable to identify their financial needs in the bog of mixed messages and other concerns, or to clarify what they can and cannot do to pursue them, they feel damned if they earn and damned if they do not. To make matters worse, they do not always recognize or comprehend the historical origin of these powerless feelings, and think it is up to them to transcend the problem personally. Moneyeluders always feel helpless and alone.*

THE PERILS OF THE YELLOW BRICK ROAD

Society, then, socializes women to believe the home is their natural habitat, and the outside world, including the marketplace, represents foreign territory. Many of the stories we heard in childhood dramatize the voyage out of secure and familiar domestic surroundings into the intriguing, but perilous "unknown." Goldilocks, for example, ventures forth into the forest and tries the lifestyle of the three bears on for size. Though she is innocently experimenting with the separation process

* In "How to Get the Women's Movement Moving Again" (*New York Times Magazine*, November 3, 1985), Betty Friedan said transitional women, whom she describes much as we have here, "are almost as isolated and powerless as those suburban housewives afflicted by 'the problem that had no name' whom I interviewed for *The Feminine Mystique* over 20 years ago." Friedan suggests that modern women return to the consciousness-raising groups of the sixties in order to "free a new generation of its new double burden of guilt and isolation," to give their problems names, and campaign for new political solutions to them.

and different roles—the momma's, the poppa's, and the baby's—the bears view this quest for adulthood as an unwanted invasion, and Goldilocks flees into the forest with her search still unresolved. Another of our favorite myths is the 1939 movie production of *The Wizard of Oz*, starring the ill-fated child prodigy Judy Garland, who herself journeyed too far from home at too early an age.

Dorothy does not leave home of her own accord; she is blown away by a ferocious tornado from her adoptive parents, who have unjustly rebuked her for misbehavior. She finds herself in a magical world where good and evil forces, in the guise of witches, vie for control of her destiny. She is frightened, but thrilled, to find herself where she has often longed to be—"Somewhere Over the Rainbow"—in a more exciting environment than her dull, but comfortably familiar Kansas farmhouse. Clad in a pair of magic shoes, she sets out on the "Yellow Brick Road," an image similar to "streets paved with gold," the nineteenth-century immigrants' description of America as a land of opportunity. The mood is one of excitement and discovery, but Dorothy is making the hazardous journey only in order to end up back where she started from: She plans to ask "The Wonderful Wizard of Oz" to return her to her home. Skipping, dancing, and singing, she meets three male companions, all of whom are frauds. Together they lack a traditional man's essential qualities: The lion has no courage, the tinman is minus a heart, and the scarecrow does not have a brain. Dorothy, however, has all three, and it is largely to the encouragement and ingenuity of this spunky little girl that these insufficient and nonrescuing, yet lovable males, make it through the trip. Once in the Land of Oz (also known as "The Emerald City") it is perspicacious Dorothy with the help of her dog, Toto, her alter ego, who discovers that The Wonderful Wizard is bogus. Toto pulls away the curtains from behind which the wizard's awesome voice comes, to reveal a little, kindhearted old man who governs his city by producing a mechanical illusion of power. The wizard is able to convince Dorothy's three companions that they possess the qualities they believe they are lacking. Dorothy herself is offered the kingdom, but she closes her eyes, repeats intently, "There's no place like home," and finds herself back in Kansas with her beloved Aunt Em, determined never to misbehave again. Her journey, of course, was all a dream—the result of getting conked on the head during the storm—but it has taught the little girl a lesson the author of the screenplay thought she needed to know, and presumably abolished her unrealistic fantasies.

From our point of view, *The Wizard of Oz* is an interesting story, with problems as well as truths. It indicates that a journey outside the home in which a young lady learns that she can use her intelligence and personality skills to overcome danger and achieve is a wonderful adventure, but strictly temporary, the stuff fantasies are made of. It tells us what many adult women already know: that men, too, suffer from the myth that they are all-powerful and invulnerable, and owe much to feminine comfort and support. But what about the glittering Emerald City? Oz reminds us of the modern corporation, which has reportedly left so many women who braved great hardship to journey there unhappy and disillusioned. Home is an important place, and wise Dorothy knows it; she does not want to be the first female vice-president of General Motors. Having flexed her talent and courage and seen a bit of the world, she has not lost her original values; she still wants to be with the people she loves, who love her in return. The problem with the story is that it presents staying at home and going out into the world as an either/or situation, dramatizing society's basic message, which discourages women from trying to do both at the same time. It is unfair that such a strong and talented little girl must choose between the home and the world, because the talents that serve her so well in one place will be wasted in the other. In the world, she is brave, smart, respected, and adored, and in the home, she must be loving, obedient, and dependent.

When women describe their career progress, they often use the imagery of *The Wizard of Oz*. They define success as a hazardous journey away from a comfortable, protected environment to an unfamiliar place, where they feel exposed and vulnerable to danger. *What are the perils, both imaginary and real, that turn women back on the yellow brick road, and how can they be recognized and avoided?*

1. FEAR OF LEAVING HOME OR "RISK-TAKING"

Many modern women have been working so long that they have forgotten their initial trepidation at setting out for the marketplace. Deanna, a South Carolina mother who put her two daughters in daycare so that she could enroll in college and earn a degree, reminded us of the fear and excitement this initial journey inspires. Because her determination to have a foot in both the home and the marketplace is less common in the rural South than it is in other areas of the country, Deanna's decision to pursue a career subjected her to criticism and her marriage to tremors.

Happily married to a construction worker at twenty-four, Deanna had settled into a rambling farmhouse, intending to be a contented earthmother and earn extra money by monogramming at home.

> I thought things were going to be wonderful! I'd stay here, have babies, a garden, and do monogramming, and I'd just love it! Instead, I was bored, the baby was into everything, and the monogramming was stressful, because once it wasn't a nine-to-five job, it seemed like I had a choice not to do it. After my second daughter was born, I thought I'd kill myself if I went on doing what I was doing for the rest of my life.

Though neither of Deanna's parents had graduated from high school, her mother had always worked and her father had pushed his children to excel in school.

> When we were growing up he always told us how horrible his life was working in a factory because that was all he could do. He wanted us to be better.

Her upbringing and strong family support allowed Deanna to contemplate the serious option of getting an education that would raise her social class. Once this determined young woman decided to set out for Oz, the sky became the limit!

> I thought about training to be a pilot, which is something I'd always wanted to do. I went out and took an introductory lesson, and I didn't tell Jackie, because I knew he would give me such hell that I never would have done it. I told him after I did it, and he said . . . "*What???!!!*" It wasn't fear for my life, I don't

think, it was fear for *our* life. If I'd become a pilot, I might have
left him.

Deanna rejected a flying career, not only because it would endanger
her marriage, but also because the training program was too long and
grueling. Her next move brought her literally back to the ground, and
because it was more realistic, it was also more frightening. She began
to take courses in soil science at a local community college.

It was a big deal, a big serious thing, and I thought, Maybe I can't
do it. . . . It's bigger than me. It's a big unknown. Oh, everybody
is going to be smarter than me. That's how I felt. Now I feel going
to college was my greatest achievement. That was one thing I did
myself. I went through the agonies myself. Nobody helped me. I
feel it was harder for me coming from where I did . . . the things
I had to overcome . . . the fears of going out on my own . . . just
going into a strange building and feeling my way around. And
going to classes! Really putting myself in there! That was harder
for me than for people who haven't been so isolated. And following through! And coming to the end!

Deanna describes the process of going to school as a journey to an
unknown environment, where she feels her way around, almost like a
blind person. More sophisticated urban women, with college well behind them, may experience Deanna's fears when they contemplate
career changes or advancements. What is "comfortable" has different
boundary lines for different women at different phases of their careers.
A familiar workplace can come to seem like a home, and a new job,
with a higher income, represents an unfamiliar territory, demanding
new knowledge and personality skills. It is the fear of continuing the
journey and finding themselves once again "exposed" that prevents
moneyeluders from making more money.

Sarah, for example, is dissatisfied with her job as an occupational
therapist in a rehabilitation department in a New York hospital. When
she contemplates quitting the secure position she has had for years,

however, and developing a private practice, she sees the move in terms of leaving a home, complete with a loving family.

> One of my friends is going part-time, and the other is quitting to have a baby. That's part of my wanting to leave . . . so many people I like won't be there anymore. I feel like I'm losing my family.

This workplace/home tolerates Sarah's flaws, much as a family tolerates a child's misbehavior:

> There's a basic flaw in me that blossoms at the hospital . . . that part of me that can be careless, or terrific at starting something but not following through. There, nobody knows whether I'm doing it or not; I blend in. But if I was working for a serious business . . . what about those days when I feel like a brainless mush, and I barely function? What will happen when my brain's not turned on, and I'm visible . . . when I'm out there?

Though she fears exposing herself to a more critical audience whose expectations are unknown, Sarah, who feels her income has not kept pace with rising costs and has no savings, chafes at these "family ties," and believes they are self-imposed by a neurotic maladjustment on her part, rather than by an understandable inability to balance cultural messages with her own changing goals.

> The fact that I'm still there and can't leave feels devastating. On my worst days I feel like I'll die at the hospital, but when I feel like leaving, it's like I'm leaving home at the point when my parents are dying.

At any stage of a woman's career, exchanging a known, comfortable job situation for a different or larger venture may seem comparable to leaving home. Molly, a successful New York fashion designer, felt she was abandoning familiar territory when she moved from a small downtown showroom, a walkable distance from her apartment, to larger quarters in midtown Manhattan.

It was shocking! I felt like I was in Chicago when I got off the subway.

This non-moneyeluder, however, had been able to weigh the comforts of home against the discomfort of losing money.

The showroom in SoHo was very comfortable. However, a recession was coming and budgets were cut, and when out-of-town buyers came in, they only had four days to cover all the showrooms. And the first appointment that got cancelled was the one in SoHo, when all the others were in the garment center. After three to six months of this, one day Jan, my partner, and I just said, "Let's move."

Women tend not only to redefine the workplace as home, but to also bring qualities that are effective in their domestic and social lives into the marketplace, sometimes with great success. High-earners in our study told us that they had created a network of important relationships on the job, and used their nurturing abilities and talents for intimacy to develop financially lucrative business relationships. The transformation of marketplace into home, however, can be self-sabotaging when domestic comforts substitute for financially necessary risk-taking activities.

2. FEAR OF "SUCCESS"

Do women traveling the yellow brick road fear reaching their destination? Many psychologists have theorized that modern women are "afraid of success." The psychologically sophisticated moneyeluders in our study sometimes cited this much touted fear to explain their income-producing problems. "Fear of success," however, proved to be a convenient catchall that summarized a number of complex underlying issues. Jeannie, for example, who was looking for a job, concluded that she hadn't found one because she was afraid of succeeding.

I'll be up against people who are going to compete against me, and I'll be better than they are, or I won't be, and my main fear is that

I will be better. I find myself in many situations where I undercut myself in order to shore someone else up. I think it has to do with my not wanting to let out my competitive instincts. I'm very competitive, and I'm terrified of that.

Int.: What would happen if you let the competitiveness out?
J.: I might be terrifically successful.
Int.: And then?
J.: I might make a lot of money, and have a great job, and love my life, and things might be too wonderful!
Int.: And then what?

Jeannie had no answer. She realized it was not really rational for her to fear "a wonderful life." What did she fear? Why was she afraid of her competitive instincts, if she saw them as a ticket to a positive goal? Her description of her feelings when a male friend got a high-paying job gave us a clue.

My male roommate, whom I like and admire enormously, just got a terrific job which he richly deserves in a field related to my field, but not the same, making $12,000 a year more than he did on his last job. And I was so jealous when I heard about it I was ready to murder him. I could not contain myself. It took three days for me to stop shaking.

According to psychologist Carol Gilligan, author of *In a Different Voice*, women project violence into fantasies of competitive success. Jeannie imagines that when she succeeds, others will feel, and direct toward her, the barely controllable envy she experiences when those close to her meet with success. She represses her competitiveness because she unconsciously believes such envy might result in her injury or death, symbolic, if not real.

Women believe that once they are envied, or experience this emotion themselves, they will be cast out of a web of all-important human relationships. Because they fear the envy of others, they find it hard to express their envious feelings, or use them to explore their conflicts

about success. Instead, they banish this "unladylike" emotion, or transform it into self-castigation or criticism of those who have achieved.

In order to learn more about the way women deal with envy, we
asked the members of our New York money group how they would feel
if a woman friend called to announce she had just gotten a great job,
contract, or commission that would net her $75,000. Most said they
would be envious if the high-earner was an acquaintance, but "happy
for her" if she was a closer friend. The envious feelings were strong and
violent:

> If it's a close friend I'm envious, but I'm still happy for her. God,
> I wish it would happen to me! If it is an acquaintance it would
> be . . . What! It happened to her! It didn't happen to me! *I* want
> that! I know one friend I could actually say that to. I'd say, "I hate
> your guts!"

Closeness, then, was one criterion of what made it safe, or unsafe,
to feel and express envy. Another was the way the success was earned.
Friends who were seen as "manipulative," "insincere," or having
achieved by using "feminine wiles" in the marketplace were entitled
to negative feedback more than those who were hardworking or "deserving." Among the deserving were the Pure in Intent, the Grateful
for Support, the Modest Souls Who Remained Good People, and the
Passive, Who Did Not Bulldoze Their Way. Those who calculated, or
"sold out," or used their talents according to current market values, also
merited the (silent) condemnation they got.

> One woman I know is extremely competitive, extremely . . . I
> would never have the nerve to come out and say to her what I
> really feel, which is that I'm really jealous. Then I can think of
> another woman who has a lot of talent, but always puts herself
> down, and if something wonderful happened to her, I'd think, It's
> about time.

In other words, successful women were expected to earn their success
by demonstrating the same qualities in the marketplace that make a

"good friend" or a "nice person." Successful men friends, however, were not expected to be quite so accommodating in a work situation. Unfortunately, the rejection of any success that is not "correct" or "pure," according to these stringent criteria, can prevent women from learning valuable lessons from female high achievers. As one woman in our group discovered, envy can be used as a resource.

> I think I've found a way to deal with the feeling of envy, which is not a nice or comfortable feeling; it's very practical. I study these women, who are my friends, and figure out how they did it, how they got what they got, and what traits they have that I can graft onto myself . . . traits that are not totally out of my ken. There are some traits—forget it!—that I can't emulate, and others that I can.

Fear of envy is not an irrational fear. Successful women experience rifts in friendships and may get the "cold shoulder" from still struggling friends. Those who repress envious feelings can manifest their envy in devious ways. We heard one didactic tale about a group of highly motivated career psychologists who gathered to celebrate a friend's $20,000 book contract with a festive dinner. During the meal many topics were discussed, but the auspicious book contract was not among them. At the end of the evening, the author-to-be's friends went home in pairs, and she found herself sitting at the banquet table alone—hurt and angry. Sometimes, those who make it to the Emerald City have to look for new friends who also live there.

Ambitious women who fall prey to the "green monster" are not neurotic or bad-tempered. They are reacting to an oppressive social and economic fact, which is that the pie to be divided up among women is smaller than the one to be divided among men. When a woman feels that another woman's success has taken something away from her, she is not altogether wrong. Because only "token" women are admitted to the top, there is simply not enough success to go around. Instead of blaming a sexist political economy for the insufficient success supply, however, women blame other women for grabbing their share, or turn the blame inward.

I feel diminished when a friend succeeds. There are people I hate for succeeding . . . though I would never say that . . . and others I feel happy for, but in either case, I would use their success to put myself down. I wouldn't think the world was being unfair, or that someone else got something I deserved as much; I would feel it was my fault. What have I done wrong? Or what have I not done?

Jamaicans say, "The higher the monkey climbs the tree the more he exposes himself." Women fear that success will expose them not only as enviable, but as different from other women. Because success in the marketplace, particularly in male-dominated professions, is attributed to self-seeking personality traits, such as ruthlessness and competitiveness, women at the top may be perceived as extraordinary, or not typically feminine, and singled out for attention that is not altogether flattering. For this reason, no doubt, Judith Resnick, the second woman in space, who died in the 1986 *Challenger* explosion, wanted to be known as "just another astronaut, period," and protested tokenism. She once said, "Firsts are only the means to the end of full equality, not the end in itself."[11] To be seen as "deviant" is particularly threatening. Successful women fear that once they are singled out as "different" or "unfeminine," they will be cast out of the pack and rejected by men as well as by other women. The top can signify loveless isolation. The "top," of course, is relative to the size of the surrounding trees. For a woman who fears the spectre of a lonely treetop, even a modest success can be seen as a threat, if those closest to her are clinging to lower branches.

3. FEAR OF FAILURE

Moneyeluders believe that in order to excel they must meet vague, but rigid ideal standards. They require an exaggerated degree of professional competence of themselves, as well as superior personality skills and a saintly character. The perfectionist who demands that she be totally deserving, sabotages herself. She may ask for less money in a salary negotiation because she secretly fears that she could never live up to the higher pay. Jeannie, our money group member who was looking for a job, worried that her imperfection would be detected the minute she stated her salary demands.

> I'm going out on a lot of job interviews, and when they ask me what salary I want, I can't get it out. I'm afraid the interviewer is going to say, *"Are you out of your fucking mind? Do you think you're worth that kind of money?"* And I think if he said that I would just expire. I've been practicing saying $29,000, and I'm shocked to see them writing it down, as if it's okay.

Fears of proving undeserving, or of seeming aggressively self-seeking, induce women to accept lower salaries than they need, and titles that represent their job descriptions as less important than they are.

Fear of failure inevitably leads to fear of risk-taking. Moneyeluders project their "inadequacies" on to unfamiliar financial activities or career challenges, and draw back from them. Highly intelligent women may have more confidence in their ability to master the skills a new job requires than to cope emotionally with change. Selena, a television producer, passed up a chance to buy her building in Manhattan, an investment that would have eventually allowed her to quit her job and pursue her real goal—making independent film documentaries.

> The fear was that I would be overwhelmed by that kind of responsibility, that it would take something away from my private life. I didn't make a decision in a rational frame of mind. There were some rational things, like how managing the building would interfere with my time, but there were irrational things like, God, what if they call me up and tell me the boiler is broken? As though I couldn't cope with that! And yet, I knew perfectly well that I could. I felt that as soon as that would happen I would panic; I would turn into a terrified woman. And if I had bought it, I'd be in great shape; I would have so much money it would be ridiculous. At the time, I had no ability to see that vision.

We asked Selena if she hadn't projected some other "terrified woman" into her fantasy of owning the building.

Down the line it was my mother, there's no question about that.
She laid that trip on me totally. She didn't believe in risk-taking!

Many women, like Selena, learned fear of risk-taking from their
hearthbound mothers. For some, fortunately, this message was
modified by their fathers, who taught them how to go into the marketplace. Some fathers, however, were inadequate instructors. Women in
our study with serious moneyeluding problems had fathers who
achieved far below the level of their talents. These fathers, also
moneyeluders, were exploited by others, or dutifully supported their
families, but were not financially ambitious; they, too, placed boundaries on the amount of money they allowed themselves to earn.

DETECTING MONEYELUDERS:
THE SIX-FIGURE FANTASY

Success is an elusive word until one attaches a price tag to it. An
unquantified financial fantasy is material for dreams or nightmares, a
source of pleasure as well as self-reproach. A woman who is unable to
calculate the dollar value of success also finds it difficult to calculate
what must be done to achieve it. Since she is also incapable of imagining the effect that more money will have on her time and relationships,
she never confronts secret fears. Once "success" has a limit, however,
the reasons for failure become clearer, or so we discovered when we
asked the women in our money study to fantasize an opportunity to
earn a very high salary.

In our Six-Figure Fantasy Game, we asked each woman we interviewed to imagine that she had been invited to a chic dinner party and
found herself seated next to a successful woman who was earning a lot
of money in her field. Next, we asked the participant to describe this
woman and their conversation. How did the successful woman relate
to her? After we heard the imaginary give-and-take, we had the rich
and powerful female tycoon make our interviewee a once-in-a-lifetime
offer—the job opportunity of her wildest dreams. We tailored the job
to fit what we felt was the ultimate career goal of the participant, based
on her questionnaire and what she had already told us in the interview.

Artists were offered mural commissions; those in the social services were given their own clinics and consulting firms, and so on. The salary that came with this job was always far more than our participant was currently earning; in some cases, it matched the salary she had named as "ideal." Usually, we offered her $100,000. How did she reply? Did she accept the offer? If she took the job, we asked her what she would do with the money, and how earning it would affect her relationships with the man in her life, with men in general, women friends, and family.

The fantasy material proved to be an excellent resource for our research. "Moneyphobic" symptoms that the rest of the interview had failed to uncover came into focus, as did rewarding reflections on the interviewee's business and personal relationships. Fears of risk-taking, envy, and loss of femininity appeared like invisible ink under a revealing light. The Six-Figure Fantasy was especially useful in helping us pinpoint exactly what was holding our moneyeluding participants back from earning more and establishing their financial identities. Here is a summary of what "stopped" our ambitious women from seizing an opportunity to make the high salaries they told us they wanted.

1. Stopped by the Successful Woman at the Dinner Party

A number of women were stopped at the start of the fantasy by the successful woman herself, who was seen, according to time-honored social stereotypes, as being cold, severe, evil, or unfeminine.

Dana, a video writer reluctantly working in another field, found it difficult to believe that a woman who was enormously successful in the visual media even existed. Once convinced, she described her dinner table companion like this:

> She's wearing black and pearls. Extremely plain and kind of severe, with a thin, slightly drawn face. I can't relate to her at all. She feels that I'm some underling that might want something from her that she doesn't want to give. I'm very reserved! I don't initiate anything! I will take an opportunity to respond to something she says and show myself as well as I can, but the idea of pushing myself

on this person and saying, "Hey, I'm a talented writer, you really ought to meet me, blah, blah, blah. Have you got any work?" I would never in a million years do that.

Women like Dee, who could not make a positive identification with a successful female, and who expected her to be forbidding and unpleasant, have placed unconscious boundaries on the amount of success they feel they, as women, can safely achieve. They cannot envision themselves as very successful, because they fear success will transform them into hard or unfeminine creatures. They reject the self-made woman, not only in the fantasy, but in themselves, and instead, angrily accuse her of rejecting them at first sight. They may also cherish unexplored feelings of competitiveness with other women. These women find it hard to see other successful women as resources or as models for achievement.

Some of the participants were envious of the tycoon or tried to "disarm" her by uncovering her "human" side; one very low-earner said she would draw her out, and get her to confide her "abortions" and "the other tragedies in her life," woman to woman. Though those who failed to see the tycoon as a resource accepted the high-paying job she offered them with alacrity, they had already revealed the unconscious blocks that were preventing them from taking the necessary steps to find a high-paying job on their own initiative.

Even high-earners rejected the successful woman. Georgette had already made more than $100,000 a year in the world of finance; for her, we had to up the ante to $500,000. She described the high roller at the dinner party like this:

She'd probably be awful. She'd be very cold, very driven, not very nice, and very snotty. I would be uncomfortable because I would feel that . . . there would be an axe coming my way at some point and it would be coming from this woman. I've always traditionally done my worst when I've had a woman in a superior position over me. They just hate me and I hate them. Once I was being interviewed for a vice-president's job—a big job—but I saw through the interviews that there would be friction with the woman boss.

And I have more trouble with women like that than I do with men with the exact same attributes. I think it has something to do with my mother.

Though Georgette's distrust of successful women is based partly on experience, her unquestioning acceptance of a negative stereotype suggested that she had trouble internalizing her own success and integrating her concept of her own femininity with her income-producing powers. A fantasy is a good place to examine stereotypes, as this woman did:

She looks happy. There's no tension in her face. My initial reaction was to make her into a stereotype, but my mind is saying it doesn't have to be that way. My mind says *no* to a business suit, cropped hair, and a hard-looking, unfeminine woman.

2. STOPPED BY FEELINGS OF LOW SELF-ESTEEM
Some of our participants were awed by the successful woman and felt their own failings more acutely in her presence. What they said to her revealed that they didn't think much of themselves. Deanna, the South Carolina mother who had overcome her fear of risk-taking to go to college, had grown up in a poor family with a "bad reputation." To her distress, she and her siblings had been pitied by condescending relatives. Soon to graduate, she had decided that she would look for a job in pharmaceutical sales. Appropriately, we seated her next to the owner of a pharmaceutical company.

She's well-dressed and you can tell she is rich. I feel I am not as good as she is. She would have to start the conversation because I would be shy. I can't do a thing when I first meet people like that.

Int.: What do you say when she asks you what you do?
D. (embarrassed laughter): I'd say the usual stuff . . . that I'm going to school.

When the pharmaceutical executive offered Deanna the coveted job, her answer came not from her present courageous self but from the insecure child who had felt demeaned by her family status.

I'd say yes! That would be ideal. I'd be thrilled. Then I wouldn't have to go out and find someone who would say that to me. Or beg for it!

Our fantasy alerted Deanna to a potential dilemma she faced when she left college (by now a comfortable home) and continued her journey toward the marketplace. She would have to be aware of the ways her feelings of inferiority could prevent her from projecting the self-confident attitude that would convince an employer to hire her.

The women in our study were surprisingly eager to confess their lack of accomplishments to a more successful woman. Some seemed to feel she would understand and sympathize with their frightened feelings as a mother would. Claire, our moneydenying set designer from Chapter 3, told the female producer of a Broadway hit all about her inadequacies.

I'm such a goof, I'd probably say, "Oh, I wish I could do something like that! That's fabulous! I don't really push, and I'm not a hustler, and I wish I had a little more of that."

Int.: So you downplay yourself right away?
C.: Yeah, probably.
Int.: Well, what if she says, "You're a set designer? How interesting! What have you done?"
C. (in comically melodramatic voice): Oh, a little show on off-off-off-off Broadway.

We doubted the women in our study would have presented themselves in quite so unflattering a light if a real opportunity with the elements of our fantasy dinner had existed. We wondered, however, how much their unquestioning acceptance of their low self-esteem caused them to crumble in an intimidating situation without a fight.

Were they alert to the presence of potential resources and cognizant of the politics of the "networking game," or did they let promising possibilities slip through their fingers? A fantasy, we thought, is a good place to prepare oneself to overcome psychic stopgaps with positive, not negative, visualizations.

Sharon, an artist, was also insecure about her accomplishments, but was able to treat the fantasy as a chance to deal with the difference between how she felt and how she should act. She saw the rich collector at her dinner table as an opportunity, and acted accordingly.

> She relates to me with reserved interest, assuming I'm where I am, and I relate to her, mixed, according to my emotional mood. Inside I feel nervous and scared, but increasingly confident, because my work has gotten better and I've gotten good responses. It's like a game. She's buying and I'm selling, so I can't act too eager, and yet I have to act confident. She would probably ask, "What kind of work do you do?" There would be chitchat and I would tell her, and I would try to be my wonderful, most intelligent self.

3. STOPPED BY THE JOB

If our participants could not get past the female fat cat, or their own low self-esteem, the rest of the fantasy was a rhetorical exercise, imaginary indeed. Yet most of those who did not pass "Go" were eager to take the job and collect their six figures, and did not foresee that having the money would cause major problems. Some, who met the successful woman with relative equanimity, however, were stopped by the job and its expectations. One moneydenier was all set to take her wad and head straight for a Caribbean paradise for an extended vacation, until we reminded her that she now *had* a job with demanding obligations. The large amount of money elicited fears of risk-taking and failure in women who had been able to overcome such fears in relation to less impressive opportunities in their real work history.

Penny, for example, who had developed new skills in order to design computer programs for doctors on a freelance basis, was stymied when offered a six-figure job running a large business of this kind.

That's when you get to my core. Can I do this? That's something
I'm struggling with now. I'd have to make her [the successful
tycoon] understand and honestly know what my capabilities are.
I don't want to be in a situation where she believes I can do
something I know nothing about.

Penny, like many women, believes she needs to know the skills a new
job requires before she accepts it. According to Margaret Hennig and
Anne Jardim, authors of *The Managerial Woman,* men take on new
career challenges, confident that they will learn on the job.

René, offered a consulting business in her field, measured her skills
against vague, self-imposed perfectionist standards she attributed to the
wealthy entrepreneur.

My first reaction is, "Can I live up to that expectation?" She
has expectations about what kind of work she's going to get for
$100,000. I would have to produce X amount of work of a certain
standard that comes out of another person's head.

Others, with a history of performance problems, feared they could not
work hard enough to succeed on the new job.

I'm scared shit. About proving that I can do it. About having to
work so hard. I don't want to work so hard. I don't want to get
myself in a situation where I'm expected to work twelve hours a
day, which is what my boss, a woman like the one we're talking
about, tells me she works. I would probably start by saying I have
a child, and I can't work that hard. Is it possible to do it given my
limitations?

It may well be that this woman's high-powered job will require long,
grueling hours, but she presented her limitations and assumed the worst
before asking the potential employer for a job description. She leaves
the responsibility of deciding whether she "can do it" up to the boss,
indicating she wants to be reassured and taken care of. In effect, this
moneyeluder has fired herself before she is hired, and revealed much

about the inner disturbances that might communicate themselves to
a perceptive employer when she applies for a real job.

4. STOPPED BY THE MONEY

Moneysqueamish women were stopped by the "filthy lucre" itself or
by the female tycoon, because she had it. Before Sue, a social worker,
would talk to the tycoon, she wanted to know how she had gotten so
rich.

> She's got way too much money. You don't get that much money
> by doing right. Somebody is getting fucked over for her to have
> that much money. I mean, nobody should have that much money.
> Nobody is worth that much. Nobody deserves it, or works that
> hard.

For Candace, who warred with genteel poverty in Chapter 2, we had
to lower the salary to $50,000, and even that was too much:

> I'm just not the sort of person who was meant to have half of six
> figures.

She was so eager to disabuse herself of her newfound wealth that her
expenses exceeded her total intake. First, she bought a new home, then
rented a vacation house in Mexico and invited her parents to visit. She
had plans for charitable donations, too.

> I'd endow a number of benches in Denver for people who are
> waiting for buses to sit on. Yes, there's now a memorial bench or
> two with my name on it. I like the idea of having money so I can
> take my friends out for dinner, send a little to my brother . . . hand
> it around. I'd send some to an old boyfriend's wife who's been
> reduced to selling falafel on the street. It's an opportunity!

The moneyblind rejected the high salary because they were unwilling
to look at its impact on their financial situation. Ann-Marie, married
to a doctor, turned down the $75,000 salary we offered her to adminis-

ter the restoration of the prerevolutionary buildings in her town because it would "put the IRS on her back."

> I would say I'm very interested in that, but don't pay me $75,000,
> because the IRS will take it all. Pay me a stipend, and put the rest
> back into the restoration.

> *Int.:* Wait a minute! Seventy-five grand is a lot of money! It's
> not $20,000. You're going to come out with something.
> *A.M.:* If she insisted on paying me $75,000, I guess I'd have
> to talk to the accountant and see what he could do about it.

Modest salary desires are not always productive. Women can be
rejected for high-powered business jobs because they ask for salaries
that are too small to convince the employer that they intend to "earn
their keep" by aggressively turning over a profit for him. For better or
worse, if a woman rejects the idea of making money, it is difficult for
her to be "successful" in American terms. There are, however, other,
more personal measures of success a woman must consider when she
weighs her financial needs against other goals.

5. Stopped by the Effect of Money on Their Relationships with Others

Women who could not imagine themselves taking advantage of an
opportunity to earn a high salary did not think money would affect their
relationships with men or friends. Those who could were able to see
potential problems. The artist who sailed through the dinner table
"interview" enjoyed the job and used the money wisely, but she was
stopped when she contemplated the effect of the huge fee she earned
for painting a mural on her love life. She saw earning a lot as a way
of undermining her boyfriend's masculinity.

> I think he would be proud of me, and feel good about it. He would
> be supportive, but he would feel some anxiety. It would represent
> a pressure. The image that comes to my mind is "stealing his
> thunder." I would be the victor, who would take away the prize

—which would be a lot more money—and he would slink off in the bushes. Money is erotic. Visually, I see the $100,000 as a triumphant erection of money, which I would have.

She was also afraid the money would "expose" her to friends.

They would look up to me and they would think, Oh, wow, she got this, and I would have to deal with my hubris. I couldn't hide it anymore because everyone would know it was there behind the humble image I like to present.

While some who played our fantasy game feared the imaginary windfall would introduce elements of competition and envy into relationships, others saw money as a means of separating from loved ones who had strangleholds over their lives. Simone, in a troubled marriage, relished the idea of the job, but saw the salary as a spectre of freedom, both tempting and terrifying.

I think Pete could live with it; it wouldn't be threatening to him. The feelings of difficulty are that the money would make it easier for me to leave. Right now our relationship is about the worst it's been. If I were economically independent, I would be more likely to say, "Fuck this!" Having the money introduces an element of choice. I would have it, and he could just leave, and I wouldn't have to have any more contact with him over money. I wouldn't have to "work it out."

Toni, twenty-four, thought the high salary would change her relationship to her parents in a "scary" way. She said she would use the money to pay her upper-middle-class family back for her college education.

I love my parents so much, but I think I'm a little too dependent. I don't think I've broken away from them in that I've never really done something I wanted to do badly, even though I knew they didn't want me to do it. That hasn't happened yet, and when that happens, I'll be independent.

For Toni, who knew her parents did not expect or want repayment for her education, offering them a large sum of money symbolized "buying" her freedom, without severing the important tie. Though financial independence facilitates the complex process of separation from the family, true emotional separation is not a commodity that can be bought. Toni, we felt, would have to look more deeply into her relationship with her parents, particularly with her successful mother, who had influenced her career choices, in order to become less dependent.

Overcoming Moneyeluding: The "Right Answer" to the Six-Figure Fantasy

One participant called after her interview to say she had been disturbed by the fantasy; she felt there had been a "right answer" and she hadn't "gotten it." There was no "right answer" to the fantasy from the therapeutic point of view, as each "wrong answer" gave us, and hopefully the participant, valuable insights into the fears that were holding her back from articulating and realizing financial goals. Non-moneyeluders, however, played our game quite differently.

Barbara, thirty-nine, an advertising copywriter who earned between $35,000 and $50,000 a year, with additional income from wise investments, was seated next to a well-known woman who ran a public relations firm that represented superstars and rich people. What was she like?

> She's got elements of the Queen Bee, as well as a fluffy Helen Gurley Brown. Like most successful women, she's patronizing to some extent, letting the conversation focus on me rather than on her. I've already read about her in all these magazines, right, so "we'll talk about this little girl who's on her way up in the world." If it seems like she's genuinely into the questions she asks, and interested in me, I'll open up a little more.

Barbara has an idea of what the tycoon is like, but her definition is flexible. She does not see her as threatening or masculine, and believes her most obvious flaw, her patronizing attitude, can be put in service to her own advantage. She believes the Queen Bee will be interested in her and is therefore approachable.

We then had The Bee offer Barbara a $100,000 a year job, helping to create "personal images" for the wealthy people she represented. Barbara was interested but reserved, weighing her desire to make money with her current needs and personal goals.

> When you first started to talk about it, I got turned off, because my reaction was that this was going to be a lot of hard work. But then, the more you described it, it sounded right up my alley, and if it's right up my alley, it isn't hard work anymore, because it's something I could do fairly easily. Hard work is when you're faking it, and you really have to sweat through a project because you don't know what you're doing.

Confident of her abilities to brave even an unknown job situation, Barbara did not want to "sweat" for money as she had in the past, because she had just gotten out of an oppressive marriage and valued her "fun time" and social life. She knew making a lot of money would prove demanding.

> My idea is to find a sinecure that pays me a hundred grand a year, and I have my weekends off! That's my ideal, but the real world doesn't work like that.

She is able to fantasize how the new job will affect not only her bank account but her social life.

> In a job like that my personal life would become the job, because I might start dating people involved—a high-powered jet set life. If that happened, it would all blend together and I wouldn't have a separate life. If I wanted a sex life, I guess I'd have to change my attitude about not getting involved with rich men. I've had my chances with guys who are rich and it frightens the hell out of me, because to me, money is power, and these guys have a lot of power, and if they turn it on me, I don't know what's going to happen.

As she weighs the advantages and disadvantages of the new job, Barbara takes her need for a "sex life" into account. Because she is aware of her conflicts between sex, money, and power, they do not paralyze her. Barbara is clear about her desire for money. She prepares to hedge her bets with the Queen Bee and make a deal that will offer her maximum financial security.

> I might ease my way into it by doing it half time, and keeping my own freelance contacts until I'm sure it's going to work out. I'd try to make that part of the deal. I want to make sure we can work together. I have other work that pays the bills, and I don't want to give it up and just drop myself into her lap.

Once she has thought about her options, planned her "deal," and decided to go for the job, Barbara turns the table on the patronizing Queen and invites *her* to lunch.

> I'd say, "Let's talk about it." I might do something amusing like, "How about I take you to lunch?" And I'd pick not Lutèce, but a pretty nice place. It would amuse me that I'm taking this woman who's worth a million bucks to lunch.

Barbara was the only participant who added a scene to our fantasy script. She was able to play with the deadly serious prospect of a job interview, letting her future employer know that she considers herself an equal, despite the financial disparity between them. She fantasizes herself in an active, creative role, instead of a passive, or defensive, position.

Once she is making more than double her current income, Barbara plans to find a female financial adviser whom she trusts and ask her to make "conservative investments that will save her on her tax bill."

> I probably wouldn't do anything terribly radical about buying a lot of things.

Did Barbara expect her friends to be envious? Having already been a victim of the Green Monster, she was realistically pessimistic.

They couldn't be any worse about this than they were about my getting married. They were really bad about that!

Almost no one is totally non-Moneyphobic, and Barbara was no exception. She was moneyparanoid, a common trait in successful women. Because she had one friend who often borrowed money, she planned to keep her high-earnings "under wraps" so the borrower would not know she had it. Since she was not planning to "flaunt her wealth" she did not think the men she was currently dating would "know much about it" either. Barbara's low-grade Moneyphobia, however, did not include moneyeluding. She ran most of the bases: She saw the successful woman as a resource, appraised her own ability to handle the job positively, and weighed her financial needs against other, personal goals. She was not afraid of risk, failure, envy, or having more money. Her moneyparanoia, however, might prevent her from enjoying her new wealth or recognizing its effect on her relationships with men.

How can a woman transform herself from a moneyeluder who doubts her own abilities and fears the multi-dimensions of success or failure, to a Barbara, who approaches the concept of making money with a positive, confident outlook? Pop psychology primers galore have tackled this problem, indicating that the way to eradicate a "poverty mentality" and become wealthy and content is to simply stop doing the wrongheaded things that we do and take other tactics. These primers instruct us on the right ways to define our career goals, sharpen our résumés, deal with job interviews and negotiations, behave on the job, and finally, manage and invest our newfound wealth. Many of these well-meaning and sometimes helpful manuals scold us for our negative attitudes, and emphasize the power of positive thinking; if we can envision ourselves as successful, they say, we have already taken an important step toward financial improvement.

We say, "Easier said than done!" For moneyeluders, the gap between hearing good advice and putting it into action can be equivalent to crossing the English Channel once someone has told you how to swim. Before a moneyeluder can take good advice about how to make money, she has to pinpoint exactly what is stopping her from hearing it. It is hard for her to envision herself as "successful" when the world has offered her so many unsuccessful images of her sex and condemned those who were successful in ways so subtly brutal we may never quite comprehend them. Before she can succeed, then, a woman must understand how her emotional blocks conspire with a sexist political economy to throw up barricades on her yellow brick "freeway." Once the fears and confusions, as well as the harsh realities that prevent us from making more money are accounted for, we have the knowledge we need to make self-aware choices about how much we want to earn, and what we are willing to sacrifice to earn it. We may find ourselves more willing to reexamine our financial needs, utilize our resources differently, and redefine success in terms of our own individuality. When we see that the messages about women and earning power are mixed in our minds, we can begin to untangle them and make informed decisions about the kind of financial identity we want to create. With a clear perception of what we want—as opposed to an impossible ideal of what we are supposed to have—we can set out for the Emerald City if we choose to do so, less at the mercy of evil forces.

CHAPTER 5

Moneyfolly

So far we have looked at the personal and social problems that prevent modern women from seeing their financial lives clearly, and the cultural messages, which once internalized, keep them from earning, or even wanting to earn, the money they need. In the next two chapters, we will turn our attention to the question of spending: What are the obstacles inside and outside ourselves that inhibit us from enjoying our money and using it wisely?

The non-Moneyphobic woman strikes a comfortable balance between squandering and hoarding her financial resources. The moneyfolly victim does not make rational or informed decisions about how she wants to use her money, but spends in order to achieve emotional goals. Because she buys to resolve emotional problems instead of to obtain goods and services, her concept of money is subjective. Depending on her mood, she views her resources as inexhaustible or insufficient, and is unable to calculate how much real money she has to spend. She may think of money as "play money."

Women with moneyfolly, like the moneyblind and the moneydenying, live in a financial present. They do not see that their everyday expenditures are part of an overall financial identity, formed by the way they earn and use money not only *today* but in the future and past. Moneyfolly, one of the most common symptoms of Moneyphobia, plagues women from youth to old age. Most of the women in our study suffered from at least a mild case of it. Divorced women often commit moneyfolly, spending their settlements on luxuries in order to compensate themselves for the emotional trials of a marriage gone bad. Single women, too, overspend, hoping a rescuer is waiting nearby. A 1971 study, conducted by an insurance company, determined that within eighteen months 80 percent of newly widowed women had none of their deceased husband's insurance money left to spend. Some had lost it to dubious investments, but many had quickly squandered it all.[1]

There are many ways to manifest the moneyfolly symptom. The average victim is simply unaware of how much money she spends and what she spends it on. A hundred dollars a week for lunch vanishes from her pocketbook in an almost involuntary spending process we call "pissing it away." She buys goods and services she unquestionably regards as "necessities," and loathes the idea of keeping track of expenses. Moneypissers see budgeting not as an effective method of taking charge of their financial lives but as a submission to outside forces that, like punitive parents, conspire to deprive them of gratification. If you want to insult one of these unconscious spenders call her "cheap," an epithet she readily applies to savers. Even as she falls into debt, she may continue her unconscious spending. She agrees wholeheartedly with Michael Todd, the Hollywood mogul, who once declared, "I'm in hock for over a million. What am I supposed to do, switch to nickel cigars?" These are the women who earn substantial salaries but never have any money—no nest egg to fall back on in the event of emergency, or "secret stash" for vacations and special projects. Though they may feel "strapped" by the way their precarious financial edge limits their mobility, they still find it difficult to take a critical look at the way they use money, or to ask themselves crucial questions such as, Are there other kinds of financial behavior my spending helps me safely avoid, like taking risks on the job market? Are my "necessities" really consolations? Am I spending profusely on small, expensive items because I don't feel I will ever earn enough to buy anything big? And last but not least, am I spending all of my money because I eventually hope to live on someone else's pile?

Moneyfolly victims can also suffer from too heavy a dose of the generous spirit. Generosity, of course, is a traditional feminine virtue, and most women, whether they are generous or not, would like to believe it is one of their qualities. Four times as many women in our money study defined themselves as "generous" as opposed to "cheap," and most said others saw them that way as well. Since society encourages us to give gifts, generosity easily becomes an accepted financial behavior we find difficult to identify as part of a destructive tendency to overspend. Gifts, like purchases for oneself, however, can have inappropriate emotional goals. Some Lady Bountifuls lessen uneasy feelings they have about relationships or attempt to manipulate others with presents. Women who believe they ought to be generous may give to make up for the extravagance they bestow on themselves. They may also sabotage the family's financial health by being overgenerous with children. One divorced mother realized that her generosity was inspired by guilt:

> My boyfriend says I should install a money machine in my kitchen, because on weekends it's "I need money for this, and I need money for that." I've let them try every class and every piece of equipment they wanted, and sent them to expensive art camps. I am very strong with them on their creative interests, because I feel I was shortchanged that way by my parents, and I feel guilty because I'm divorced and my children don't have a nuclear family. Now I think that I've done to them what my parents did to me in a different way—that is, I haven't been particularly honest with them about life's financial deal. My daughter wants to be a photographer and has no interest in earning money. She thinks Mommy will always be around to give it to her.

Those who commit moneyfolly can also be moneybingers, who submit to uncontrollable urges to spend. Unlike the woman who knows what she needs and why, and sets out for the marketplace to buy it, the moneybinger has a less concrete goal—to spend and keep spending. Her closets overflow with clothes she seldom wears; she buys Vuitton luggage for trips she cannot afford to take after she buys it, and antiques she can barely squeeze into her jammed studio apartment. Shopping is a necessary and often pleasurable activity, but the overspender does not really enjoy either the process or the purchases. Once in a store, she feels she is at the mercy of dictatorial forces, and she emerges package-laden, frightened, and guilty. One extreme moneybinger in our study described one of her emotionally draining "rampages" like this:

A couple of weeks ago I had a really bad day. I was in a total rage. I work across the street from Bloomingdale's, which is an unfortunate place to be situated when you're somebody like me. I ran in there and breezed through the place, grabbing things like a maniac in the Perry Ellis department. I was so completely loaded down I could barely walk. I didn't try anything on or look at the price tags. I handed it all over to the saleswoman and said, "Send it!" I was feeling kind of tired, so I went back to my office. Then I thought, I have to go back there! I have to get some more! So I raced back to the same department and started grabbing. I didn't even know what I bought. This time I took the package with me. A few days later the UPS parcel arrived. When I hung up the clothes I noticed that I had two Perry Ellis skirts—$150 each—side by side and they were exactly the same! The same color, the same style. I was freaked. Even for me, buying the same skirt twice on the same day was going a bit far.

Bingers like this one are actually addicts. Though we tend to think of an addict as someone who is hooked on a drug, experts now say that any substance or behavior habitually used to alter a negative mood can be regarded as an addiction. A woman addicted to overeating learns that putting something in her mouth at a stressful moment makes her feel less anxious; the overspender buys a new pair of slingbacks and gets the same transcendent feeling of relaxation. When she finds herself having to spend more money more often to get the good feeling she craves, her diversion has become an addictive habit. When she goes into debt and keeps on spending, her addiction is out of control. Many moneybingers, we learned, are binge-eaters, too, and suffer from unshakable debts as well as pounds.

Some moneyfolly victims binge on bargains, attempting to control the marketplace, even as they lose control of themselves. The bargain hunter will never pay full price for anything, but may spend a great deal more by buying dozens of reduced items she does not really want or need. More than other shoppers, she is susceptible to the allure of the Almighty Brand Name: Norma Kamali, Anne Klein, and Ralph Lauren are Holy Grails, and she both undermines and enhances their status by her much-prized ability to outwit the system and obtain them for less than their "real" value. She can recognize her fashion icons even without their identifying tags, and scoop incredible "steal deals" from flea markets and thrift shop tables. Her house and closets may be filled with junk she eventually returns to the Salvation Army. The bargain hunter does not decide what she wants, but bases her desires on the relationship of the label to the price. The time and money she wastes, however, get undervalued in her obsessive wheeling and dealing.

Even high-earners are not immune to the bargain's fatal lure. Karen Valenstein, the previously discussed first female vice-president of E. F. Hutton & Company, first demonstrated her financial savvy by purchasing reduced clothes at Filene's Basement and selling them to college classmates for more, a process she now gleefully calls "arbitraging Filene's." Karen, whose salary approaches $250,000 a year, still bargain-hunts at Loehmann's, a cut-rate clothing store. She told *The New York Times Magazine:*

I have enough money for the finest stores in Paris, and I go to them, but it's more fun in the basement.[2]

For this successful woman, bargain-hunting symbolizes the control she exerts on the Wall Street marketplace; for her it is "fun." For women with little or no financial clout, bargain-hunting can temporarily assuage feelings of powerlessness and is all too serious.

According to analysts of consumer trends, women spend most of their money on themselves and their homes. Many moneyfolly victims are moneydeniers who overspend on goods and services—like clothes, makeup, beauty treatments, and self-improvement courses and plans—that enhance female sexuality and make them more appealing to potential rescuers. No wonder so many use a sexual term to describe the overspending experience—*blowing it*! Moneyblowers perform a vital service for the American economy, for without the insatiable female consumer, multimillion-dollar industries would fall to the wayside, among them cosmetics, fashion, furs, diet centers, perfume, exercise studios, beauty salons, home furnishings, and cosmetic plastic surgery. It is in society's interest, then, to perpetuate female moneyfolly and wage advertising campaigns that convince women of the necessity to purchase an endless stream of products. Advertisers play dirty pool: They indicate that without their goods we will be unfeminine and subtly prey on our fears of ending up alone. A Bill Blass ad for a new perfume, to cite one among billions of possible examples, shows the ruggedly handsome Blass posing between lists of "What he likes and doesn't like so much in a woman." Among his dislikes are "A woman who talks about money all the time" and "A woman who won't spend her last few bucks on perfume." The advertising message, like society's, is mixed, offering us conflicting fantasies of what material goods we need to be "real women" at any given moment. One season we are offered the man-tailored look and the next, "a return to femininity." Unlike some feminist writers, we do not believe that women are necessarily victimized by this fashion game, provided that they also spend money on freedom and security. Shopping for "femininity" can be an enjoyable pastime with its own rewards. Many of the industries we support with our shopping, moreover, are owned by or employ women (though not always in the most influential slots). It is when the shopping game, and the nearsighted intensity with which we play it, begins to sap our financial strength and becomes a joyless obsession, limiting other, important life options or preventing us from dealing with our real deprivations and fears, that it becomes a dangerous symptom of Moneyphobia.

The Moneyfolly Myth

This is the age of moneyfolly, and plenty of men suffer from it, too. As moneybingers rack up debts on credit cards, the national debt threatens the nation's economic health. Individual predilection for moneyfolly mirrors the upswing in government spending. In 1983, 535,000 Americans were officially bankrupt, and experts say that one in twelve is overwhelmed by debt. As we spend instead of save, we are banking a smaller portion of our incomes than at any time since the early fifties. Economists find this phenomenon alarming, because savings provide the capital that finances the modernization of the production base, and are one of the nation's primary economic resources.[3] The decline in real income—or what our salaries can actually buy—is, in part, responsible for our desire to concentrate our cash in consumer goods and services instead of banks. Since the end of the Second World War, the middle class has been defined by its ability to own one's own home, educate one's children, and afford amenities such as family vacations. Today, the price of the middle-class family's lifestyle is increasing, while the share of the national wealth it receives grows smaller. A family needs an income of $37,000 to afford a medium-priced home. According to new census figures, the median family income in 1985 was $27,735—almost $10,000 too low.[4] As the value of money shrinks in the marketplace, it shrinks in our regard, and we want to exchange it for things that do not alter their worth, or for services that give us immediate gratification. As the average earner becomes less able to afford his own home, a new car, or a magnificent vacation, he compensates for his feelings of financial powerlessness by buying raspberry vinegar, VCRs, and Giorgio Armani suits. Women, who earn less "real" money than men and have traditionally spent on "little things," suffer even more from this syndrome.

Most of the women in our money study did not learn moneyfolly from their mothers. Though some from upper- or upper-middle-class homes had mothers whose main occupation was shopping, wives from the middle and lower classes were not usually bingers and blowers. During the depression and postwar years, it was our mother's astute management skills that got our families through lean times. They let down hems, made pound cakes with only one egg, and transformed Sunday's leftovers into Monday's lunch. They knew where to find two cans of tomato sauce for under a dime. It was thanks to these thrifty mothers that many of us were able to go to college and become independent professionals. They budgeted not only for our educations, but also for vacations, camps, and lessons. Seventy-eight percent of the women we asked to describe their mothers' attitudes toward money said they were practical.

Our mothers' expenditures tended to be very concrete. They bought *things* they could touch, cook, and see, and saved for definite expenses in the foreseeable future. They did not engage in speculative or abstract economic activities, nor did these interest them. They did not invest, unless it was to switch the family savings account from one bank to another in order to get the free toaster oven. Fathers most often took responsibility for major financial decisions.

Women suffering from moneyfolly learned some spending lessons from their mothers, but rejected others. They learned what women spend money on, and that shopping can be fun. Some were taught the art of bargain-hunting, and others found out that luxuries can provide rewards or consolations. What they did not learn (or want to learn) was how to budget and save. Growing up in a more liberal economic climate, most of us did not identify with the deprivations that history imposed on our middle-class parents. We did not have to survive crashes or provide for families in the face of depressions. We may have witnessed our parents' struggles, but we did not have the alarming experience of having our own earning ability suddenly and dramatically restricted. As we went to the marketplace, then, we did not see the same need to conserve what we had or to curtail our desires. For those who grew up in an atmosphere where money was handled very carefully, the macaroni casseroles of the early fifties, the hand-me-down clothes, and penny-pinching messages in general represented a depressing, colorless wasteland we wanted to flee.

More important, our mothers' careful spending symbolized their fundamental economic powerlessness and dependent state. Though they often controlled the family resources, the money they managed was not their own, nor did they get paid for the hours of work they did to conserve it. Some felt they had no right to squander their husbands' hard-earned salaries or spend it on themselves. Those who had money of their own were often self-sacrificing, and spent it on their children. One woman told us her mother's "money secret."

My mother, who comes from a poor rural family, still lives in the depression era, though my father earns more than $70,000 a year. She called the other morning at a quarter to eight so she could save money on the long-distance call to tell me she had seen miniblind cleaners on sale for $2.98. She wanted to know if she should buy one for me. For her, $2.98 is still the kind of money you have to think about before you spend it. I always thought I would have to call the rescue squad if I told her how much I blew on clothes. I was very surprised when she recently told me that before she was married, and earning her own money, she was a spendthrift, too. She didn't earn much, but she bought a skunk coat on credit, and sometimes got behind in her rent in order to buy furniture and clothes. It's only since she married my father, and has been supported by him, that she has become a non-spender like he is. She said she always felt it was his money.

Once we began to earn our own money, our mothers' careful management techniques represented a financial and emotional claustrophobia. We wanted to spend in a way that conveyed the journey we had taken—or hoped to take—to govern our own lives. We had crossed difficult barriers in order to achieve financial independence, sometimes at great cost; we did not want barriers around our ability to spend. We saw the things that money could buy as tangible proof of our success and as rewards for our struggles. It was in a spirit of positive exploration, then, that some of us progressed from the pleasure of spending our own money on ourselves to the perils of moneyfolly. What began as financial behavior that expressed our positive feelings about ourselves outgrew its original intent and became an expression of what we felt we were lacking. For better or worse, society provided those with the tendency to overspend with role models who were quite the opposite of their frugal mothers—the heiresses, daughters, and wives of rich men, and glamorous stars of the stage and screen. These women received much attention for spending as if there were no tomorrow, and their moneyfolly became part of the mythology of American wealth.

The daughters of the robber barons who made millions by building railroads with exploited labor after the Civil War helped "launder" their fathers' disreputable earnings by marrying impoverished European aristocrats and raising conspicuous consumption to a high art form. Barbara Hutton, the Woolworth heiress, one of the last of this line, was perhaps the most famous moneyblower of all. In 1924 she inherited $28 million (worth twenty times as much in today's currency), which her father doubled with astute investments that were able to survive the stock market crash. While breadlines formed during the Great Depression, Barbara incurred the national rage (and also envy) by throwing extravagant parties, buying the jewels of deposed princesses, villas, palaces, Cadillacs galore, and European ne'er-do-well princes and barons. Throughout her life, Barbara, who was wed seven times, used her capital to purchase good sex. When she got tired of men she paid them fabulous sums to quietly decamp, knowing her huge fortune would soon draw another. Her fifth husband, Dominican playboy and renowned superstud, Profiro Rubirosa, collected approximately $2 million in gifts and $2.5 million in cash in their fifty-three-day marriage.[5]

Barbara is by no means the only goddess in the moneyblowing mythology. The moneyfolly of prominent women is inevitably a major feature of their publicity profiles. The press eagerly pries into the closets of the rich and famous: It tells us that Jacqueline Onassis has the same garment in every color, and that Dolly Parton owns 2,400 pairs of shoes and 410 wigs. Jewelry designer Elsa Peretti, we learn, once tossed a $35,000 sable coat into Halston's fireplace in the heat of an argument. Mae West, actually a smart investor, is more famous for her swansdown-marabou stoles. Female moneyfolly is rampant on a grand international scale. Recently the spendthrift wives of foreign dictators helped topple their husbands' corrupt regimes. Michele Duvalier kicked off protests that forced Baby Doc into exile when she blew several million dollars on a shopping spree, depriving Haiti of the foreign exchange it needed to pay for fuel for public transportation. After Ferdinand Marcos was forced out of power, journalists and poverty-stricken peasants were led through the Malacañang palace to marvel at his wife Imelda's loft-sized closets, trunks of girdles, and shelves of unused Gucci bags. We know less about the way the power-hungry dictators themselves spent their filthy lucre; they seem to have invested it in real estate, or salted it away in discrete Swiss banks. In fact, we seldom know the intimate details of how rich men dispose of their discretionary cash. We almost never see what they have in their closets!

Moneyblowers, then, embody a popular American fantasy—unlimited wealth—and their excessive spending remains part of an ongoing legend about what women do when they have money to burn. Wealthy women who use their money wisely or donate it to charity, do not get much media attention. Good sense, it seems, makes bad copy. We may despise the way infamous moneyblowers misuse their wealth, especially if it is ill-gotten, but we cannot help imagining ourselves with equal sums at our disposal.

Most of our own lives are defined and controlled by financial boundaries, which often seem to restrict our emotional freedom and creativity. In fact, it is when we feel financial restrictions limiting our options that we are most tempted to imitate not our mothers, who unplugged the iron when they answered the phone to save on electricity, but women who live what we perceive as glamorous, sex-rich, romantic existences. Unfortunately, we are not offered intriguing prototypes of women who both manage wisely and enjoy their money.* Our experience and culture give us an emphatic either/or.

It is easy to forget that the majority of classic moneyblowers, whose unlimited options we envy, are not in the same financial position as most of us. They are not self-made or independent. They were either catapulted to wealth through fame or are the beneficiaries or wives of powerful men. Many are not responsible for their financial futures, and many do not manage their own resources. Some, like Barbara Hutton, never worked a day in their lives. The women in the moneyfolly pantheon, moreover, are seldom happy or well-adjusted. Barbara Hutton was one of the unhappiest. Placed in boarding schools after her mother killed herself, she was a lonely child, ignored by her father and shunned by schoolmates who envied her money. When the girls at Miss Shin's School told Barbara that people would always hate her because she was so rich, she asked her aunt if she could give her money away. After her aunt said no, Barbara proceeded to cut up all her clothes with a pair of scissors. Her deprived childhood condemned her to repeat this

---

* Some of the new women's magazines such as *Working Woman* and *Savvy* are attempting to correct the myth by presenting portraits of sensible high-earners who live interesting lives.

self-destructive act throughout her life, which she passed with no higher purpose than trying to prove she could give her money away or destroy her resources. She died alone and almost penniless, addicted to alcohol and drugs.[6]

Detecting Moneyfolly: The Little Match Girl Who Earned Six Figures

Moneyblowers may strive for money and fame to compensate for a lack of love and attention in troubled childhoods. It is often when a woman has struggled up the ladder of success, and finally has money to burn, however, that her real anxieties are illuminated. When efforts to overcome financial difficulties, which take so much energy and time, are no longer necessary, she may find herself falling apart. For women we envy because they have inherited money or achieved their ambitions, overspending can be a symptom not of success, but of a deep dilemma.

At first, Tiffany did not seem Moneyphobic, but a candidate for the Six-Figure Fantasy come true. At twenty-four she was an all-American beauty with a heart-shaped face, blue eyes, and curly blonde hair. She had a boyfriend who was understandably crazy about her. Not only was she beautiful and adored, she was also successful: Her ingenue role in a television comedy series netted her $100,000 a year. We were not surprised to find that she radiated self-confidence and charm.

We had asked Tiffany to volunteer for an interview because her questionnaire indicated big financial trouble brewing beneath her enviable exterior. Though she earned much more than our other participants under thirty, she had no savings, and owned no stocks, bonds, or real estate. She indicated that her inability to save was an "emotional anxiety."

Now that I am at the point I've worked so hard for, I know I have to start thinking smarter and learn to invest. I find if I have money saved I can be a completely happy person. And saving money for me is rare. Some people are born just plain spoiled, and I will always spoil myself if I can.

Why did a simple financial activity like saving represent a happiness this high-earner felt unable to achieve? *Spoiled* can mean both "destroyed" and "damaged by overindulgence." Was Tiffany unconsciously trying to ruin herself, and if so, why? What had she learned about the meaning of money in her family? We discovered that the smiling, gracious young actress who had worked her way from a Miami nightclub to New York City's brightest lights, had a persona she often referred to as *you*, as if she was somebody else, while the real Tiffany was a deprived little girl who saw herself as a bag lady from a fairy tale.

Tiffany's rise had been meteoric. By the time she was a senior in high school, she was completely self-supporting and living in an apartment of her own. She was going to school, and dancing in a local nightclub on weekends. A year later she was discovered by a Hollywood agent and moved to the West Coast. After going to drama school Tiffany was soon making $800 a day playing small parts in TV shows, sometimes written in especially for her. Eventually she was offered the important role in the New York–based series. When we met her, she had been making six figures for almost a year and was due for a raise. What was she doing with all this money?

It was not easy to find out. Like many spending addicts, Tiffany hid her habit, even from herself. She did not want to look at, or talk about, the way she managed her money. She rejected investment advice from her manager and boyfriend, and felt humiliated by our questions about her spending. She said they made her feel that she was on "the gynecologist's table." She said:

You just pretend you are somebody else.

She denied she was a "shopaholic":

I spend a lot of money on myself, but nothing big. I don't have a lot to show for it. I think I treat myself fairly okay. Anytime I want to get some things I do. Play things. Um . . . gifts for friends.

Whenever I'm out, if I see something someone would like I grab it . . . things . . . you know, a new pair of sneakers . . . whatever. I don't like to feel deprived. I was never the type to leave $100 sitting in the bank. If I saw a wonderful new $80 red jacket that I had to have . . . well, I would have to have it.

We pressed Tiffany for details on how much all these "little things" cost:

Int.: How much a month do you spend on clothes, would you say?
T.: Not that much—$500.
Int.: You keep track then?
T.: No. . . .
Int.: So you spend about $6,000 a year on clothes?
T.: More than that.

Tiffany "grabbed" anything that caught her eye, showered her boyfriends with $600 carpets and $800 exotic plants, and indulged in "nice $100 dinners." She did manage to save for a trip to Europe; she told us she needed $2,000 "just to shop."

I got a nice paisley silk jacket . . . no, two silk jackets. I got some luggage, real nice luggage that was very expensive, and, of course, makeup and perfume of every scent . . . lots of things like that. Outfits and shoes, lots of shoes.

Did all these new presents give Tiffany pleasure? Like most moneybingers, she wasn't sure.

I had fun, but now these things are all thrown about, and I can't even enjoy them. [Tentatively] Of course I had fun. . . .

The reason Tiffany had no place to put her purchases, we learned, was because she did not have her own apartment. Though she had been in New York for more than nine months, her reckless spending had prevented her from accumulating enough cash to pay a broker's fee, deposit, and first month's rent on a "decent place." Feeling "thrown about" (like her purchases), she had lived at a hotel for six months, then moved to a sublet when she fell behind in the bills. When we interviewed her, she was staying in a "little rathole" someone had loaned her.

A home was extremely important to Tiffany, despite the fact she had not yet managed to find one. She told us that once she had a desk, and a place to organize her checks and bills—a "center"—she could begin to manage her money better. Home also represented a center of emotional tranquility.

> For what I do, for how I get my work done, it calls for a whole lot of concentration. I need a home, and to know that my desk is there, and the TV, and the VCR, so I can sit down for hours upon hours and study my part.

If home was such an important place, why had Tiffany invested in homelessness? Unlike the moneyeluder who finds it difficult to leave the safety of home for the insecurity of the marketplace, Tiffany was like a modern Dorothy who had gotten stranded in Oz and could not find her way back up the yellow brick road to Kansas.

As she began to open up and reveal her real self instead of her starlet persona, we realized that home had never been a place where Tiffany felt cared for or secure. Her childhood home had been "broken" by her parents' divorce when she was seven. Her father was an unreliable gambler, who cardsharped the rent money away.

> He's a high roller. He never had a job in his life.

Although Tiffany and her two sisters visited him every summer, he never paid regular child support. It fell upon her mother to take care of her family by working as a secretary until she remarried four years later.

> She did it on her own. She's a very tough lady.

After she remarried, Tiffany's mother continued to work. She raised her daughters to believe that they would be responsible for their own support.

> I had a very strong mother, and I watched her all those years, working really hard. She said, "I want you to do well, to do what you want to do." The trick of it is knowing that you can't depend on someone else.

From her hardworking mother, then, Tiffany learned how to go out into the world and become an independent risk-taker. Unfortunately, she was taught this important lesson at a high emotional cost. Her father was not there, and her mother had little time to spend with her children.

> It was hard being away from her during the day, and having to do all the things she had no time to do. She was tired on the weekend.

Tiffany, then, felt neglected by her mother, who had no choice but to work during her children's formative years. When her mother remarried, home became a threatening place. Tiffany confided that her mother's second husband, her stepfather, was abusive and beat her mother when he was drunk.

> He wasn't too cheery to be in a household with. I always saw my mother staying with him because she couldn't keep doing it on her own.

When Tiffany talked about her stepfather, her voice dropped to a distracted whisper. We wondered if he had abused Tiffany, too. She also told us that homelessness went back a generation in her family. Her mother had been placed in a Catholic home by her mother, who said she could not afford to keep her. Tiffany, a sensitive child who loved her mother and identified strongly with her, suffered for her as well as for herself.

Deprived of the attention and sense of security a child needs to feel loved, Tiffany learned that money could be used to buy consolation or communicate emotions.

After she remarried my mother's income was really play money for us girls. I think it was my mom's way of saying that she was sorry she was away all day. Or that she had been poor and she wanted us to have all the things she didn't have. Even though my family didn't have a lot of money, my sister and I always looked like a million bucks. We always had new clothes, makeup, and all the things that make it fun to be a girl. So I found out that having new things made me feel good. If you don't want to wake up in the morning, but you have a pretty new sweater (in bright red) to put on, you are out of bed in two seconds, looking at the sunshine.

The real Tiffany, then, missed having loving, responsive parents. But the Tiffany persona could put on a new costume in a color that did not express the way she felt inside, and become someone else—sunny and confident. She began her adulthood, then, with all the psychological ingredients to become an ambitious high-earner, unafraid of risk or success, who binged and blew the money she made in order to block out deeply rooted feelings of deprivation.

Though she had no home of her own, Tiffany's fantasies were all about houses. She wanted to buy a house for her mother. She planned to donate money to a home for abused children, with whom she also identified, when and if she could put a halt to her compulsive spending. She fantasized about homes of her own—villas in the South of France and California, and apartments, reminiscent of the luxury palaces of thirties' screen stars.

In California I was struggling and working for something, and when I got it, I expected it to be glorious. A penthouse, you know, with white carpets and a white marble fireplace. To be living somewhere fabulous! That didn't happen. The opposite happened.

For Tiffany, a home was a fantasy she expected success would make real. It symbolized the emotional security she so desperately needed and did not have. This young actress, earning more money in one year than most women her age could earn in four, told us:

I feel just like the Little Match Girl.

Tiffany had chosen a homeless character from the saddest of Hans Christian Andersen's fairy tales to identify as herself. The Little Match Girl, who is also beautiful and abused, wanders the street barefoot on a freezing New Year's Eve, afraid to go home, because she knows her father will beat her for failing to sell her matches. In order to warm her fingers, blue with cold, she begins to light match after match. In the brief glow of each, she sees a tempting fantasy of holiday cheer in a warm, secure home—a roast goose, a Christmas tree with thousands of lighted candles gleaming under its branches. When the match goes out, this youthful bag lady's fantasy fades with it. Finally, her dead grandmother, who loved her, appears in the glow.

She hastily struck a whole bundle of matches, because she did so long to keep her grandmother with her. She lifted the little girl up in her arms and they soared in a halo of light and joy, far, far above the earth, where there was no more cold, no more hunger, and no pain. . . . In the cold morning light the poor little girl sat there in the corner between the houses, with rosy cheeks and a smile on her face—dead. Frozen to death on the last night of the old year . . . with the ends of burnt-out matches in her hand.[7]

Home, for the Match Girl, is more than a place; it represents a positive emotional state where one feels loved and secure. Ironically, those who get insufficient love in childhood may continue to deprive themselves of the people who could give them love, or not be able to take it in, because they want it from those who denied it in the past. Tiffany also deprives herself of the *place* that symbolizes emotional contentment—dramatizing her internal plight. Like her poignant fairy tale role model, she burns her inventory, forgetting that it may be limited, as she fantasizes secure and comfortable homes.

Unlike the Match Girl, however, Tiffany has the financial resources to get what she needs. She spends on "little things" in order not to feel pain, but material consolations fail to console her. In order to give herself a "home," she must unite the two Tiffanies and face the neglected child, frozen at the center of the beautiful and successful actress. She cannot change her childhood, but with the help of psychotherapy, she can explore its deprivations, mourn for herself, and then accept them. She can learn to provide a good mother and a warm hearth for the sad little vagabond she harbors within.

Moneyfolly Fantasies

Though few moneybingers are as emotionally deprived (or as successful) as Tiffany, all spend in order to experience brief, glowing fantasies. All see visions of a different, better, or more interesting life as they spend. Though women commit moneyfolly in numerous ways, it is easiest to pinpoint their anxieties and fantasies when they spend on jewelry and clothes—the most logical props for an imaginary drama.

Shoppers and bargain hunters set out for the stores in response to anxious feelings. Usually the shopper defines them, if at all, as anger, boredom, or restlessness. The shopping, like any addictive habit, momentarily relieves the troubled emotions and prevents the shopper from exploring them further. The more compulsive and destructive the habit, it seems, the more deeply buried are its emotional causes and the less able the shopper is to see them. Little Match Girls, like Tiffany, with debilitating out-of-control spending addictions, are expressing feelings of deprivation and emptiness that began in childhood. Other, more moderate moneyblowers may be responding to the frustrations of their adult lives. As they shop, the anxieties give way to pleasurable fantasies, which offer a real, if brief sensation of relief. If these women remain alert to their feelings while shopping, they can learn much about their real emotional needs.

A writer who worked alone at home, said she had been leading a dull, celibate life while trying to make a book deadline. Though she said she shopped mainly because it got her out of the house and relaxed her, she confessed that she was spending all of her discretionary income on clothes. What was she really shopping for?

> Every night I dream about sex, usually with strange men. In the morning I feel satisfied, more than deprived, but by the afternoon I'm usually shopping, whether I want to or not, and buying things I don't really need. Once I bought a white silk faille dinner suit —the kind of thing you wear to a Florida bar mitzvah. I remember looking at it on the rack and fantasizing being out to dinner with a handsome man in a tropical setting. Just like a scene from *Casablanca!* It was a great bargain, so of course I bought it. I think I wore it once to my cousin's wedding.

This writer is actually shopping for the sex and adventure she believes her work schedule denies her.

Clothes furnish costumes for a woman's fantasy life and also deck out her fantasy persona—the different self she might like to be. A working mother told us:

> I have this dress I bought a while ago, thinking of a slinky image. It was a beautiful champagne knit with a **V** front. . . . And I pictured myself walking into a room . . . sexy . . . I never took the tags off because it's not me . . . I'm not sexy, I'm not slinky, I'm your basic . . .

Shopping can also provide transportation from a demanding modern life, where a woman is responsible for her own support, to a more romantic era, where her rescue fantasies would be fulfilled. One single corporation executive who hedged her shopping habit by buying collectibles she could resell at a profit, said:

> When I'm feeling depressed I'll go on a shopping binge. My passion is antique jewelry. When I look at these beautiful things,

done in such detail, so feminine, so delicate, I kind of get away from my reality into the Victorian era. Then I have to own it. It takes me out of a rotten, painful life into a soothing world, and gets me out of my depression temporarily.

Sometimes it is the relationship of buyer to seller that offers emotional relief. One harassed mother, who was nursing an ailing relative and maintaining a large suburban home, as well as working, shopped for attention and help.

I have trouble with sizes, so I find myself in a specialty store where someone will help me. I enjoy having somebody help me . . . "Oh, try this! Try that!" That last paycheck I blew at Ms. Bazaar . . . what intrigued me there was this little girl who kept pulling things off the rack and who knew by looking at me what would look good. If it looks good, I'll buy it, and if it comes in three different colors, I'll buy three.

These shoppers are using money to solve problems through illusion; with imagination and a willingness to change a pleasure-giving habit, they might use their resources to provide real solutions. The writer, for example, might spend on an adventurous weekend trip instead of clothes; the harassed mother might "blow" her paycheck on a part-time housekeeper.

Shopping habits, we learned, are not always ultimately destructive. Sometimes shopping can put women in touch with buried skills, as well as problems. For one of the participants in our suburban money group, bargain-hunting was a way of using familiar behavior to recognize and develop latent abilities. Kit, forty-three, had been a high school teacher since college graduation and was thinking of changing professions—for her, a major step.

My parents wanted me to be a teacher. They felt it was a respectable occupation for a woman with a family. In 1965 you listened to them. Now, I'm burned out. I've been a successful teacher for twenty years, and I'd like to try something new.

In our group meeting, Kit confessed she was an avid bargain hunter.

> I want to die next to a clothes rack. I'm serious. I love it. I just love to shop.

One of the reasons that Kit loved shopping is that when she hit the stores she used business skills that she had no opportunity to employ in her teaching job. She hunted for clothes with the same high-powered intensity with which Wall Street brokers buy stocks, researching the market, and as Shearson Lehman Brothers advises its clients, "investing her time before she invested her money."

> I like to go to Loehmann's, but before I go there I want to check out Macy's, Bloomingdale's, and a couple of others so I know the quality of what I'm getting when I hit Loehmann's. It's not like I go there and don't know what I'm buying. I know the inventory.

She used her shopping time with maximum efficiency; like the frenzied broker, she grabbed a quick lunch on the job.

> I can set out in the morning, plan my day, and hit five different places. Sometimes I pack lunch and eat it in the car, so I don't waste any time.

Like any successful businesswoman, Kit prided herself on her astute eye for value.

> If I don't get it on sale, I feel like I've betrayed myself, that someone's putting one over on me. The other day, I saw the same Cathy Hardwick jeans I bought at Clothing Town for $27.90 for $48 at Macy's. I wanted to shout, "Look what I found!" I mean, I felt great!

Sometimes she left the domestic market to invest in foreign commodities.

Last year I went to London, determined to get a good-quality camel suit. A Jaeger suit. And I don't know what the hell I paid for it. I think I paid 90 pounds for the skirt alone. I have to admit I went to England mainly to shop. I could have cared less about the crown jewels.

Like stocks, bargains have seasonal ups and downs, and Kit accommodates.

There are seasons when I have a low period—when nothing's on sale, and I know I can't wear the stuff I'm seeing in the stores for a couple more months.

Though Kit is proud of her shopping expertise, she guiltily smuggles her purchases into the house.

I bring them home and slither them into the closet. I feel, Why get my husband all upset? Why aggravate him? There's no need for this. And eventually he might see it on me, and he might say, "Gee, when did you get that?" and I'll say, "This? Oh, I've had it for a while."

On her questionnaire, Kit had confided that her husband was jealous when she went to New York for a job interview.

I could sense the jealousy in my husband. I know that if I do change my profession, he will feel threatened.

Kit's husband's jealousy gives her ambivalent feelings. On the one hand, it confirms her own success, and on the other, it threatens their relationship. Her husband, she told us, would not object to her spending the money she earned on clothes. Why, then, does she hide her bargains from him? We felt that what she was hiding was not the clothes, but her ability to match wits with the marketplace, and her desire to turn her consumer savvy into income-producing power. It may have been the fear of transgressing career boundaries, imposed first by her relationship with her parents, then by the one with her husband, that kept this talented, assertive woman in a profession that had ceased to challenge her for so many years.

Kit drove us home after the money group meeting and told us a secret. She had just been offered a new job as a sales representative for a large office furniture company and was considering quitting her teaching job to work partly on a commission basis. We suspected that shopping would become less of a preoccupation once Kit gave herself the opportunity to exercise the skills she had shown as a consumer in a seller's marketplace. Kit was using shopping as a training program: As she hunted for bargains she expressed and enjoyed abilities that had not been encouraged in her career-planning years. Traditional feminine behavior was helping her pinpoint her career fantasies and develop the confidence she needed to take new risks.

Overcoming Moneyfolly: The Moneywatch

Stopping moneyfolly, like stopping overeating, calls for a twofold approach. First, moneyfolly victims must step outside their spending behavior long enough to see how they are using money, and label the anxieties and fantasies they bring to the process. If they are moneybingers, once they see that what they are shopping for is love, comfort, or self-esteem and not a red sweater, they have taken the first step toward limiting the addiction's control. Moneypissers, too, must examine the emotions that influence their spending. Most important, any woman prone to moneyfolly must develop "moneywatching" techniques in order to observe when, and under what conditions, she is inclined to spend, and how much money passes from hand to store. Organizations like Debtors Anonymous, based on the principles of Alcoholics Anonymous, give overspenders group support and specific methods to help them halt their rampages.

The moneyfolly victim in search of a cure must prepare herself to experience what will at first seem like deprivation as she trades in her habitual overspending pattern for a higher goal—getting a grip on her financial life. Some, like this Los Angeles woman, resort to unique and drastic measures to curb their moneyfolly:

> I took my credit cards, put them in an ice cube tray, and froze them. Since I don't have a microwave, I'll have to think for quite a while before I use them.

A financial diet, like a diet that restricts the intake of food, is most likely to become a permanent way of life when it feels like a positive expansion of the entire self, rather than a temporary or one-dimensional punitive act. Overspenders in our money group who went on the "moneywatch" and wrote down their daily expenses in a notebook, reported that not only did their expenditures drop, but they also learned interesting facts about themselves and other people.

Andrea, who wanted to save so that she could buy her apartment and travel, saw that she could exploit others when she was not exploiting herself—a character trait she found "disturbing."

> I wrote down so much for subway, so much for drinks, and so much for this and that. I told all my friends I was doing this. I didn't stop going out for drinks at first, but I'd bring $10, and that's all I'd bring, so I wouldn't spend more than that. I have one male friend, whom I sense wouldn't mind being more. He's an easy prey in a way; I know him well enough to know that he has a thing about taking care of women. When he said, "Have another drink" and I said, "I can't, I don't have the money," he'd say, "Oh, that's okay. I have money." I discovered a willingness in myself to let someone else pay, to take advantage . . . a feeling that if he wanted to throw his money away on me, let him do it. That made me feel uncomfortable. This guy isn't rich; in fact, he makes slightly less than I do. To be a real friend to him would have been to say, "Don't do this! You shouldn't be spending your money either."

Another participant on the "moneywatch" began to see a man she was dating in a different light.

When I looked up the year my ex-husband's maintenance payments end, and began keeping a mental record of my expenses, I began to realize that Dave has terrible money problems, too. The minute he has it, he blows it all, and then he's broke again. I liked it when he spent on me, but I asked myself, "Do I need a man with my binging problem?"

Ridding oneself of moneyfolly does not imply a life devoid of the pleasures of spending. Women who learn to control their spending really enjoy the things that they buy. They make consumer decisions, instead of responding to hidden anxieties. Ilona, a New York psychoanalyst, decided to celebrate her graduation from an analytic institute by buying herself an expensive bracelet to replace a piece of heirloom jewelry that had been stolen from her apartment. She budgeted between $500 and $700 for the piece, got dressed up, "like the kind of person who could pull out a checkbook and write a check for a large amount," and went to a Fifth Avenue jewelry store. She promptly ran afoul of seller sexism. When she hesitated over one bracelet and asked to see more, the salesman suggested, "Why don't you come back with your husband?"

The idea was that I hesitated because I needed my husband to approve of the bracelet, aesthetically as well as financially. I said, "Sir, there is no husband, and it is time you realized that women are buying their own jewelry and paying for it with their own money." I walked out of that store and felt great, like I was flying down Fifth Avenue.

Ilona is not shopping for love, but for a bracelet. She is not blowing money; she has decided to spend it in order to reward herself for a significant accomplishment. With this clear purpose in mind, she is not about to allow anyone to deter her from the full pleasure of spending on herself. For her, spending symbolizes the control she has over her life, not the lack of it. A sexist salesman would most likely have made a moneyfolly victim in a similar situation feel guilty and alone.

When a woman cures herself of moneyfolly, saving, as well as spending, becomes a source of satisfaction. While earning and spending are an integral part of our financial present and past, savings determine our financial future. Savings also increase our wealth, because investing—an important facet of the earning process—cannot be undertaken without an initial sum of saved money to invest.

As women become less Moneyphobic, they tend to look in the future direction, and translate savings into financial goals with a place and a name. When they can do this, "putting money away" seems less like a deprivation. Time often helps women to see the necessity to save, but if they have been big-time spenders, they have to help themselves modify their financial behavior. Let's look at one moneyblower as she begins the painful process of starting to save.

Molly, a New York fashion designer who worked hard to develop her lucrative career after she was divorced, now earns more than $50,000. Until she was forty-one, however, she spent every cent she made on herself and her two children.

> What gave me the desire to be ambitious and make money was the desire to spend it. I feel like I can now look at my house and see the things that I bought and that feels good to me. I don't want to wear overalls anymore. And when I take the kids out to dinner, instead of taking them to McDonald's and spending $10, I take them to Hamburger Harry's and spend $25. That's the way I've always been. I'm not cautious about money and spend pretty much whatever I have.

As Molly starts to save, the new experience is uncomfortable, like a diet.

> I don't like it that I have to take the money I've really worked hard for and put it away instead of spending it, so I'll have money when I'm sixty-five or seventy. But if I don't do it, there's not going to be anything there. When I turned forty, I started to think about some of this stuff.

Her new financial experience makes her question her rescue fantasies, often at the bottom of moneyfolly.

I've recently given myself a budget for the first time in my life. The reason I never had a savings account was partly because I was afraid that if I had one I would really save. It was that part of me that says, "Why do I have to do it all? Why doesn't someone come along and take care of me . . . ?" There's not much there yet, but I like having the savings.

Though Molly is about to marry a man she loves, as she puts money in the bank, she realizes that taking full financial responsibility for herself is satisfying as well as necessary. She begins to see her savings account more positively.

I would like to have investments . . . I would like to own property, and have a house in the country. I want to buy art . . . stocks!

As her savings begin to represent exciting images of resources that will make her future life not only more secure but also more enjoyable, this ambitious and successful high-earner joins the ranks of the very few women who are finally Moneyphobia free.

CHAPTER 6

Moneyparanoia

Moneyparanoid women believe others will rip them off, or that by overspending, they will rip themselves off. They use their money to build protective fortresses that make them feel secure.

The moneyparanoid may be moneyholders—female Scrooges who are obsessive savers. Lady skinflints are seldom generous with others or even with themselves. Friends term them "cheap," and they fear exploitation. It is hard for the moneyholder to distinguish between dollars and pennies or to part with her "secret stash." She may sock away money for a specific goal, denying herself creature comforts she can well afford, but she never buys or does what she is saving for. Sometimes she spends freely on one thing, then withholds on another, buying an expensive dress, then punishing herself by making chicken soup with backs and necks for dinner. She equalizes assets and debits to keep the fortress strong, and her cheapness causes conflicts with those she regards as "spenders."

Not all who suffer from moneyparanoia are cheap, however; some fear others more than themselves. They are afraid that friends and threatening strangers are plotting to borrow or steal their money, lean on them, live off them, or "suck them dry." These Fortress Women can spend, but they may do so in the wrong places, on the wrong people, or at the wrong times, making their moneyparanoia a self-fulfilling prophecy. As irony will have it, they *do* get ripped off, often by the men in their lives.

The moneyparanoid may be obsessive savers who salt away modest salaries (some of the women in our study with significant assets earned much less than moneyfolly victims who spent it all), but usually they are successful, with highly developed financial identities. Unlike the moneyblind, they understand the power of money and zero in on their financial horizons. Though the most paranoid are hush-hush about finances, and maintain money secrets, because they do not want potential exploiters to get wind of how much they have, many speak frankly about the subject that occupies a central role in their thoughts and feelings. Unlike eluders and the moneyconfused, the "paranoid" are good at earning, managing, and especially negotiating; they know how to fend for their financial rights in the marketplace. These future-oriented women never imagine that anyone will rescue them—quite the contrary! In many ways, the moneyparanoid appear a step ahead of other women in terms of financial behavior and have accomplished some important financial goals. But they use money to sabotage themselves emotionally.

Moneyparanoid women cherish deep feelings of insecurity about their future well-being and often suffer from low self-esteem. Even if they are successful, they may not have internalized their success or identified themselves with it. They feel the slightest wrong move will topple their fortress, which for them is bogus, like an illusion of Oz. A vice-president of a large financial conglomerate who earned more than six figures told us:

It's one step from the shithouse to the penthouse, and vice versa.

Because they have little faith in the fortress's foundations, the moneyparanoid do their utmost to increase the thickness of its outer walls. They try to accumulate as many assets as possible, and their insecurity may be mistaken for greed. One real estate tycoon said she felt that her success was "luck with a marshmallow."

What is enough? I need a million dollars. With a million dollars I will feel that I have achieved something. My worry is that if I do get there I won't be able to stop. When one deal goes down and I don't have another to jump into I feel horrible about myself. When does it end? When do I stop? That's what I ask myself.

These women invest the dollar sign with magical powers and believe money will take care of their emotional needs.

Because they feel their position is precarious, it becomes important for the moneyparanoid to control others and themselves. Money—a symbol of power and security—is seen as a mechanism of control. While bingers and blowers succumb to uncontrollable urges to spend in order to satisfy emotional needs, the moneyparanoid solve emotional dilemmas by maintaining financial control at any cost. Some save, controlling themselves, and others spend (or do not spend) to control those they fear may exploit them.

The financial behavior of the woman who suffers from Deadly Symptom #6 is rigid. Instead of seizing opportunities to vary her financial modus operandi according to her needs, she sticks to narrowly defined ideas of how, why, and when she should use money. She can live behind the unyielding walls she constructs with her dollars and feel more or less in control, but the minute a crack appears, or someone arrives who might tear the wall down, she panics and becomes even more inflexible. She puts so much energy into fighting off the enemy—and the enemy can be within—that she loses touch with her own internal experience.

Ann, one of the withholders in our study, for example, felt too guilty about spending on a new hairstyle to enjoy it.

> I went to Bendel's and blew $100 on a haircut and perm. Afterwards, I was so guilt-stricken I couldn't sleep, and woke up at night for a week thinking about it. Even though I'm looking for work, and feel more confident with curly hair, I thought I could have done something cheaper to make it look better. I got no pleasure from it. I couldn't decide whether I liked it or not. I've been feeling like a failure lately, and I don't feel like I deserve anything. I only feel I deserve to reward myself when I'm working hard . . . killing myself!

Ann also told us that she was considering delving into her savings to buy a personal computer, but was afraid that once she started spending, she would never stop. This moneyholder feels she lacks control over her life, and tries to restore law and order by refraining from spending.

The moneyparanoid may recognize their symptom as inhibiting behavior and try to eradicate it. However, they tend to do so in a way that confirms their suspicions that others are trying to rip them off, and their fears distort their instincts and perceptions. One Fortress Woman loaned $300 to a boyfriend who had never been reliable.

> Originally I offered to loan him $100, but he asked me for more. I agonized over the decision. I knew that he—and a lot of other people—think I'm a tightwad. We were getting back together and I wanted to show him I could be there for him. I thought, He needs me to express my feelings with money; am I capable of giving him what he needs? Secretly, I thought that if he realized I cared about him enough to loan him money—a big move for me —maybe he'd respond by being a better boyfriend. When I thought about it, $300 didn't seem like so much. I thought I could afford to lose it. I only saw him once after the loan; he disappeared and never paid me back, and never contacted me about the money. The three hundred began to seem like three million. I couldn't forgive myself. I decided I'd never loan money to anyone again.

This woman had attempted to control a man who had already proven untrustworthy. Now, armed with evidence that others will indeed try to rip her off, she can justify her real desire to remain a "tightwad" and close herself off to the possibility for change.

The most severe cases of moneyparanoia, however, never made it into our study. These women inevitably expressed more than passing interest in our subject, and enthusiastically offered help and information. Naturally, we contacted them and asked them to fill out the questionnaire—a prerequisite for an in-depth interview. Suddenly, we encountered serious resistance. A Florida lawyer, earning six figures, refused to participate for fear of leaving "a paper trail for the IRS." A twenty-seven-year-old Texas entrepreneur sent us names of experts on the money question, told us about money seminars in her state, and described her job developing real estate with a new lover. She graciously offered to "share her knowledge about money with us." We sent her two questionnaires, at her request, but never received either of them. A Boston woman sent the questionnaire back blank with a letter criticizing our "scientific method." Later, she confided to the mutual friend who had given us her name that the idea of revealing information about her financial behavior had evoked anxieties. These women were in positions of control, and they wanted to stay there. Opening up about money would have made them feel vulnerable and exposed.

The Case of "The Yellow Duck"

Often it was not money per se that elicited fear in the moneyparanoid, but the way money was entangled in their emotional lives. We approached one friend, a high-earning New York cosmetics executive whose questionnaire we had not yet received, and said we hoped she would soon find time to complete it. Somewhat precipitously, we told her that we were anxious to interview her about her experience supporting a man for fifteen years. She panicked immediately, saying she did not want to talk about *that*—she did not like it, but had had no choice —and she hoped our questionnaire didn't ask questions about *that!* She would, however, be delighted to tell us how her moneymaking goals had become more concrete in her thirties—a subject our readers would want to hear about. We said that for better or worse we had developed certain rules, and before we could interview her, we needed the questionnaire. She retorted that no woman in her right mind would provide such personal financial information and sign her name to it! What if the IRS saw it? Or someone else? We explained that anonymity was guaranteed, and respondents were welcome to eliminate any question that made them uncomfortable, provided they explained why—including those that asked for details about salary and assets. She allowed that maybe she would fill out the questionnaire, but she would never sign it with her real name. "I'll use a pseudonym like . . . Yellow Duck!" she told us.

We thought *Yellow* stood for "chicken" more than for "duck," and that *Duck* was for "ducking out." By telling this powerful woman that we wanted to discuss an aspect of her financial behavior over which she felt she had lost control, we had obviously blundered into a terribly touchy emotional area and deprived ourselves of a valuable case history.

Why Women Are Moneyparanoid

No discussion of moneyparanoia could exclude Sigmund Freud, who linked frugality and parsimony with the anal stage of human development. According to this famous theory of infant sexuality, the infant sees his feces as his most treasured possession, and its elimination gives him erotic pleasure. During the toilet-training process, he comes to view what to him is precious, and to his parents "filth," as a gift, or an object to hoard—a symbol of the power struggle between himself and his parents. Money eventually takes the place of excrement, Freud said, and in the adult mind may evoke the same responses and symbolize the same conflicts.

If the infant is toilet trained gently and persuasively at the appropriate time (that is, when he is physiologically and emotionally ready), he learns that he can have control over himself as well as his parents' approval. If he is trained too early and punitively, before he is able to perform this important developmental task, he experiences shame and self-doubt, which he brings to the next stage of his development. He may grow up with an exaggerated sense of the importance of control, not trusting himself or others to "let go" and resenting submission to authority. In a society that values money, he comes to see money as a symbol of control, and may use it to control himself and others. He may believe that people are conspiring to take his money away, just as his mother took away his feces, and as a result, he hoards and saves.

Though nothing in the Freudian theory leads us to believe that girls are less likely to be harshly toilet trained than boys, most of the money-holders we know from life and literature are male. Dickens's Scrooge had to be visited by groaning ghosts on Christmas Eve before he could dig into his coffers to help the crippled Tiny Tim. Howard Hughes, despite his fathomless wealth, borrowed tuxedos, packed his possessions in cardboard boxes instead of Vuitton trunks, and never picked up a tab if he could help it. John Paul Getty, another famous miser, once installed a pay phone in his mansion, and John D. Rockefeller, charged for two chickens instead of one in a restaurant, demanded that the bones be reassembled as proof before he would pay.

History provides more examples of moneyparanoid men for the simple reason that men have always had more money to fear losing. Before women had money of their own to withhold, however, they practiced the principles of moneyholding in their housekeeping roles. Traditionally, a good housewife was frugal, mending, cleaning and repairing to stretch money as far as it would go, and controlling the family's day-to-day expenditures. Often she had a "secret stash," saved from her housekeeping money, which her husband knew nothing about. (Even today, one in five wives keeps a cache hidden from her husband.)[1] Some wives treated food as a resource to be withheld and guarded protectively. One woman told us that her mother's refrigerator was her "safety deposit box."

> She saves all the leftovers in labeled containers. Only she knows what's in there, and is allowed free access. If you open the door, looking for something to eat, you feel you're invading her territory. She watches you suspiciously, saying, "Don't eat that cheese! It will spoil your dinner," or she says, "You can have an apple and some iced tea, if you want it." You get the feeling you shouldn't be anywhere near her refrigerator. God help you if you eat something for lunch that she was planning to serve for dinner.

Though female misers are viewed in a negative light—because women are expected to be generous, open, and trusting—anal practices in the context of the middle-class home have long been viewed as a feminine virtue.

When women earn or inherit money of their own, however, moneyparanoia grips them just as it does their successful male counterparts. But not all moneyparanoia harks back to our toilet training; fears of exploitation accurately reflect the social and economic status of women in our society today. According to *Working Woman* magazine's November 1985 survey, "Love and Money in the 1980s," one out of two affluent, well-educated women fears ending up destitute and suffers from "bag lady" nightmares. As *Working Woman* pointed out, there is a real basis to the bag lady fear; one-fifth of all older women live in poverty.* What *Working Woman* didn't explain is why high-earning women with retirement plans and substantial assets should continue to fear eventual destitution. Older women in our society are not only poor but socially devalued, cast aside by employers or sometimes by husbands, and deemed "undesirable" by men. A bag lady is a useless, discarded, lonely, isolated, unattractive outcast! Women with money who are afraid of becoming homeless and carrying their belongings around in bags, are reacting to the *emotional state* that the bag lady symbolizes. They believe that no amount of money in the bank will decrease the vulnerability of old age. Given the harsh realities that confront American women as they get older (including those who are not bag ladies), it is a wonder that more women do not become moneyparanoid withholders.

Most of us, however, prefer to deny our fears and fantasize that others will take care of our futures. Moneydeniers binge and blow to obliterate the painful bag lady vision. The moneyparanoid woman, on the other hand, believes a store of money will combat her feelings of emotional as well as financial precariousness. She can never have enough! Somewhere in the middle are the women with non-Money-phobic financial identities, who use investments and savings to hedge their financial futures, and seek other solutions for emotional insecurity.

Successful women who fall victim to moneyparanoia may also be responding to the same fears that prevent the moneyeluder from earning. Having achieved success, they now believe that they have been indelibly marked as "deviant" or "enviable," and that others will try to reduce them to a more typically feminine lowly status by taking what they have away from them. If they feel their success is a fraud, as many do, they may believe they deserve a comeuppance; but they project their own unconscious desires to descend to a more comfortable rung

---

* According to the National Organization for Women, because women earn less than men, they also receive about 60 percent less in social security benefits, or $4,226 for women as compared to $7,342 for men.

of the ladder on to others and feel afraid. In fact, rich women *are* often the target of envy, manipulation, and even violence. Did Claus von Bulow marry his wife, Sunny, for her $75 million, then try to kill her with an insulin injection so he could go off in style with another woman? Even though he was found not guilty, Von Bulow's saga must have fueled many simmering cases of moneyparanoia in women far less wealthy than the Pittsburgh heiress.

THE FIRST OF THE BIG-TIME WOMEN WITHHOLDERS: HETTY GREEN

Hetty Green, "The Witch of Wall Street," is the world's most notorious moneyparanoid woman. Born to a wealthy New Bedford whaling family in 1835, Hetty grew up reading stock market quotations on her father's knee and following him about town as he conducted his business. She had little positive feminine influence: Her mother, whose own sizable fortune had been removed from her hands by her husband, took to her bed after the death of her infant son and stayed there. Hetty's aunt, also rich, was bedridden, too, and bequeathed much of her fortune to a manipulative doctor.

When Hetty grew up, she continued to follow in her father's footsteps, amassing a personal fortune of $7 million by 1900. (At that time, the national average income was $490, and the tab for a nine-course meal at Delmonico's was less than 75 cents.) By 1908, her real estate holdings, stocks, railroads, and other properties had increased in value to $150 million.

Hetty, however, did not enjoy her wealth; she merely accumulated it and fought off those she believed were conspiring to take it away. Throughout her life she dressed in dingy rags, did not bathe, and lived in cheap, working-class boarding houses in Hoboken instead of in the mansions she could well afford. She dined on cold oatmeal, which she heated on the radiator of her Wall Street office. (In 1888 her weekly expenses were estimated at $9.) She sacrificed health, as well as comfort, to her moneyparanoid fears. Her son Ned's infected leg was eventually amputated because his penny-pinching mother dragged him from clinic to clinic, pretending to be a poor immigrant, in hopes of obtaining free medical care. Hetty herself suffered from an enormous hernia for twenty years rather than pay a surgeon to remove it. Stories about her cheapness are endless. She once spent half a night searching for a misplaced two-cent stamp. She was not beyond shady dealings to save and obtain either. She forged a false will in order to garner more than her share of her dead aunt's fortune, and evaded taxes by moving furtively from state to state. When she died in 1916, the richest and most detested woman in America, she left not a single penny to charity. Her withholding tendencies, however, were partly responsible for her legendary wealth. When others panicked and sold in stock market recessions, Hetty tenaciously held on; the properties she saved eventually became worth millions of dollars.

Unfortunately, Hetty's moneyparanoia undermines her accomplishments as a financial pioneer. This original "Supermom" was one of the first women to invade and conquer the all-male Wall Street domain. Being a "first," however, was part of her problem. Like many ambitious women today, Hetty had no role models to teach her how she could preserve the positive traits of her sex and still pursue her professional interests. Having seen her neurasthenic female relatives succumb to illness and financial control, she grew up disassociating femininity from her ambitious drive and fearing male dominance. As a result, she forged her personal, primitive financial style, which included denying herself and her family. Determined to out-man the men in a male capitalist world, she evolved into an iconoclastic "economic animal" who played by her own unique rules. Though few women are as withholding—or as wealthy—as Hetty, the same forces that shaped this nineteenth-century tycoon shape moneyparanoid women today.[2]

Detecting Moneyparanoia

Moneyparanoid women were difficult to detect on the basis of their questionnaires. Often they appeared to be earning high salaries and have clear financial goals. In our money groups they were regarded as being "together" about money, and provided constructive advice to the moneyeluders and the moneydeniers.

In our two-hour personal interview, however, the Fortress Women were easy to detect. The "rip-off" theme entered the interview in the first five minutes and was repeated throughout. Usually they told a story involving exploitation (of themselves or somebody else) immediately. Some of those who feared exploitation tried to break the rules and rob others before they could be robbed; others tried to gain power by making the rules work to their advantage. For all, money was magic— an almighty power that, if worshipped devoutly, could control and protect. And yet, money magic had failed them; our moneyparanoids had all been exploited at one time or another.

Moneyparanoid women, we learned, had a number of common factors in their backgrounds. They grew up believing that they were responsible for their own support, and although they cherished vague hopes of finding a man who would at least share expenses, they basically did not believe that marriage would make them feel financially secure or enrich them. Most had a male ne'er-do-well (often an alcoholic) in the family and a female relative who had been left impoverished by her relationship with him. Though this "bag lady" may have been a remote cousin or aunt, her misfortune became part of the family myth, cited as a reason that women should be financially independent. Sometimes family hardship had made the moneyparanoid fear poverty or dependence on others. As a result, moneyparanoid women grew up with the belief that they could control their own lives and shield themselves from unpredictable male behavior by having their own money. Often the moneyparanoid woman's parents were "cheap" or gave her money on an inconsistent basis. Sometimes she had parents who encouraged and helped her use her abilities to produce income. Most of the moneyparanoid were financially independent at an early age and earned while they went to college. The amount of money they had or earned was their most important measure of career success.

"THE HORST SYNDROME": HOW ONE FORTRESS WOMAN RIPPED HERSELF OFF

Gabrielle, thirty-nine, had no practical problems with money. She had developed a highly successful direct-mail advertising company, and earned more than $75,000 a year writing and designing promotional brochures. Her company promoted many products, ranging from quartz watches to Caribbean vacations. She had invested her money wisely in a Long Island house (which doubled as her office), and in bonds and limited partnerships, yielding high rates of interest. She said money was "very important to her," and she saw it as a "security blanket."

Gabrielle's anxieties seemed centered on men, but we soon learned that money was part of what troubled all of her relationships. When we interviewed her, she had just gotten out of a ten-year traumatic marriage to an abusive alcoholic, and her lawyer was warring with her husband's lawyer over the divorce settlement. Her husband, it seemed, was claiming a portion of her business, in which he had never been involved, and refused to sign divorce papers until she paid him his share. She was dating two men: a SoHo artist who worked as a carpenter and was bitter about his sporadic success, and an Italian antiques dealer, whom she had met on vacation and saw whenever one of them could make the transatlantic trip. She was already worried that the painter was also a rip-off artist. She had given him $150 in exchange for a lithograph, and now two months had gone by and he had not produced the work or returned the money. At his request, she had purchased one of his paintings, and unsure whether she had succumbed to manipulation, could not decide whether she liked it or not. Gaby was confused. Why did she always choose "roller-coaster guys"—men who were poorer than she was or financially unstable?

> It could be that because I'm steadier making money, I feel a sense of power. I feel I can deal with men better when I have a source of power that they have traditionally had. A man with money might think that what I was making was chickenshit, and want me to give up what I'm doing and play all the time. I feel more in control of guys who are very up and down with money.

Gabrielle was moneyparanoid. Money was instrumental in her desire to control men and to maintain her own autonomy. Her focus on money, however, kept her from focusing on her emotions. She told us that she was good at "fooling herself" and often felt "numb":

But I don't feel numb when I'm making money.

Uncomfortable feelings of emotional numbness had led her to marry the man she was now in the process of divorcing. At twenty-nine, Gaby had succumbed to her mother's pressures to marry and have a child.

When I went home for Christmas, my cousin, who's my age, was pregnant. I thought, Jesus, I'm almost thirty. If I ever want to get pregnant and have a kid, I'd better find myself a husband. That's step number one.

Like many women, Gaby found it difficult to integrate her own ambitions with her mother's traditional script for her life. Cut off from her own feelings, she chose the wrong man.

I knew him about nine months before we got married. It was a stormy courtship; we fought all the time. He did bizarre things, but I swept them under the rug and forgot about them. If you knew what they were, you'd think I was crazy for not dumping this guy immediately. Living alone, I'd started to feel numb. I couldn't feel anything at all. My emotions ran the gamut from A to B. He came along and he was like fire all of a sudden. Even though a lot of the feelings were negative feelings, at least I was feeling. And one of the reasons I got out of the marriage was because I had become totally numb again. The only way I could deal with his tirades and tantrums was to just block them out. In a way, I have him to thank for my success, because I blocked him out by locking myself in my room and working really hard.

Once in a difficult marriage to a man she did not trust, Gaby used money to protect herself. Like many moneyparanoid women, she was excellent at devising "systems" for sharing expenses.

For the first six months he just sort of paid for things. That created a lot of friction. I think I was the one who hit on the system that we finally used: There would be certain things that would be joint expenses, like rent, and others that would be separate, like clothes. And we would write all of our joint expenses down in a book with a column for him and a column for me. At the end of the month we'd total everything up and figure out who owed whom.

At the time, Gaby's husband was earning a good salary, and she was copywriting on a freelance basis for publicists. Her career had not taken off, and she was barely earning a living wage. Gaby feared her husband would exploit her because she earned little and constructed her system so that it would work to her advantage.

I thought because he was older, a man, and had more experience, he would always be earning more. This is where I outmaneuvered myself. I said, "The only fair way to do this is for whoever makes more at the end of the year to pay more of the expenses. Let's say you make a third more than I do. Then you have to cover a third more of the expenses, and vice versa." Shortly after that he got fired, and from then on it was practically always vice versa, and I would end up giving him money at the end of the year. That was a real dumb move on my part!

Later, when Gaby started earning high fees working for prestigious clients, she feared her husband would exploit her because she had much more than he did. She bought land in another state so he could not spend her money.

As time went on it became clearer and clearer he couldn't be trusted. He thought I was paranoid about the money, but all I could see was that here was a man who hated women, and he was going to get me. He knew that money was important to me, and that's what he'd go after if he could.

Her divorce problems, too, were due to financial maneuvers in which she had outsmarted herself. At one point her husband had suggested that she apply for a $20,000 bank loan to get her direct-mail business off the ground. Afraid that he would spend the money and she would be responsible for repaying the loan, Gaby made him sign a partnership agreement, stating that he had invested $5,000 to capitalize the business and owned a percentage of it. That way he, too, would be responsible for repayment.

> We never got the bank loan, but he's got his name on this piece of paper. He now *believes* he actually put $5,000 into my business. He can't come up with a cancelled check because there isn't any.

After a separation Gaby came back to her husband, on condition that he sign an agreement stating that if they split up, neither of them would have to pay the other any money.

> So when I wanted to get out of the marriage, the only thing he had to hang his hat on was his so-called stake in the business. He's still got the general partnership agreement saying he owns a percent of it and that he put money into it, which he never did.

Gabrielle, then, married an untrustworthy man and tried to make the relationship safe by establishing complicated and rigid financial arrangements. Her belief in the magical powers of money led her to give money a job it could not do—protect her from her husband's abuse and take care of her emotionally. Since her husband's abuses were not only financial, and she had other reasons to distrust him, her arrangements did not save her from pain. By becoming "numb," she managed to stay in the doomed relationship. Gaby's systems failed to offer even financial protection; because they were inflexible, they rapidly outmoded themselves. Nevertheless, she continued to put her faith in money, working hard to earn as much as possible; but money could not give her the supportive relationship she wanted and needed.

Why did Gaby choose "roller-coaster guys" and let money stand between her and the closeness she craved? Her family background, we learned, provided fertile soil for moneyparanoia to grow.

Her parents were married during the war and divorced soon thereafter. Her father, angry with her mother, paid almost no child support, and her mother abandoned her nursing career to run a small nursery in her home, so that she could keep her infant daughter with her while she earned a living. When Gaby was five, her mother married a stable man, but did not make Gaby feel part of the secure new household. Instead, she told her that her stepfather supported her out of the "goodness of his heart."

> She emphasized that my father was behind in his payments, and that my stepfather was paying for things he shouldn't have to pay for. She said the only things she could ask him to provide were the food on the table and the roof over our head. When she sent me to dancing school she made a big deal about how she was paying for that out of her own money, and how it was her money that was going to put me through college. I was made to feel that my circumstances were different than my stepsister's. She just complained that my parents were tight.

Gaby, then, grew up feeling insecure about her financial well-being and source of support. She learned early on that she would soon have to take care of herself.

> My mother made it clear that I was going to get an education out of her, and that's all I was going to get. Then you're on your own, baby.

Though her mother forced her to be aware of financial realities, she sheltered her emotionally.

> She thinks children shouldn't know what goes on in the world, about evil things, like sex. Money is practical; you can know about that.

Gaby also learned that men were not to be trusted. Not only her father, but also her uncle, left women "high and dry."

> My aunt was a secretary who got screwed financially by her husband. He went bankrupt and she had to go back to being a secretary.

Her stepsister, too, suffered from what the family now jokingly calls "The Horst Syndrome."

> Every woman in the family so far has managed to come up with a man who's a bum. And that includes me. My stepsister married this German guy who has absolutely no responsibility about money. His name is Horst. So we refer to it as "The Horst Syndrome." The reason it didn't get labeled "The Jack Syndrome" is because my husband at least felt guilty about not making money. Whereas Horst never felt guilty about it at all.

In the clutches of a family myth, which stressed that men were financially unstable, and with unique feelings of personal insecurity, Gaby grew up yearning for closeness, yet afraid that men would rip her off. She also learned moneyparanoid defenses, which helped her to become a high-earner and protect her financial interests, but she did not learn to let her emotions help her decide whom she could trust. Ironically, as an adult, she chooses men who give her a reason to maintain the strong defenses that have helped her survive and function in the world. These men confirm her worst fears and validate her mistrust. Since her defense system includes a high-paid career and financial autonomy, Gaby is afraid that a responsible man who also makes money would compromise this important and positive aspect of her identity.

Gaby desperately wants to break this vicious circle. But moneyparanoia is not easy to shake. Some time after our interview, she told the money group she joined that she had spent a month with her Italian boyfriend and was planning to marry him. He would live with her and look for a job in the States. Since he had less money than she did, she wanted to ask him to sign a prenuptial agreement stating that if the marriage did not work, each partner would leave with only the assets he came in with.

> I thought, If you've ever met a man you could trust it's this man. So why are you putting him through this little exercise? And I finally decided that the reason I'm doing it is to make me feel more comfortable.

Though it is reasonably self-protective to ask a fiancé to sign a prenuptial agreement, Gaby felt her request symbolized mistrust and guiltily tried to compensate. The agreement, she revealed, would apply only to the money each partner brought into the marriage and would state that after marriage, they would "share the pot." The group reacted strongly to this information: What if her new husband, a newcomer to America, failed to earn any money at all? Gaby's career was thriving. Wouldn't the agreement entitle him to half of all the money she earned after they were married? But Gaby still believed in the power of money, and was now using it to convey positive emotions:

> How I felt about money when I married Jack was symbolic of how much I distrusted him. And the symbolism now is that it's really time to trust somebody. Because money is so important to me, I'll let money be the thing that says, "Okay, I trust you, and this is a symbol of my trust."

Gaby believes that money talks, but she has to learn to speak for herself and to hear the replies. She is relying on a purely external criterion to express trust and mistrust. How does she know what money means to her fiancé? Does it symbolize the same emotions? Before she tries to control him with financial agreements, she might enter into a dialogue and find out in what language money speaks to him.

In order to find a trustworthy man, Gaby must be able to trust herself to choose one—difficult, because she was raised to mistrust men. As long as she believes in the magical powers of money to protect her, she will cut herself off from the emotional messages that are telling her whether to trust or not, and in hopes of outmaneuvering the untrustworthy, outmaneuver herself.

Overcoming Moneyparanoia

Moneyparanoia is one of the hardest Moneyphobic symptoms to overcome. Because the moneyparanoid believes in money and the way she uses it, anxiety is created when her financial behavior is defined as a problem. She may feel as if she is disavowing her faith in God, and as if any change would jeopardize her lifestyle and future well-being. Her problem is compounded by society's tendency to reward the money-paranoid. Women who are focused on money are hardworking and know the rules of the marketplace game. They can look at money with understanding, value its importance, and negotiate deals. As a result, they accumulate money and assets, which our materialistic culture commends. In fact, we believe a mild case of moneyparanoia is good for women.

What the severely moneyparanoid do not understand is that market-place rules do not apply in the home, and when practiced there, can sabotage their personal lives. It is only when a Fortress Woman becomes aware that money is coming between herself and her emotional goals that she can take a critical look at her financial behavior. Even then, in order to renounce moneyparanoia, she has to closely examine the way she uses money to solve nonfinancial problems. With hard work on herself, she can become less moneyparanoid.

THE 69¢ BREAKFAST SPECIAL: HOW ONE WITHHOLDER LEARNED TO SPEND

Moneyparanoid women who are capable of spending focus their suspicions and fears on individuals; withholders, however, believe in an almost cosmic conspiracy to rip them off. These are the cheapskates and misers, who try to outwit the marketplace by keeping their money far away from it. They, too, use money protectively.

Sheilah, like Gabrielle, was raised in a perfect climate for the cultivation of moneyparanoia. Her parents, first-generation immigrants, had lived through hard times and become confirmed withholders.

They didn't have much money, and they were very careful about spending it. In my entire childhood we never ate out in a restaurant—that was absolutely a waste of money. To save 10 cents we would walk several miles to the subway instead of taking the bus. My mother still buys reduced rotting vegetables on sale and cheese ends and ham ends.

Like many withholders, Sheilah's parents saved for goals they never accomplished.

> My father's dream was to make a great trip around the world, because he really was a geographer by training, but he ended up working for the telephone company for forty-five years. He wanted to travel someday, and do it really big, but he also never wanted to live through the depression again. My mother is too afraid and generally not strong enough to make such a trip. So they accumulated all of this money which they can't spend, and which they saved all their lives so they wouldn't ever have to worry about money again. But they really haven't done anything with it. After my father retired, they finally bought a house and paid for it in cash, so their expenses are minimal.

Sheilah got lessons in low self-esteem as well as withholding. Her parents, themselves insecure, continually told her that she was unattractive and that "nobody would want her." She grew up believing she would never marry and would have to take care of herself. The family myth was that she was untalented as well.

> When I was about fourteen my mother was told I had a low IQ and was an overachiever—a thought which she shared with me shortly thereafter. I've always thought of myself as an overachiever who isn't very bright. They did spend money to counterbalance my natural deficiencies. I was given every kind of lesson possible, and I had orthodonture work done for seven years. So they made choices as to what was important to them, and they spent money on those things very generously. It was just a question of where the choices were made.

Despite her "deficiencies" Sheilah had achieved a great deal. She had earned a graduate degree in biology and had done laboratory research at a university hospital for fifteen years. She was an excellent musician, a competent photographer, and lived out her father's dream by traveling extensively. She did not, however, manage to overturn the family moneyholding pattern and followed her parents' financial footsteps, saving and making rigid choices about how money should and should not be spent. She spent freely on travel, but exactly like her parents, refused to spend on restaurants or local transportation.

> I stashed away everything I made, and had a lot of trouble—and am sure I still have—parting with nickels, dimes, and quarters. There's a part of me that would still rather walk to the subway. I'm comfortable doing it. I'd never take a cab! In psychological terms I was anal retentive. I just wanted to hold on to it all.

Her inflexible holding created "loads and loads" of problems between herself and friends.

> I tended to spend much less than anyone I knew, so it prevented me from eating out a lot as a social activity. At one point I'd just refuse. I would back off or express a lack of interest. And I made sure that if I traveled with anyone, they would travel in the style I wanted to go. Very, very low budget! When I was dating in my twenties men tended to pay for everything anyway, but I had trouble accepting covering my own expenses. If a man wanted to go out to dinner, my feeling was, I wouldn't go out to dinner if I wasn't with you, so therefore you should pay. They paid, even graciously, but I was always uncomfortable. My parents said, "Don't be a gold digger. If you go out and someone pays for you, be sure you always take the cheapest thing on the menu." All these goofy things with money—a real source of tension.

Sheilah sought help with her moneyholding when it broke up an important relationship.

> What finally split us up and drove me into therapy was we were visiting Washington and he found a place where they had a $1.99 breakfast special, and I knew a mile down the road there was a 69¢ special, and I insisted I wasn't going to eat at the $1.99 place. We had this incredible battle scene about it. He decided that I

was a bit too much for him on this kind of thing, and I decided
to go into therapy to try to sort some of this out. Money had not
been an issue in other relationships because I usually went out
with very poor people who couldn't spend.

In therapy, Sheilah learned that her childhood feelings of low self-
esteem had not been diminished by her many accomplishments. Her
fears of ending up alone, coupled with an inherited moneyholding
pattern, had led her to use money to protect herself emotionally, as well
as financially.

I wanted to make sure I was covered for all kinds of contingencies.

As she began to understand that her focus on her own fears had
prevented her from understanding others' needs, or empathizing with
them, she saw the financial aspect of her most recent relationship in
another light.

When we went to a play, and he wanted to sit in the orchestra
and I wanted to sit in the balcony, I would get totally crazy and
torn and wracked with upset because I didn't want to spend $30.
I'd be hostile and guilty. He said, "Look, one play we'll sit in the
orchestra and the next we'll sit in the balcony." I was not feeling
that this was a reasonable compromise, but *shit*, you're forcing me
to spend every other time on something I don't want to spend on.
I wasn't looking at it from the point of view that I was forcing
him to sit in the balcony and be uncomfortable half the time.

When Sheilah was asked to vacate her rental apartment and realized
it would be both more economic and practical to buy a co-op, she was
faced with a major spending dilemma. Such an investment seemed to
signify the onslaught of the lonely vulnerability she had been saving to
avoid and created an emotional crisis.

I needed a place to live; it made a lot of economic sense and would
give me a lot of freedom to buy. But it was an immense commit-

ment. Here I am, buying a house alone! It meant that in some way
I was an absolute failure. I remember throwing myself on the floor
of the therapist's office, crying hysterically. I really had it in me
that single women don't buy, and if you were to buy a house, that
was an admission that you would never get married.

Her therapist helped her to see that buying the co-op was an accomplishment rather than a failure, and Sheilah began to understand that
she could take care of both emotional and financial needs in ways other
than saving. Owning the co-op gave her personal as well as financial
satisfaction when it rapidly doubled, then tripled in value. Gradually,
Sheilah was learning to spend.

Now I wouldn't risk a relationship over $1.99 bacon and eggs.
When I first started to spend, I wouldn't have risked it because
I would have realized it was crazy, but I would have still been
unhappy about spending the money. In the last few years, something has snapped that makes it easier.

Sheilah found that in many ways her compulsive saving had paid off.
She had turned a modest salary into more than $200,000 worth of
assets. She had a pension, a valuable home, and was drawing a full-time
salary, as well as interest on long-term CDs and money market accounts.

I looked at what I had and thought, It doesn't make sense to be
crazy over money at this point. I have so much coming in regularly
that I can't begin to spend it; I can get more comfortable with
it. My knee collapsed a couple of years ago, and I spent a lot of
time in the hospital. I also watched two friends die, and I realized
time was passing all too rapidly. I began to look more and more
at how other people spent money, and how they lived.

With these revelations, Sheilah could loosen her rigid criteria about
when and how money should be used, and spend it in new ways:

I did a three-week African safari for $3,000. I've never done
anything like that in my life. I do very easily pick up and tootle
off to Mexico for a month now to the tune of $700. I bought a
$100 sweater last year that was on sale from $200. *Never* would
I have dreamed of doing that before.

Sheilah had come a long way, but the family moneyholding legacy
continues to plague her. She had seen an expensive piece of camera
equipment she wanted, but had been unable to buy it. She asked, "How
do you get yourself to spend when you know you have the money?"
Ironically, her co-op had replaced her savings account as a secure
fortress, and was standing between her and the love relationship she
wanted.

Having a really super place of my own has made me feel real good
about a lot of things. But the package, in some way, seems to have
removed me even more from the average male, because I have—
at least in material terms—gathered so much together, and built
myself such a strong little world, my feeling is that it would be
overwhelming to an unputtogether male. I feel that me, plus
everything I have around me, is such a strong statement that if
ever I was to live with someone, we couldn't live here, because it's
so strongly *me*. There's no way anyone could come into my space.

When Sheilah takes the next step, and sees that her co-op, like her
savings account, symbolizes the protective fortress she has built inside,
she will be able to open the door and invite a man in.

CHAPTER 7

Moneyconfusion

When a woman suffering from Moneyphobia enters a negotiation, moneyconfusion strikes. Unable to see money clearly, feeling that talking about it is crass or wanting it is greedy, and believing that someone else should take care of her, she flounders in a process she fails to see as a game. Whether the negotiation is minor (who is going to pay on a date) or one that may affect her well-being for the rest of her life (a bid for a pay raise or a fair divorce settlement), the moneyconfused woman is unable to separate money from pressing emotional issues. Like the fairy tale heroine, she expects to be rewarded for being good, hardworking, feminine, or even needy, and neglects to strategize. Instead of arming herself with information and support in a systematic way, as she would for any other job she recognizes as important (researching an assignment or planning a wedding), she tends to hope the negotiation will "turn out all right." With her focus fixed on her own and others' emotions, she does not formulate concrete financial goals. When negotiating, she tries to cooperate and make the process comfortable for her adversary. Because she wants to emerge from the negotiation certain she has not compromised herself or her ideals, she tends to take a passive position and let others assume responsibility for the outcome. Sometimes she avoids negotiating at all. Though she may not have been sufficiently self-protective during the negotiation process, the moneyconfused woman takes her failure too hard: She castigates herself for getting "screwed," and dwells on her ineptitude instead of analyzing the negotiation to learn what went wrong and why. Unfortunately, our sexist society does not always help women with Deadly Symptom #7 obtain financial justice. They must help themselves, and their confusion prevents them.

Throughout this book we have tried to show how our financial attitudes have been formed by historical programming and personal relationships, and how they reflect the difficulties facing ambitious women today. To succeed in a negotiation, however, it is essential to *depersonalize* money and see financial issues as a separate problem. Because every economic act, including spending and saving, involves some type of negotiation, we have already discussed this important process in other contexts. Now, we would like to look closely at the negotiation game itself and examine the factors that make it hard for a moneyconfused woman to accomplish her goals.

Why Women Are Moneyconfused

Most of us grew up ignorant of negotiation strategies; in the traditional home environment in which we were raised, women did not negotiate because they did not work for pay. It was assumed we would follow in our mothers' footsteps and that our financial needs would be taken care of by men.

Our middle-class mothers were dependent housewives who earned their keep by doing a demanding twenty-four-hour-a-day job. Cleaning, cooking, sewing, nursing, childcare, and managing the household money—arduous and necessary tasks—were not regarded as income-producing or assigned a monetary value. Nor was the maintenance our mothers received regarded as "pay." Since a housewife's job had no description, her responsibilities were unlimited, and she was often overworked. She was given no raises, overtime, unemployment benefits, or Social Security plan for being a homemaker. Though wives who were supported by their husbands' salaries earned their keep, the myth was that they worked for spiritual or emotional reasons and were valued, not for their labor, but for gloriously representing an idealized role—the institution of motherhood.* As mothers and wives they were both above and beneath the baseness of the marketplace. On the one hand, their work in the home was "priceless," too great to be measured in monetary terms, and on the other, economically valueless—worth nothing at all. Since their work was not perceived as a job but as a kind of voluntary activity, inspired by love or a sense of duty, there was no objective measure to evaluate or reward their success. Hardworking wives received gifts, chosen at their husbands' discretion ("Promise her anything, but give her Arpège"), which were doled out, not as bonuses for a job well done, as in the corporation, but for admirable personality and character traits, such as loyalty, lovability, and self-sacrifice. Their wives' labor, however, enabled men, whose basic domestic needs were taken care of, to pursue successful careers. Yet, no matter how skillfully and devotedly a woman filled her housewife position, she could still be "let go" without any notice and legally deprived of an equitable portion of her husband's wealth. Novelist Carolyn See has described the effect of watching her mother, who worked like a "sled dog," get "fired" by her father on her own financial philosophy:

My mother was devoted to, and furious with, my father, and insupportably shocked when he left her. Shocked? She was blown out of her mind. Nothing had prepared her for this. Still, after a few months spent on her (rumpled, unmade) bed, she enrolled in business school, brushed up on her typing, learned shorthand and went to work as a secretary for a series of other men. This was double work and utterly futile, because *he* had gone. "I *folded* his shorts, I *stacked* his socks. . . ."

* Ironically, as modern women begin to define work and success in male terms, those who opt for homemaking roles can no longer claim the automatic respect motherhood traditionally inspired. They feel their important jobs are regarded, especially by other women, as irrelevant or "boring." Mothers in our suburban money group, who had temporarily stepped out of the marketplace to raise young children, felt defensive and guilty about not having jobs. One told us that she accepted a badly paid part-time teaching job so she would be able to answer, "I teach college" when people asked her, "What do you do?"

Here is what I taught my daughters: Become women of substance. Work for yourselves if you can. That way you won't have
to take any lip, and you can work the hours you want. . . .[1]

How did our powerless mothers negotiate? Because the work they
did was perceived as providing emotional satisfaction for themselves
and others, they also bargained in emotional terms. A housewife who
wanted something from her husband often resorted to tactics such as
nagging, complaining, pleading, martyrdom, or clever manipulation;
she learned to make her husband believe that he himself had decided
to give her what she wanted. The breadwinner, however, did not have
to negotiate if he did not want to. He could make unilateral decisions
about how his money would be spent, and give or withhold as he saw
fit. Not all fathers, of course, chose to exercise their power of non-
negotiation, but those who did humiliated their wives and taught their
daughters that unheeded requests for money were associated with
shame or blame. A woman in our Boston money group described her
family's negotiating game like this:

My father gave my mother a budget and an allowance. Decisions
about money were made by him, and he decided what was a
reasonable amount. The amount he gave her was actually *un*-
reasonable. As prices went up, he became very anxious, and he
compensated by not giving my mother a raise. They would fight
all the time because she fell short. She would argue that there just
wasn't enough, and he would say, "You must have blown it; you
must have done something wrong." It really did affect her self-
esteem.

Mothers who were unable to negotiate at home often felt helpless when
they had to negotiate with the outside world. Some learned negotiating
skills, but used them to earn money, not for themselves, but for charitable organizations. A New York woman with a history of negotiating
problems described the lesson in "selflessness" she learned from her
mother:

My mother runs everything and talks all the time. She handles the books. She's always complaining, "How we managed on what your father was making, I don't know." She was real active outside the home, but not for money. Everything was for the Good Will. She was president of the woman's club, president of the library, and raised more than anyone had ever raised to build a new one. She knows a lot of very important people. For years she's been talking about getting a Tofutti franchise or a car wash franchise. I say, "Go do it! Get the money from your rich friends. . . ." But no. She's a tycoon for everyone else, but not for herself.

Mothers who did work outside the home usually had sex-stereotyped jobs at the bottom of the ladder. Confined to these low-paying positions, they were unable to negotiate pay raises or better working conditions on an individual basis. In fact, women have historically been most successful at negotiating when they formed powerful unions and political groups, which made their collective influence apparent to male power brokers.

The middle-class daughter, then, learned that negotiation involved trading personality characteristics and devotion for an undefined amount of material support, hardly a good lesson to bring to the marketplace. Instead of seeing negotiation as a means to obtain a specific amount of money for a specific amount of work, she sees it as a complex process involving not only money but also her own self-worth and the emotional well-being of others. Because she is trading partly in intangible emotional bonds she may find it difficult to attach a price tag to them or judge the economic value of the services she provides. In her concern for others, she bypasses her own self-interest, yet feels exploited. When asked to divorce her emotions from money in a negotiation, however, it seems to her that she is sacrificing a vital facet of her feminine identity and she becomes anxious. Finally, she finds it frightening or unsuitable to confront men and compete with them. For these reasons, many women can negotiate successfully for others but not for themselves, or win a negotiation game when they do not really want what they are negotiating for.

Actress Joan Collins, for example, turned down a solid $350 a week offer for an exclusive contract with 20th Century–Fox when she was only twenty-one and asked instead for the unheard of sum of $1,250. The reason: The new contract would have taken her away from a local lover. Her agent tried to persuade her to accept the first offer. "You can always find a good *shtup,*" he said, "but a good contract is a once in a lifetime thing. I hope you're not blowing your career, Joanie."

"You can't cuddle up to a career at night," Joan replied, expecting to lose the negotiation by not "selling herself short," and was "thrilled —but dismayed" when Fox accepted her terms.[2]

HOW PARENTS DEPRIVE CHILDREN OF NEGOTIATION SKILLS

Some parents prevent their children from mastering the negotiation game by the way they handle their requests. When a parent greets a child's demands with a non-negotiable "yes" or "no," the child does not learn how to bargain effectively. A woman with a father who said "no," for example, found it difficult to negotiate with men in both her personal and professional life.

I have a lot more trouble negotiating with men than with women, and that's because my father always said "no," whereas my mother would mostly say "yes" if it was within her means.

If the parent made the child feel guilty for asking, indicating that her needs were inconsiderate, greedy, or burdensome, a woman may bring the same guilt, as well as a sense that she is undeserving, to adult negotiations. She may feel she has to work harder than others to merit a salary or a raise. A Massachusetts woman told us:

I saw my father sweating over the checkbook. I had a sense that I had to watch to know what it was okay to ask for. I remember asking for a bike, and my father telling me how many loaves of bread he would have to sell in his grocery for me to have it. That was when I stopped asking. I learned to baby-sit, and from that moment on, I bought my own clothes.

When a daughter associates asking for what she wants with family economic distress, she is likely to go off on her own and take care of her needs—the first step toward forming an independent financial identity. Going off on one's own, instead of negotiating, however, is not always possible or effective in marketplace or personal relationships that demand the power to stay and persuade.

Detecting Moneyconfusion

PERSONALIZING MONEY

Moneyconfused women also personalize money. They may project their feelings about the context in which they earned it on to their pay and use it accordingly. A Washington architect told us she "cared more" about the money she got for projects she believed were worthwhile:

> The money I got for designing a museum almost embarrassed me, and I felt calm and sober about the check. But the money I earned for doing a McDonald's inspired immediate visions of a fur and red boots.

A woman physician personalized the debt she had incurred for her medical education. She could not take in her financial planner's sensible advice not to clear the debt, but to pay only the interest, which was then tax deductible. The planner argued that as the value of money decreased, the doctor would actually be paying back less than the amount she had borrowed. This economic truth, however, fell on deaf ears. The doctor was afraid of her debt, which she saw as a kind of vicious wild animal, and wanted to "get rid of it."

> I want to clear my debts. Every time I clear one, it's like striking a piece of my past away, getting rid of another reminder of how

hard I had to work, how little I had to work with. That constant, constant struggle. I truly don't resent paying it off on a month-to-month basis. It's worse to know the debt is sitting there, ready to leap on me and eat me alive.

The personalization of money can also extend to the people and places that handle it, and women may develop transferential relationships to financial advisers and institutions. Some feel "comfortable" with a bank and leave their money in a low-interest passbook account. Others develop affection for a stock, loyally holding on to the shares, even after they drop in value. Women may give a stockbroker too much power, maintaining a "little girl" relationship, or remain ambivalent, giving him money, but refusing to trust him. Stormy relationships reminiscent of the kind a rebellious adolescent daughter has with her parents may develop, too. A woman in our study threw tantrums in a "horrible" bank she "hated and despised" because she regarded it as having an uncooperative staff. When it was suggested that she close her account and deposit her money elsewhere, she told us she "didn't know why" but she "couldn't do it." Instead, she formed a passive-aggressive relationship with the bank and got even with it by removing her money little by little, spiting the bad institution, while maintaining her power over it. Needless to say, personalizing money and its institutions makes it difficult to accomplish objective financial goals.

UNCONSCIOUS BARTERING

During feudal times money was not an important means of exchange. Instead, people bartered goods for goods, services for goods, and services for services in a network of ongoing complex relationships. The development of a monetary system allowed for more mobility and flexibility (a trader no longer had to carry his bushels of wheat), but short-circuited personal contacts between seller and buyer. When used consciously, bartering is still an effective form of negotiation. In the corporation "good old boy network," important favors, leading to increased income, are routinely exchanged. Networking, in which career information is traded, is also an effective form of bartering. For an equitable barter to take place, however, each party must know what he is giving and getting in exchange, and the goods and services traded must have equal and measurable value.

Like their mothers, moneyconfused women tend to exchange services that have monetary value for emotional assets, such as affection, loyalty, or respect. Because the terms of the barter are never established, and the participants are unaware that a barter is taking place, one party may feel ripped off. A working mother told us that her boyfriend, who earns half of what she does, vacuums and does laundry instead of contributing his share of household costs. Though this is theoretically an equitable barter, since his housework spares her the expense of hiring a cleaning lady, she feels it would be bitchy and aggressive (or destroy closeness) to set specific times to do these tasks, and the unvacuumed floor and dirty laundry still occupy her long list of anxiety-producing responsibilities. By keeping the terms of the barter unclear, she is preserving what she regards as important feminine qualities (gentleness and understanding), and trading her anxiety for closeness.

OVERCOMING MONEYCONFUSION: WINNING THE NEGOTIATING GAME

When a woman faces a negotiation in her personal or professional life, she must first be aware that she is playing a game. As in any game, the other player also wants to win. Furthermore, the game itself has built-in obstacles, and she must know in advance exactly what they are and develop the skills to overcome them. Some obstacles, she will find, are coming from a society that has traditionally discriminated economically against women. Others come from her own lack of training to play the game. Sometimes, however, the obstacles are confused emotions, which prevent her from seeing that the game *is* a game or deciding to take the necessary steps to win it. Let us now analyze three important negotiation games that affect women's lives and identify their obstacles: (1) negotiating for pay; (2) personal negotiation over money issues; and (3) negotiating a divorce settlement.

1. NEGOTIATING FOR PAY

Society's Obstacles   Though women are now legally entitled to get the same pay for doing the same job as men, the law is often abused, even by white-collar employers. Nationally, women make about half of what men do. College graduates, professionals, and technical specialists command about two-thirds the salary of men in equivalent positions. Inequities continue because the 1963 Equal Pay Act, which established the principle of equal pay for equal work, regardless of sex, is not always enforced. Employers get around this law by giving women low-paying job titles or more responsibility than their title indicates. For example, a female secretary, doing the same job as a male purchasing agent, receives the "secretary's" lower pay.

The Equal Pay Act also provided discriminatory employers with loopholes: It specified that one sex could legitimately be paid less if a seniority system, merit system, or a system that measures earnings by the quantity or quality of production existed. In court cases challenging pay inequities, employers have repeatedly invoked these exceptions to justify pay differentials. They also argue that they must pay men more to induce them to take a job, or set wages on the basis of the prospective employee's previous salary. Some have said, and supposedly proved, that women have turned down competitive jobs, or jobs dealing with materials or areas of expertise with which they were unfamiliar. In 1986, Sears won a court case by showing that women did not want high-paying commission sales jobs because they feared or disliked "dog eat dog" competition. The judge concluded that differences in the number of men and women in a given job could exist without discrimination by an employer.

In some cases, women receive lower salaries because they work in professions dominated by their sex. Pay scales for jobs that employ mostly women have not been rising as have those for sex-integrated jobs. One-half of all women work in sex-segregated jobs, to their economic disadvantage. Experts say that low-paying women's jobs are expected to increase, not decrease, in the future, which means that unless pay differentials are equalized, women will continue to receive lower pay.

A concept that proposes to rectify salary differences is called "comparable worth." Slightly different than pay equity, the comparable worth idea holds that women should get the same pay for doing different, but equally difficult jobs, requiring equivalent skills, responsibility, and working conditions as jobs that are male-dominated. In Los Angeles, for example, a union contract based on achieving equitable pay will now award a female clerk or librarian the same salary as a male gardener or maintenance worker. A conservative administration and conservative groups, however, are marshaling their forces to oppose comparable worth, and to prevent it from becoming a legal basis to uphold complaints of job discrimination. Nevertheless, this concept has been gaining momentum in some states, which have appointed commissions to study the basis on which salaries are determined for different jobs and have raised the salaries of some women workers.

Unfortunately, women often unwittingly collaborate with a system that conspires to pay them less than men. Uninformed about salary differences, or comparing themselves to other women, instead of to men who earn more, they unconsciously accept and perpetuate the status quo. Research has shown that women expect to work harder than men for less money, and that they undervalue their contributions.

A Harvard University study indicated that women who were asked to do as much work as they thought was fair for a fixed sum, worked longer, accomplished more, and did a more accurate, efficient job than men. Though the women's performances surpassed the men's, both sexes believed they had done equally well on the job.[3] A survey by Olsten Services revealed that female college seniors expected to earn about half of what men do after ten years in their field. In other words, their low expectations coincided with the national statistics.[4] A study done at the State University of New York at Buffalo, however, showed that women who allotted themselves half of what men did for the same job, paid themselves an equal salary when they were made aware of the going rate.[5]

Companies prevent women from evaluating their objective economic worth by encouraging all workers to keep wages confidential.

This practice allows the employer to negotiate salaries with new employees on the basis of their credentials and experience, and to give merit raises without causing dissension. Salary secrets also permit companies to violate the Equal Pay Act with impunity. Moneyconfused women keep their salaries a secret, however, because disclosing the amount they earn seems a question of establishing personal trust, instead of necessary strategizing to meet mutual goals. A woman who had worked for a large publishing conglomerate told us:

> A colleague who did an identical job and I were going to tell each other what we made. At the time we related to each other as kindred spirits, which turned out not to be true at all. (Since then, she has gone on to a very big job in a totally dollar-oriented field.) But there was this moment when we agreed to trust each other that much. It became this huge big deal. And something happened and we never did it. It was so frightening to ask, "What did they offer you? What did you come in at?"

In a salary negotiation game, of course, lack of knowledge about what one's services are worth is a severe handicap.

Women who avoid confrontations over pay may be unconsciously reacting to another marketplace reality: sexual harassment. Though reports of harassment have risen nearly 50 percent since the Equal Employment Opportunity Commission started keeping statistics in 1981, estimates are that much workplace violence goes unreported. According to a 1981 survey, one out of every hundred female federal employees reported actual rape or attempted rape or assault on the job.[6] Harassed women are often told they will lose their jobs if they refuse or complain, and sexual assault in the workplace is difficult to prove in male-biased courts. In corporations, a woman executive's job description may include resisting attacks by clients. In her excellent negotiation primer, *Games Mother Never Taught You: Corporate Gamesmanship for Women,* Betty Lehan Harragan warns women executives about the perils of male associates who drink and attack them, and advises that it is up to them to handle this "delicate problem."

> You have to get rid of him, but he may be aggressive, nasty and physical. . . . Usually it happens when you're alone and he's forced his way into your apartment or hotel room. . . . You can't be "nice."[7]

According to Harragan, the price of being "nice" and submitting in any way to sexual harassment will cost the woman executive her influence and work relationship with the harassing man, who will realize he made a fool out of himself and project his self-hatred on to her. Psychological violence and intimidation, as well as the threat of physical violence, are real, not imagined obstacles for women who are perceived as aggressive competitors in a game some men want to reserve for themselves.

The Obstacles Within   The marketplace, as we have described it, is an ideal backdrop for moneyconfusion. In a discriminatory and sometimes violent atmosphere it is easy for women to confuse the goods and services they have to offer with traditional definitions of their female role. What forms does moneyconfusion take in a negotiation for pay?

First, those who do not understand that negotiation is a game may be naïvely unaware of its most basic rule—no expert player ever asks for the amount of money she expects to win:

> The guy before me was making more than forty-five. So I go in there, and I figure I don't have the experience he had and they're not going to pay me what they were paying him, but they should give me at least forty. He said to me, "How's forty?" and I said, "Fine." Then he turned around and said, "Well, the big boss won't give it to you; he'll probably say thirty-eight with a raise in six months." I was hot and tired and I agreed. Later I thought, What a jerk I am! *Stupid! Idiot!* I should have known he would screw me down right away. So I got thirty-eight and every time I went back to him for more money he'd say I wasn't doing a good enough job.

Women who have seen their mothers working for free may find it difficult to distinguish time for which they ought to be paid from time devoted to caring for other people's needs. A computer programmer who designed studies for private clients, became moneyconfused when asked to evaluate a study for a potential customer—a task that proved more time-consuming than she had thought it would be.

> I went home and looked at the data. The study was ridiculous—terribly set up. I wasn't responsible for the study, only for telling him what I thought of it at that point. So what is the price I should put on this? Finally, my husband asked, "What's it worth for you to be sitting in your house on a nice day, trying to make sense of it?" What is my time worth? That was the question. I had to get real angry and tell myself, This is set up wrong, not me, before I could decide to charge him $25 an hour for the evaluation.

Moneyconfused women, who see their salaries as a symbol of their total self-worth, may be unable to negotiate on days when they feel insecure, or when they are troubled by personal problems. They may also confuse employer-employee relationships with friendship. Patricia, a magazine editor who had recently been fired from her job, undersold herself when a friend, the publisher of an industry house organ, asked her to work on a per diem basis. Before she offered Patricia the per diem job, she had given her a writing assignment. The research had been difficult, and Patricia felt that she had written a piece that was not quite what the publisher wanted. She was prepared to be "open and honest" with her employer-friend, instead of fending for her own self-interest.

> I was going to tell her that it wasn't so good, but my husband said, "Then you'll be putting it in her mind that you didn't do a great job. Just give it to her."

Feeling nervous about the article she had written, doubting her competence because she had been fired from a job, and worried about outstanding bills as well as her appearance, Patricia blew a negotiation that took her off-guard.

So I was thinking, Oh God, this piece is going to be killed. I'm never going to get the money, or be able to pay my sheriff's fine for overdue parking tickets. And I felt fat, and my stomach hurt because I had cramps. I was dressed nicely, but not like I was going for a job. I turned in my assignment and she said, "Come and see me before you leave." When I went into her office she said, "I'm ready to start work on those projects I mentioned. Can you come in?" And I said, "Sure." She asked, "What's your rate?" I said, "I don't know," like a fifteen-year-old dope. Then I told her $150, and I should have said $175. I was so excited, I just didn't think. I wanted to work with her. I wish I had said, "I want to think about it. I'll let you know tomorrow."

Any negotiation is a contest between adversaries, even if the two parties were friends before it and go on being friends after it is over. Moneyconfused women, however, may feel estranged from their femininity when they have to take an aggressive role and fight a winning battle. A law student in our Boston money group, who had left a low-paying social work job to train for a money-making career, described winning a large settlement in a mock negotiation assignment as "devastating."

I was defending an imaginary plaintiff who had gotten injured from a wrongful discharge. We researched the case for two months, and I finally sat down at the table with the other lawyer to try to settle out of court. I came away with a very large amount of money—higher than anybody in my group, and way above average. In a real case, I would have gotten to keep a third of the settlement. So I exactly fulfilled what I wanted to happen. And I came home and felt devastated. The other lawyer was a man, younger than me and very nice. I felt like I'd been cruel to him . . . a monster. It felt lonely to know that I couldn't be friends with him. In my previous job, I had made little money helping people. I had never been an adversary.

As an adversary who won by being more aggressive than her male opponent, the law student felt cut off from a network of all-important human relationships. Fortunately, she was able to put herself back into a supportive, personal context by discussing her feelings with a female teaching assistant:

> Everybody was buzzing about the negotiation and asking me, "You made that much?" I took her aside and said, "I really feel guilty and really stupid for having such an inappropriate reaction to my success." She told me she'd had the exact same feelings the first time she'd negotiated a very high settlement. It was validating to know a woman associate who had similar issues doesn't have them anymore.

Women who do not play the negotiation game to win, or try to help the other player, may underprice goods and services. An artist who had sold a drawing to a friend for less than it was worth, told us:

> When he wanted to buy it, well, he was a friend, he was in school, and I know he doesn't make that much money. He was surprised it was so cheap. I think I should have charged him $50 more, but when I sell to friends, I always deduct at least $10 so that it's more personal.

On the one hand, the moneyconfused artist made herself feel comfortable by making the sale "more personal"; but since she had done so by putting a lower price on her drawing, she felt she had "cheapened" herself and her work. Though the amount she had undercharged her friend was minimal, it symbolized painful self-betrayal.

> I went as low as I could go for my self-respect. I think I should have sold it to him for what *it* was worth. I was too emotional. I was thinking for the work, and for him—I was doing everybody's job.

Some moneyconfused women, then, try to take care of their opponents. Others, who bring their traditional feminine personas into the negotiation game, may expect their adversaries to take care of them. They want their opponent to provide them with information about how much money they should bargain for. Instead of researching pay scales for their particular area of expertise, they wait for the other team to hand them the ball.*

If someone says, "Come to me with a price," I'm always stymied. I indicate that they should give me a guideline, and they won't tell me anything. I don't find it difficult to negotiate if what I'm offered isn't enough, but to name a figure . . . ? I go through such anxiety. Somebody once suggested I could ask a crucial question like, "What ballpark are we talking about?"

The slang commonly used to describe failure in a negotiation process —"fucked over" or "screwed"—has a special meaning for women. It signifies a financial rape by a sexist system in which they cooperated. One woman who failed to negotiate an appropriate salary for a new job, described her feelings in these sexual terms:

I felt like I'd just slept with someone I shouldn't have slept with.

Losing a negotiation game, however, is not necessarily the same as "getting screwed." Moneyconfused women may not understand that risk is an inevitable part of every negotiation. Those who associate the outcome with their total self-worth may feel ashamed and humiliated when they do not win. A word processor who played the game skillfully but lost, told us:

The company kept asking to have me back. I told the agency I could no longer work there for $12 an hour and asked for $15. The agent hemmed and hawed and said the boss did not like to renegotiate fees and made a tentative offer of $13, which she later withdrew. I said I might accept $14 and asked if the $13 was firm; it wasn't. So I decided to leave. Afterwards, I felt extremely anxious—worthless and guilty for failing to get more money. I

* The U.S. Department of Labor's *Occupational Outlook Quarterly* publishes salary guidelines for different jobs. Professional publications also publish salary surveys.

thought the reason they wouldn't give me the $15 was because I wasn't a good enough word processor—even though the company and the agency had said I was good.

Overcoming Obstacles: Getting What You're Worth   These examples of women who played the negotiation game, and did not win, partly because of inner obstacles, offer some important suggestions. The computer programmer and editor both asked their husbands for advice. Men, who associate self-worth with the amount of money they make, know how to play the game and can be good coaches; but it is important to choose men who do not see themselves as competitors to play this role. The lawyer who won a mock negotiation was able to play her game on a practice court, and in the process, became aware of emotional "injuries" that might occur when the game was for real. Her sympathetic woman adviser provided reassurance and understanding, and let her know that her feelings were neither unique nor inappropriate, but predictable responses to her socialization. Mock negotiations and women mentors, who have already conquered the hardships of the game, help us win and enjoy success. Most important, all of the women were able to look back at a failed negotiation and analyze what went wrong; their self-reproach did not stop them from considering new strategies to bring to the next negotiating tournament. As they reviewed the "plays" and examined their feelings, they were able to take a step toward depersonalizing this important process and acting in their financial self-interest.

2. PERSONAL NEGOTIATION

The Obstacles   Other symptoms of Moneyphobia prevent women from negotiating equitable financial arrangements with those they love. Moneysqueamish women feel it is "petty" or "not nice" to discuss money, or to demand their financial rights in the context of a relationship. Struggling to integrate their traditional "ladylike" side with their quest for modern independent selfhood, even those who desire equal financial relationships may feel confused. One moneysqueamish woman described her difficulty negotiating with the man she lives with like this:

I am very squeamish dealing with Lionel about specific amounts of dollars and cents. I look at the phone bill and check his long-distance calls, and then I don't say anything to him. I feel it's not nice to say, "You owe me $1.50." I feel guilty about making an issue about such a small amount—like I'm moneygrubbing.

Women who believe they ought to be generous may feel it is "selfish" to keep track of expenses in a love relationship, and may become moneyblind in order to avoid feeling "ripped off."

He's very generous, and I'm very generous, and we get to the point where we're out-generousing each other. And then I ask myself, "What actually went down there?" and I get uncomfortable thinking about it. He plays right into my discomfort by teasing me and saying, "Don't worry, it will all come out even in the end." It may be that I'm spending $2,000 a year more than he is on our relationship, but I'd never know, because I have no idea how much I earn and spend in a year.

Moneydeniers, who secretly want a man to take care of them, may feel angry and resentful when asked to pay their share on a date. When they get involved in nominally equitable relationships, they believe a loving partner should automatically be just and fair, and fend for their financial interests; they do not think they should have to negotiate.

It annoys and bothers me that I have to ask him to contribute groceries or rent money, but it bothers me more that he can't or isn't more compelled to offer.

"Systems" for dividing expenses, or keeping them separate, may symbolize an emotional separation to the Moneyphobic woman. When inequalities develop, however, she feels "ripped off," furious at the man for creating them and at herself for failing to seek redress. A Boston woman, unable to negotiate with her husband to have her name put on joint assets, felt angry and powerless:

There's a whole lot I do as a human being in this marriage that should give me more say as to how the money is spent and how it is earned. I should have as much leverage with the property equity as he does, so I can go to the bank and say, "I'm going to take out a $50,000 loan so I can go to school," and not have to check with anybody. My husband doesn't have to come to me and say, "I'm going to sink $150,000 of *our* income into my business." He just does it. It's mine as much as his.

This woman, who associated negotiation with emotional manipulation and futile tantrums, found it difficult to imagine the language she would use to bargain for her financial rights.

If I imagine asking I hear this very bitchy voice that doesn't sound competent. One must be able to ask in a civilized, rational way. If I go in screaming like a banshee, I won't get what I want either.

Inequitable financial arrangements can also occur when a woman uses money to barter for power. Transitional women may reverse the old formula, in fact, and take care of men. Forty-two of the 123 women in our money study had at one time supported a husband or lover— a surprisingly large number. Some (who did not believe in financial equality) did an about-face and married another man who supported them; others felt they had been exploited and swore they would never support a man again. For most, the inequitable arrangement had proved unsatisfying, possibly because they had never accurately defined what it was they were "buying" with their money. One of the women we interviewed was aware that she had traded economic inequality for a position of control—a barter that backfired.

I supported us. It wasn't a decision. It sort of evolved. Part of it was the philosophy of the hippie era—what's yours is mine and what's mine is yours—and the traditional applications of the male-female role were smothered. I didn't think about it. When I look at it in retrospect I think our arrangement emasculated him from my point of view and from his point of view. Our sex life went down and became nonexistent. I think he looked at me as a mother, and I acted like one. I would never support a man—or *anyone*—again, now or ever. It gave me a kind of power, but it became a double bind, because I had the power and then I lost it.

This woman is now married to a man with whom she adamantly shares all expenses, even when it feels "uncomfortable"; in fact, the night he proposed in a candlelit restaurant, they split the bill.

Overcoming Personal Negotiation Obstacles In order to negotiate successfully in a relationship, a couple must establish a tradition of discussing money. In a 1984 *Playboy* article, "The Dow Jones Emotionals," Philip Blumstein and Pepper Schwartz listed thirty financial issues on which relationships "rise and fall." Most of the disputes defined by the two sociologists, who studied 12,000 couples for their book *American Couples: Money, Work, Sex,* involved quarrels about when, how much, how, and on what money should be spent, differences in spending and saving styles, problems with record keeping, and unclear property titles. Almost all the issues could have been avoided or settled peacefully if the couple had evolved a diplomatic financial style early in their relationship and learned to negotiate flexible "deals." Blumstein and Schwartz, who blame interpersonal financial arrangements on moneysqueamishness, observed that courting couples discuss prior sex lives, but ignore mutual economic histories, because "it is not very romantic or interesting to talk about net worth or projections of income or one's indebtedness."

> . . . money becomes the last frontier of self-disclosure, even though each partner may hold strong feelings about how money should be dealt with.[8]

Once a couple institutes a solid bargaining tradition, individual transactions do not seem "petty," nor does an unacknowledged code of secrecy about money matters have to be broken before they can be discussed.

In order to talk about money with any loved one, however, a woman has to let him or her know that the topic is important, and find her negotiating voice—harder in a personal relationship, in which the other party is not defined as an opponent, than in the marketplace. To find her voice, she must become aware of issues that silenced her in the past.

Andrea, in our New York money group, was able to negotiate with her sisters for a larger portion of an inheritance once she realized that her peacemaking role in the family had kept her from asking for what she wanted. Andy's mother had died nine years before and left a bank account to be divided between her four daughters, with the lion's share going to the one who had cared for her most before her death. A younger sister contested the will and then died, too. Andrea, who needed money to buy her co-op apartment, had to examine her relationship with her two surviving sisters before she could speak in her own behalf.

> My older sister called and said, "Now about that account. . . ."
> I began to do what I recognized as my typical number in the family, which was to say, "Oh, anything, just so long as we don't have fights. Anything you want." And what she wanted was essentially to grab the biggest hunk.

Weighing her financial goals against her traditional emotional role in the family, Andrea hung up the phone and thought, No, this is not okay. Her first attempt to reopen the issue with her sister, however, failed; she wrote a hesitant, conciliatory letter that began, "I'll never mention this again, but. . . ." Her sister, of course, ignored this self-effacing plea, and Andy realized that a one-sided statement was not an effective bargaining strategy; she would have to confront both her sisters and play the negotiating game. For all successful negotiations—in the marketplace or personal sphere—the timing must be right. Andy took advantage of her sister's personal happiness to make her first move.

> Very conveniently, my older sister got married, and as I was flying to the wedding, I thought, Well, this is your opportunity. If you're going to confront this, you have to do it now, or you're going to hate yourself. At one point the three of us were alone in the hotel

suite, happy and gay and drinking champagne. I thought, Now or never, and I plunged right in. I caught my older sister at the right moment, because she's in a marriage and she's happy. I knew my younger sister would go along with what the two of us decided. I said that what I wanted was to be given my dead sister's portion of the account. That way, neither of them would get a penny less, and I would get a little more. They're both married and they both have two incomes, whereas I am self-supporting and live in New York alone—and I have to deal with that. But I didn't say all this at first. I just laid out what I wanted. And they both said, "That's okay with me."

Since Andy's relationship to her sisters was based on an emotional tie, she did not feel that she had achieved her goal until she brought the negotiation back into a personal framework. She used an expression of positive feeling after she had won the game to reinforce her relationship with her sisters and make them feel good about her victory:

I sat there for a moment, still feeling like a sulky kid, and then I thought, This is really important to you, Andy; let them know this. I hugged my one sister and then I started sobbing, "I've just begun to realize I have to take care of myself. . . ." I felt she understood, because she's a loving person. So we hugged and cried, and then I went to my other sister, and we hugged and cried. And it was this incredible moment of true intimacy between us. It was wonderful, and yet, it was one of the hardest things I ever had to do.

Andrea, then, was able to separate the personal aspect of the negotiation with her sisters from the strategies necessary to win the game. In retrospect, she realized that she had mastered new skills she had never been taught and altered her traditional family role. She understood that she had taken a risk and won, but that her self-worth would have been damaged more if she had not negotiated at all than if she had lost. She learned that assertiveness is an essential component of self-esteem.

I was terrified. The only way I got myself to do it was to have a stern talk with myself. "Andy, if you don't do it you're going to be really disappointed in yourself. What are you afraid of? That maybe they'll say no? What if they do? It's a learning experience. You'll live through it. It's not going to kill you, and you'll feel a lot better for having done it."

Her new knowledge of negotiation is one Andy should be able to transfer to the marketplace, as well as to other personal relationships.

3. NEGOTIATING A DIVORCE SETTLEMENT

The Legal Obstacles   When the time comes for a woman to negotiate a fair divorce settlement, she may discover that despite the lip service society pays to the importance of women's role in the home, her work there is worth little in real economic terms. Though divorce laws have theoretically changed to favor women, courts continue to discriminate against them when parting couples litigate to divide the wealth. Leonore Weitzman, a Stanford sociologist, found that divorced women suffer a 73 percent reduction in their post-divorce standard of living, whereas divorced men enjoy a 42 percent increase.[9] The sharpest drops are suffered by older women who do not work outside the home and by women with young children.

Until the 1970's, the majority of states gave ownership and control of property and income to the spouse who had acquired them and whose name was on the assets. Under these old laws, if the savings account and other properties were in the husband's name, they were his, no matter how much his wife had contributed to the marriage. Patriarchal judges, however, assumed wives were dependent on their husbands, and usually awarded them the family home and lifetime alimony as well as child-support payments, provided the wife was not seen as the "guilty party" in the dissolution of the marriage. In 1970, California passed the first no-fault divorce law, which allowed divorce on the grounds of "irreconcilable differences." In the next ten years, forty-four other states adopted some version of these reforms.

In a no-fault divorce, marital property is theoretically divided on the basis of need and the ability to pay. A judge who applies equitable distribution laws is supposed to distribute the family assets "equitably" (which is not the same as "equally"), taking the ages of both divorcing partners and their future prospects into account. Decisions about child custody, as well as property division, are made with the assumption that men and women are social equals. With this in mind, alimony payments have been replaced by temporary maintenance awards to help women who have been dependent on husbands become self-supporting.

Though equitable distribution laws were expected to help women, the results have proved disappointing. The new divorce laws are less sexist, but the judges who interpret them are not. They tend to disregard marketplace sexism, and assume that a woman who has been a homemaker for years will be able to get a high-paying job and support herself. As a result, they grant short-term maintenance awards, which are taxable, or nothing. In deciding who has a right to marital property, they continue to undervalue nonmonetary contributions to the marriage by the wife as a spouse, parent, and homemaker, and bestow the larger chunk of the goods on the husband whose income acquired them. In a recent study of seventy court decisions, two women matrimonial lawyers found only five in which there was a roughly equal division of assets.[10] Though many divorce suits are settled out of court, the settlement usually reflects what would have occurred if the case had been tried. Some states are now reviewing divorce decisions and drafting amendments to serve as judicial guidelines for equitable property distribution.

Under the new laws, the burden of proof rests upon the woman, especially if she has not been working outside the home. If she does not hold title to property, she must prove that she deserves it, and hire accountants, appraisers, tax pension specialists, and a first-rate lawyer to help her. The husband, on the other hand, often benefits from hiding income, and divulging as little information as possible, for which he, too, requires expensive professional help. As a result, the cost of contesting a divorce has skyrocketed to as much as $70,000.[11] A contested divorce, then, may be financially prohibitive to a woman who emerges from a marriage with insufficient capital to fight for her rights. The more equitable custody laws have also given husbands another weapon. Because judges often assign children to the man in a contested proceeding, some fathers now raise the possibility of fighting for custody as a bargaining tool. They use "custody blackmail" to intimidate their wives into accepting lower settlements and child-support payments. Terrified of losing their children, wives agree to a bad deal.[12]

The Inner Obstacles   Divorcing women, then, face a complicated and unfamiliar legal process that still favors husbands, despite changes in the law. Their moneyconfusion may make it difficult for them to separate the legal and financial aspects of the divorce from its intense emotional ramifications. Whereas women who are left by their mates may be too shell-shocked to strategize, those who are leaving may feel too guilt-ridden to fight for their rights. The divorced women in our study whom we interviewed had left their husbands, or had parted by mutual agreement.* They, too, felt desperate and confused. Said Darlene, who divorced her husband in 1981:

> I knew I had to leave to survive, but I couldn't really face what I was doing. I had to have blinders on everything. Everybody's life, it seemed, was crumbling because of what I was doing, and I had no way of supporting myself. I couldn't look. I had to shut my eyes, and nothing seemed real.

The first mistake a moneyconfused woman makes is to choose the wrong matrimonial lawyer. Feeling helpless and frightened in the face of an uncertain future, she may look for a lawyer who will comfort or take care of her—a father figure. Darlene, who "had blinders on everything," said she was "looking for a saviour, not a lawyer," but chose one who insulted her with his patronizing attitude:

---

* Because most of the participants in our money study were part of the baby boom generation, we encountered few who were old enough to have been left by husbands for younger women.

When I asked about the settlement he patted me on the head and said, "Don't worry. If it wasn't for divorced women we wouldn't have waitresses." And I ended up using him, even though I didn't like him. I had all my signals off because I was so confused and scared about what I was doing.

Whatever the reason for the divorce, women tend to feel guilty and responsible. Their guilt makes it difficult for them to see their husbands as legal adversaries, and they may choose a lawyer who reinforces their feelings of failure and low self-esteem, or one who will help them take care of husbands they believe they have wronged. Molly, a New York woman whose husband moved out after they amicably agreed to separate, chose a lawyer who "spoke softly" instead of one who "carried a big stick."

I had feminist friends who said, "Go to a lawyer; you can't not do anything." I went to a woman matrimonial lawyer who is now well known, and she said, "Okay! We're going to send him papers for desertion because he moved out, and we're going to say he deserted you and the two children. We're going to nail him to the wall! He's an engineer; we'll get a lot!" And I said, "Oh no, no, you can't do that! He's a nice guy! I don't want to kill him. He's got to have a life!" I think I felt very guilty because I hadn't been happy in the marriage. At that time he was giving me $600 a month, which fourteen years ago was more money than it is now. Two years later we decided to get a legal separation, and we both went to lawyers. He became the aggressive person then and served me papers for adultery—which was a lie. He had a woman lawyer who was a real fucking bitch! I had a nice lawyer, and he was not good. I got scared the kids would be called in to testify against me. So I made a very bad settlement because I didn't want to deal with it. I still get only $600 a month.

As Molly discovered, a divorce negotiation is not one you can learn through a process of trial and error. She had only one chance to fend for her rights.

I recently talked to a lawyer because I wanted to reopen the idea of getting more money. But because my ex-husband has his own business, he probably can prove he doesn't earn very much. The lawyer said, "Don't waste your money."

Divorcing husbands, too, experience deep emotional trauma. They are more adept, however, at separating the financial from the emotional issues and bringing marketplace games into the interpersonal arena. When Rebecca, a New York woman in our study, felt that her marriage was falling apart, she gave her "macho" husband an ultimatum: Either he went into therapy or she would file for divorce. He did not go to a therapist, but immediately started hiding income and removing money from joint accounts. When litigation began, her husband, vice-president of a large corporation, changed lawyers and reneged on verbal agreements—excellent strategizing, which prolonged the proceedings —and wore Rebecca down with his "tremendous stamina."

We would sit down and go over all the costs, and he would say, "I don't want to hurt you," and there would be all this tenderness. Then we'd meet with the lawyers and he'd say, "I only discussed that; I didn't agree to anything." He kept bringing in new legal blood, whereas my lawyer had already done the work (and raised his fees for new clients), and didn't really care about my case anymore. I couldn't afford to get a new lawyer.

While this husband wheeled and dealed to his own advantage, Rebecca continued to confuse her caretaking and adversarial role.

My husband kept saying, "You're taking my family away." He was a macho guy and that part of him was breaking down. I felt caring about him. At one point I even interviewed a men's rights lawyer, thinking we could have joint custody. I didn't hate him yet, or want to destroy him. Why I ever thought I might have the power to do that, I now don't know. I wanted to believe the best, and couldn't believe what he ended up doing to me. And I still can't believe it, because I know he really did love me. When I look back

I realize I should have gone to court. I shouldn't have been so honest; I shouldn't have given him the house—all these "I should haves" which make me sick.

Many divorcing women eventually "give up" and accept unfair settlements because they find it too emotionally painful to go on fighting aggressively. Beth, who gave the husband she was leaving half the worth of a house she had paid for with her earnings, said:

The house was in both our names, and I was referred to as *et ux* (and wife) on the deed. At the time, I remember feeling furious about the *et ux*, but I was unaware of what it would mean. He really shouldn't have gotten any part of the house, but my lawyer said, "Common law . . . a couple. . . ." He said we couldn't fight it, but now that I think about it, I don't think the lawyer particularly wanted to fight it. I don't think I wanted to fight it, or had the strength to fight it, because all I really wanted to do was get out of the marriage. So I left him the car, the dog, and the house and took my freedom and independence.

As in any negotiation, getting "screwed" in a divorce leaves a wake of low self-esteem and bitter chagrin. For this reason, many women choose to deny that the negotiation failed or that they made mistakes. Beth still feels she had "no choice" than to give up half of her house without fighting for it. A larger settlement, however, would have increased, not decreased, her newfound freedom.*

Overcoming Obstacles   A divorce settlement usually reflects the way the "business" of a marriage has been conducted. If a couple's financial arrangements have been equitable and flexible, the divorce settlement will tend to be the same. On the other hand, if financial roles within the marriage have been rigid and traditional, the husband will fight to

* Beth might have benefited by familiarizing herself with the divorce laws in her state before consulting a lawyer. The NOW Legal Defense and Education Fund (99 Hudson Street, New York, NY 10013) will send its booklet, "Planning for Divorce," upon request.

preserve his control during the divorce, and his wife may not have either the emotional or economic wherewithal to change the balance of power. For example, if a man owns and acquires all the property during the marriage, and gives his wife an "allowance," he is likely to want the arrangement to prevail when the marriage ends. Couples who both earn and keep property separate or equal, or who have flexible systems that enable them to share financial power, are more likely to emerge with a mutually satisfactory settlement.

If a woman learns to negotiate for her financial rights within the context of her marriage, she will be better able to obtain them in the event of a divorce. Many women, however, believe that to negotiate a prenuptial agreement, or make self-protective financial arrangements, indicates a lack of faith in the future of the marriage. To confuse the emotional and financial clauses of the marriage contract may be to set oneself up for a fall if the marriage fails. Though no one who marries "plans" for a divorce, learning and practicing personal negotiation about money matters is excellent preparation should one occur. Couples with a history of discussing money and creating equitable financial arrangements are more likely to benefit from divorce mediation—a new social service that offers a nonadversarial, much less expensive method of making divorce and separation agreements outside the court.

Once a divorce is in process—or a settlement has been made—a woman can accomplish her financial goals by keeping business issues separate and clear. Molly, who had gotten an unfavorable settlement because she chose a "soft-speaking" lawyer, found divorce an incentive to earn. After experimenting with various careers, she finally started a fashion design company. Once she was experienced in business negotiations, Molly was able to apply the concept to her divorce settlement. Her ex-husband rarely sent her child-support check on time.

We played this game which was that I called him and said in a cute, wheedling voice, "Oh, hi, Justin, how are you? Could I please have my child-support check this month?" And he'd put it in the mail. Then I decided I really hated doing that. Why should I have to ask him for the money? So now I have this new system, which is that I call his secretary and say, "Tell Justin I'm sending a messenger tomorrow." My business pays for the messenger service to go to his office and pick up the check, and there's always an envelope with the money in it waiting.

By using a businesslike approach to collect her child-support check, Molly lets her ex-husband know that she knows the money he must pay her is not a favor or gift. When a woman clarifies the difference between "business" and "personal" in her life as well as in the marketplace, she ceases to be moneyconfused.

CHAPTER 8

Life Without Moneyphobia

The time has come to stop describing our problems with money and identify the happy woman who does not have them. How does a woman with a healthy financial identity live her life and relate to money?

The non-Moneyphobic woman, it may surprise some to learn, is not necessarily earning megabucks, or rushing off to Wall Street or to some high-powered business with briefcase in hand. She is, however, getting paid what she is worth for the work that she does, and making the amount of money she considers necessary for a meaningful lifestyle, security, and flexibility. She takes advantage of financial opportunities, works hard, and uses her resources wisely, spending neither too much nor too little to satisfy her needs. She knows she is responsible for taking care of herself in the future, as well as in the present, and plans accordingly. She adapts her financial behavior to her age, to changing goals, and to economic trends in her society.

If she is sharing her goals with a man, she still sees herself as a financial individual, with power over her own economic life. Even when she takes time off from earning to do a job at home, she believes what she is doing is important and productive, and knows her work, too, contributes to her family's financial well-being. Because she is comfortable with her financial identity, she seeks out information and advice about money matters without feeling squeamish. She performs financial tasks, makes decisions, and talks about money with equanimity.

When she has to negotiate, she does not confuse emotional and economic issues. Most important, she understands the meaning of money; she neither fails to acknowledge it or overemphasizes it. She has learned how much is *enough* for her, and does not strive for more. Her realistic appraisal of the value of money, however, allows her to handle a windfall (like an inheritance) with creative aplomb. Perhaps the best evidence of a well-formed financial identity is the enjoyment of money. The non-Moneyphobic women in our study *enjoyed* making, spending, and investing, and took pleasure in their financial independence.

The few non-Moneyphobic women we found were happy women, who communicated undeniable feelings of satisfaction. Because money in our society spells *power*—and a power women have long been denied—those who had learned to deal with it effectively radiated an aura of confident self-assertiveness. What gave the financially healthy women such high self-esteem was that they had *feminized* the meaning of money in a positive way. They understood how to integrate the desire for money and financial independence with activities that have traditionally held meaning for women. They had not sacrificed their relationships with others to become driven workaholics. Our non-Moneyphobic case histories were not earning what a powerful man would call *money,* but unlike many powerful men, all enjoyed rewarding relationships with other people and active sex lives. *For women, we found, there was a definite connection between a healthy financial identity and a healthy sexuality.* Contrary to what many women fear—that earning power and competence with money will make them unattractive to men—the women in our study who were "good" with money, as we have defined that, tended to have good relationships.*† In gen-

---

* A woman can be "good" with money without being completely Moneyphobia-free. Those with fewer symptoms, who were open to acknowledging their problems with money and working on them, seemed to enjoy better relationships than those who were willing to analyze their financial woes, but resisted change. In the course of our study, several women who had satisfying relationships with men *improved* their relationship to money. Flexibility, and willingness to change, make for progress in any area.

†The relationship between economic power and sexual satisfaction has been noted by psychologists and feminists. In a study that measured women's sense of "well-being," Grace Baruch, Rosalind Barnett, and Caryl Rivers, authors of *Lifeprints: New Patterns of Love & Work for Today's Woman* (McGraw-Hill, 1983), show that the

eral, it was the seriously Moneyphobic who either had no men in their lives or who had troubled marriages and love affairs.

Why should this be so? A healthy sexuality, like a healthy financial identity, requires the ability to create flexible and practical options to satisfy one's needs. Modern women who enjoy sex as well as money have a strong sense of self-esteem, freedom, and control over their destinies. They have been able to negotiate viable solutions they find personally meaningful, instead of succumbing to passive fantasies of an ideal romance or subscribing to traditional definitions of women's sexual role. In other words, they are successful sexually for the same reason that they are successful financially—because they have taken responsibility for taking care of themselves. The definition of a satisfying sex life, like a satisfying financial life, of course, varies from woman to woman. The non-Moneyphobic women in our study had evolved different sexual as well as financial styles. Some were involved in a traditional monogamous marriage or lived with partners, and one enjoyed a number of lovers simultaneously. All, however, had in some way altered the original "script" society and parents had drafted for their lives. And all were equally emphatic about their sense of independence in the context of the relationship, *and defined that independence in economic terms*.

The Queen of Non-Moneyphobia: Mae West

One of the most outrageous personalities of the stage and screen provides a good illustration of the joys of non-Moneyphobia. Known for

---

money a woman contributes to her family's income has a strong impact on her sexual satisfaction. According to these psychologists, a woman who earns money ranks higher in the area of "mastery"—that is, self-esteem and sense of control—than one who does not. Feminist writer Betty Friedan, who believes women are "still more economically dependent on men than they would like," has commented:

Whoever said that feminism shouldn't be sexy! . . . As long as sex is distorted by women's economic dependence, or fear of it, it can't be truly, freely enjoyed" ("How to Get the Women's Movement Moving Again," *The New York Times Magazine*, November 3, 1985, p. 98).

her famous one-liners and physical charms ("My measurements are the same as Venus De Milo's, only I got arms"), Mae West was also a financial whiz. From her early days as a child vaudeville star, she earned, negotiated, and managed wisely, eventually becoming the wealthiest self-made woman of her generation. She also led a full, if extravagant, emotional life, and claimed to have had an orgasm a day for most of her eighty-seven years.

Sometimes it seems to me I've known so many men that the FBI ought to come to me first to compare fingerprints.

From childhood Mae knew what she wanted and was determined to get it, and her mother recognized and took pleasure in her unusual daughter's talent and individuality. Mae's mother indulged her whims, never holding her back from accomplishing her ambitions or suggesting more traditional goals. By the time she was in the third grade, Mae had quit school, and was performing suggestive dances and singing songs, mimicking the accents of New York's immigrants, to the delight of the audience of the vaudeville stage. Even as a little girl, she was aware of the financial aspect of show business. In her autobiography *Goodness Had Nothing to Do with It*, published when Mae was sixty-six, she remembers and notes the amount she received for each of her first performances. She also had an instinctive knowledge of the negotiation process. She refused to pick up money that was thrown on stage, as was the vaudeville custom, knowing that "stooping for money" was not an effective posture in the negotiating game. Later, an agent treated Mae and her dancing partners contemptuously, offering them a trial gig in South Norwalk for no remuneration, except $10 in traveling expenses. Mae refused this pittance, knocking the agent's hat down over his eyes before she exited from his office. Outside, her partner protested, "Gee, Mae, maybe we should have taken the $10," and Mae replied, "Don't worry, that $10 will get us more from Mr. Bohm." The act was a huge success and the agent was soon groveling, as Mae had predicted he would be.

Her awareness of the value of money led Mae to make a timely move from Broadway to Hollywood. Sentenced to ten days in a New York jail in 1927 for her obscene language and "coochie dance" in her own play, *Sex,* she took the opportunity to ponder economics. In her cell Mae read reports of Hollywood films' high earnings.

In 1925 Paramount reported earnings of $21,000,000; Metro $16,000,000; and First National $11,000,000. Nice, solid, round figures that I liked. I gave some real thought to motion pictures and how they could use my style and personality.

Once in Hollywood, Mae, who proved adept at studio politics, convinced conservative producers to do her kind of film. Eventually she earned $300,000 a picture—the highest salary paid to a star—portraying a lusty woman who knew what she wanted and always got it, and was never dependent on or at the mercy of men. She was soon involved in writing and helping to produce her own films, in which she also starred, delivering unforgettable lines like, "Is that a gun in your pocket or are you just glad to see me?" She also learned judo, how to fire a six-shooter, and insisted on entering the lion's cage herself when a stunt man got sick in the filming of *I'm No Angel,* which grossed $85,000 in the first week of its New York run.

In 1935 the flamboyant star earned $480,833. Only William Randolph Hearst, who earned $500,000, made more. The wealthy newspaper publisher wrote vindictive anti-West editorials. Mae, who recognized the forces of sexism but was not affected by them, took an indulgent view:

He hated to see a woman in his class. I didn't hold it against him.

Mae not only earned great sums but also enjoyed her money and invested it wisely. She was famous for her glamorous clothes, furs, and fabulous diamond jewelry. She bought real estate (which she managed herself when Jim Timony, who played many roles in her life from lover to financial adviser, died) and parlayed a $16,000 investment in Van Nuys, California, into $5 million. She bought stocks, horses, and ranches, too.

What makes Mae our non-Moneyphobic Queen, however, was not

only her exceptional earning power and intelligent use of money, but the way she achieved balance in her unique lifestyle.

> Hard as I worked, I would be lying to say I neglected all of my emotional side. I'm a girl who likes balance in everything. . . .

At times she turned down lucrative deals because she wanted to cater to spiritual or emotional needs:

> Money is a splendid commodity . . . and everybody should have lots of it. But money to burn does not necessarily produce the flames I need right now.

At other times, the star took on new challenges, not because she needed the money but because she loved her work.

> If I'm not convinced that what I do is great entertainment, I would rather do nothing at all but sit home and polish my diamonds.

Not surprisingly, this extraordinary woman's need for sexual pleasure could not be filled by only one man. Independent, and in charge of her own destiny, she saw no reason to marry, curtail her desire, or fashion a life (which in no other way resembled the typical female lifestyle of her time) to suit conventional morality. She satisfied her sexual needs with the same self-reliant assurance with which she took care of herself financially, often to the dismay of her partners, who were asked to call her "Miss West" in public and "Honey" in bed.

> The men who had so far loved me were strong and important citizens who had been attracted to me because they had become aware I was not like the other women they knew. They soon discovered I would not conform to the old-fashioned limits they had set on a woman's freedom of action. Or the myth of a woman's need of male wisdom and protection. This baffled men. Often made them angry, but oddly enough, once they knew they

could not change my philosophy or dominate me, none of them left me. My problem was actually how to get rid of *them*.

Mae did marry once, when she was only seventeen, but kept her husband a secret, locking him up in hotel rooms so she could enjoy sex with fellows outside. Much later, he sued her for alimony. The judge ruled in her favor, but Mae felt "a little sorry" for her husband, now toothless and old, and made him a settlement of some blue-chip stocks.

Like modern non-Moneyphobic women, Mae enjoyed. She relished the life she had designed to suit her needs, and even in old age worked, loved, and radiated a sense of power, self-control, and youthful vitality.

I got fun out of being a legend and institution.

In only one way was Mae West deprived: She failed to form close, supportive friendships with other women with whom the "legend" (perhaps understandably) did not identify.[1]

Detecting a Healthy Financial Identity

The women in our study who were non-Moneyphobic bore little resemblance to the inimitable Miss West, yet they conceived their lives as creatively as the thirties star conceived hers. These non-Moneyphobic women, who were also leading very different lifestyles from one another, came from different kinds of families from different parts of the country. All had arrived at their healthy financial identities via different routes, and had been able to separate from their parents' messages about women and money through outright rebellion, or by modifying the script they had been given over time. All had been able to incorporate positive elements of the family message into their adult lives, however, and, in retrospect, felt grateful to or accepting of their parents —a sign that they saw themselves as separate from them, and were comfortable with their own individuality. All had found "money mentors," or people who had helped them achieve personal and financial goals, and seized available opportunities to advance their earning power. All had taken risks. Though our non-Moneyphobic women were earning better-than-comfortable amounts of money, none were rich. All, however, took pleasure in their financial independence and used money to create harmony in their lives. Let us now look at brief profiles of three women who enjoy money, work, and love.*

PRISCILLA, WHO SAID NO TO POVERTY AND DEPENDENCE

Priscilla, forty, was born in Savannah, Georgia. Her mother was a housewife and her father a truck farmer who barely earned enough to support his large family. The second youngest of eight children, Priscilla decided at an early age that she did not want to grow up without any money.

> We always had the necessities of life, but we never had extras. I didn't want to always be poor!

By the time she was in the eighth grade, she saw economic independence as a way to avoid her mother's subservient life.

> I always felt sorry for my mother. She's very religious, and before she went to church my father's meal would be on the table. And when she came back she'd have to clean up the dishes. I never wanted that! And I always felt that the only way you didn't have to behave like that was if you could be independent.

Unusually clear about her goals, Priscilla found a "money mentor" in a rebellious older sister.

> She's very self-centered. I guess that's one of the reasons why she's been so successful. And she really was a role model. She told me

---

* The three non-Moneyphobic women we are profiling range in age from thirty-nine to forty-two, indicating that, given the obstacles in our culture, it takes time for woman to achieve a healthy financial identity as we have defined it here.

the facts of life and paid a lot of attention to me. I wanted to be like her, not like my mother.

Priscilla's family money mentor encouraged her to get financial aid and go to college. She even paid for a semester in the dormitory so Priscilla could have a taste of independent life away from home. Like many women her age, Priscilla had considered a career in education, but revised her plans when she learned that teachers made only $5,800 in her state—hardly a ticket out of the poorhouse. She changed her major to accounting, a field few women of her generation braved.

I got into it for the money. That's the pure reason.

When she was twenty-three, Priscilla married a nuclear physicist who had also fought his way free of a family background similar to hers, a man very unlike her father.

He never put any restraints on me at all. He was always very supportive.

Priscilla and her husband left the South and moved to Westchester, where she worked for the state tax office and he was employed by a large private firm engaged in government research. When the Equal Employment Opportunity Commission began pressuring Priscilla's office to promote more women, she took advantage of the opportunity. Though the EEOC was on her side, Priscilla still had to fight. When evaluations from a sexist manager were not what she thought she deserved, she requested counseling sessions.

I said, "So what should I do differently?" And there wasn't anything.

Though Priscilla's husband makes a lot of money and could easily support her, she prefers to work, and share financial decisions and goals. She proudly considers herself self-supporting and knows emotional dependence is not the same as financial dependence.

Although he is not chauvinistic, I just like the fact that I don't have to depend on him financially, though we do have a very close relationship. To be self-supporting gives me security, confidence, and lots of positive feelings.

Like many non-Moneyphobic women, Priscilla, who earns between $45,000 and $50,000 a year, feels she has enough money. Though she works hard and enjoys her job, she recently turned down an opportunity to apply for a position with a higher salary because she felt her present job offers her more personal time and flexibility.

We're not interested in buying an expensive car or a bigger home. We travel once a year, and there's just nothing else we want to do or buy. What we have is adequate, actually more than I ever anticipated.

Priscilla's sense of personal satisfaction has enabled her to make peace with her mother, whose traditional role she rejected.

For the first time I can really tell my mother that I love her. The distance between us has brought us closer together. Nobody's perfect, and I guess she did give us as much love as she knew how to give.

The same delight with the status quo led Priscilla to question the wisdom of having a baby when she realized her biological clock was ticking. Like other non-Moneyphobic women, she sought balance in her life and rejected the desire to "have it all."

I knew I would never give up my career. I would put my child in daycare, and I wondered if I would blame myself if it developed problems. I also think I was concerned with altering what I had. I hate to keep saying this, because I guess it sounds artificial, but I'm really happy. Not everything is perfect, but I'm very satisfied. My husband doesn't have a desire to have children, and I wondered if our relationship would deteriorate if I had to take total responsibility for an infant.

Instead of depriving herself of the opportunity to enjoy motherhood or giving birth to a baby, which might have interfered with her job and her marriage, Priscilla continued to rewrite the traditional script. She and her husband adopted a seven-year-old girl.

With an older child there are fewer unknowns. And there are so many older children like Cathy in orphanages who don't have homes, that nobody knows about or wants to adopt.

CONNIE, WHO INHERITED HER HEALTHY FINANCIAL IDENTITY

Priscilla achieved a healthy financial identity by forming goals in opposition to what she saw at home, with the help of a family mentor. Connie, on the other hand, was one of the few women lucky enough to inherit a positive financial identity directly from her parents. She took what she had learned at home, however, and used it to create a modern lifestyle that was very different from family expectations.

We knew we had uncovered a rare bird when we read Connie's questionnaire. She wrote that her parents had taught her that "Financial planning is important and fun; investing is necessary, and don't be afraid to take a chance, and it is a parental obligation to instruct children about financial matters." We interviewed Connie to learn exactly how these important messages had been transmitted and how she had incorporated them into her life.

Connie was born in Illinois. Her father owned his own lucrative business, and her mother, a housewife, participated in all the family's financial activities and played an equal role in decision-making.

My parents would talk in a very disparaging manner about families in which the wife didn't know what was going on financially. They both thought that was really terrible.

Though her parents fought, they never argued about financial matters.

> They bickered a lot, but I don't remember a fight about money.
> I saw them as a team.

Early on, her parents taught Connie to be assertive about money. When she was a child they asked her to collect for the Community Chest:

> I never had trouble asking for money.

They neither deprived her nor used money to control her behavior.

> If I asked for something frivolous—like a certain doll—and talked about it a lot, they would realize it was important to me. I got the doll, but not immediately. It was delayed gratification, but I don't remember feeling resentful about the delay.

When she was in high school, Connie started her first business— teaching art to neighborhood children, for which she charged their parents a fee. She was the only high school student with her own checking account; her parents gave it to her and taught her how to balance it. In college, Connie continued to work. She got a waitressing job, even though her upper-middle-class parents would have been glad to provide her with discretionary cash.

> I didn't tell my parents at first because I didn't think they would understand. The college situation was so artificial; I had to have a taste of the real world. I liked having my own money. It was freedom. For me, economics is the bottom line.

Having inherited a sense of the value of money and the experience of accomplishing financial tasks, Connie used this sound training to fly away from home. Instead of remaining in Illinois and teaching art, as her parents expected her to do ("a narrower kind of life"), she set off for New York to become an exhibiting sculptor. She taught part-time to support herself and also went to school.

I got support from my parents to be an artist, but not to leave Illinois. My father was even more upset than my mother. He tried to bribe me to stay by buying me a car. Since he had never before used money to control me, I viewed it as a joke. What did I care about a car? When I enrolled in graduate school, it made coming to New York more acceptable to them.

Later, Connie, who had learned how to take financial risks from her parents, bought her own co-op with their ongoing help. When a couple in her building threatened to purchase her unit out from under her, because they did not think, as a struggling single woman, she would be able to buy, she called her father for advice.

I said, "Daddy, they're trying to steal my apartment!" He said, "Don't let it bother you. You're worth more than they are." He was talking about his money, not mine. I had a few hundred in my checking account. What he was saying was, "You have my complete support."

When she felt she was not making enough from teaching to have a comfortable lifestyle and support her art, Connie continued to expand her parents' original script. Positive money messages she had grown up hearing enabled her to take a bold, innovative step: She started her own construction business with another woman.

My father had always talked to me about his business and investments. When I had my own business, we had more to talk about. He would tell me about estimates and competition.

After a television talk show personality, intrigued by the idea of women in the building trades, invited Connie and her partner to be guests, her business boomed. By now a full-fledged financial adult, Connie invested the profits in land and stocks, consulting her accountant, her brother, an MBA, and friends for advice. She also continued to pursue her dream career in art, as well as her money-making business. In order to have two careers, however, she had to curtail her desire for money, and use what she had to buy herself security and time, instead of material things. She finds her salary of between $35,000 and $40,000 a year sufficient.

> Sometimes I work for very wealthy people, and I see what it would be like to be rich. I have moments of envy, but they don't last long. It takes a tremendous amount of energy to maintain that lifestyle. Wealthy people tend to be nervous and demanding. I'm glad I'm not obsessed with getting more and more stuff.

Still single at thirty-nine, Connie does not plan to marry. Instead, she has designed a romantic life that is as untraditional as her dual career. When we interviewed her, she was involved with a number of men. Her love life, and personal feelings of self-esteem, she said, had improved as she had become financially self-assured.

> Sometimes I think, Gosh, who would have ever thought my life would be like this? For years I had no boyfriends, and now I have five or six men in love with me. To me, that's a miracle. Sometimes I feel like I'm on the fringe of society, but I don't really care. When I do think about settling down with one person, I feel not any one person could give me everything I need.

Though Connie is grateful to her parents for giving her a healthy financial identity, she stresses that her relationship with them was not in every way ideal.

> I can feel angry about, "I didn't get this. Or if only they had done that, this would have been different." But money is an area where I can say they did a really good job, and feel great about that.

MOLLY, WHO CHANGED HER FINANCIAL IDENTITY WITH TIME

Both Priscilla and Connie, in different ways, were able to develop the foundations for a healthy financial identity at an early age. Molly, our third non-Moneyphobic woman, struggled against obstacles that face many women when they deal with money and earning power, but was able to change. By learning to use money mentors, and gradually discovering her ambitions and talents, she achieved a healthy financial identity over time.

Molly, now forty-two, was born in a New York suburb. Her loving and indulgent middle-class Italian parents raised her to be a moneydenier, and marry a man who would rescue her and give her a luxurious life. They sent her to college, in hopes she would find a rich husband there. Molly, who was not rebellious, tried to fulfill her parents' expectations, but felt stifled.

> I grew up feeling I wanted to have contact with all this stuff out there in the world, and knew if I didn't figure out how to do it, I wasn't going to have it. But I also wanted to be a good girl and I wanted my parents to love me. I wasn't strong enough or rebellious enough to make a break with them and do my own thing.

When she graduated from college Molly married her high school sweetheart, instead of a handsome prince, and they moved to New York and had two children. After several years of being a mother and a homemaker, however, Molly grew bored and her marriage foundered.

> I wasn't happy because I wanted to go back to work. I knew I had to be doing something, and I don't think that was necessarily making money. *Career* was not part of my vocabulary then. I just didn't want to stay at home, taking care of two children and making dinner for my husband. I wanted to do something that was for me. When he couldn't do it for me or with me, I did it myself.

Molly and her husband were divorced, and she slowly began to discover the money-making part of her identity.

> I think I am a very ambitious person, but I don't think I knew or felt that until very recently. The process I went through from the time I separated was a slow one.

An inadequate divorce settlement made it imperative for Molly to earn:

> If I didn't have children when I got divorced, I could have partied and partied and made barely enough money for myself. I needed more; it was a reality. Having the children made me feel I needed to earn money, and find ways to do it.

Molly quickly learned that she was not afraid of risk and saw starting a business as an exciting adventure. From the first she chose an independent career path, creating jobs for herself that offered the flexibility she needed to work and take care of her children. Intuiting a profitable real estate market in downtown Manhattan loft buildings, she got a salesman's license and convinced a broker to let her set up a "loft desk" in her office. She rented and sold the "trendy" new living spaces, doing business on her bicycle. Next, Molly, who had a bent for fashion, "did flea markets," selling antique jewelry and clothes. When she decided to open a boutique, featuring both antique clothing and her own designs, in the up-and-coming SoHo district, she learned how to negotiate with her father, and use him as a money mentor and financial resource. Her father had already refused to loan her the money she needed to buy a loft of her own.

> I told him the part of SoHo where I would be opening the store would soon be booming. "Look at that loft I could have bought for $18,000 that's now worth $100,000," I said. He asked me how much I needed. In my mind I had no idea of money. I spent it, I earned it, I spent it—I didn't even balance my checkbook then. I took a guess and said $10,000. He hesitated, and I reminded him about the money he said he'd put away for my

sister and me to have as an inheritance. I asked him if I could have $10,000 of it now, and he said okay. I think that since I was supporting myself, he felt I had some retail talent.

Once Molly demonstrated that she had a financial identity, her father started to treat her like an adult, instead of like a fairy tale princess. When she got "bored" with her store and decided to open her own fashion design company, she was able to ask her father to invest in her again. Unafraid of risk, she was not stopped by lack of knowledge or experience in this new field.

I think when my marriage ended I felt like such a failure that after that taking risks was easy—what did I have to lose? I didn't know anything about the fashion business, how it worked, how to market my designs, write orders, net terms, delivery dates. . . . I knew nothing. But it was a new project and I was very excited. It was a challenge.

To help her realize her goals, Molly took a seminar sponsored by American Women's Economic Development Corporation (AWED), designed to help women start their own businesses, and formed a network of money mentors. She took on a partner, another woman, whose talents complemented hers.

The things I do that make our partnership successful are very different from the things Jan does. She examines everything very closely and pays attention to the big picture. But she's always a little bit scared of the next step, and I have to shove her along and convince her.

Molly and her partner also employed an accountant, who helped them negotiate with each other, and with a bank when they needed a loan to move their business to larger quarters in the garment center. Forming this new financial relationship with an institution also expanded Molly's financial identity.

I never felt so nervous and so grown up as the day we signed the loan.

Her business now nets Molly a personal salary of $50,000 a year. She has come a long way from the rescued princess her parents wanted her to be and the penniless divorced mother who needed to earn. Like many entrepreneurs, she needs to push on to new and more challenging territories in order to feel emotionally satisfied, and is already restless in her profitable business. She is considering ideas to expand and change it. An unfortunate event—her father's death—enabled her to separate even further from her parents' money message and to contemplate earning more.

> My father had a secure job, but he wasn't aggressive and he didn't make a lot. Something happened to me when he died; it kind of freed me to make more money. I had a strong relationship with him, and wanted his approval. There was a part of me that thought, I can't be more successful than my father, because he's a man.

Like many non-Moneyphobic women, Molly has brought the financial awareness she has gained in the marketplace into her personal life. She has started to save for retirement and is thinking about the money messages she is giving her children.*

After many years of single life, Molly became involved with a man whom she at first thought was not her "type"—a personal money mentor. Shortly after we interviewed her, she married for the second time. Unlike her first husband, this one takes pleasure in seeing her as an equal and encourages her ambitious goals.

> He's younger than me. And when we met, he told me he was tired of women who felt he should take care of them, and support them,

---

* We wrote about Molly's saving experience in Chapter 5 in "Overcoming Money-folly" (p. 170) and discussed the way she collected child support from her ex-husband in "Negotiating a Divorce Settlement" in Chapter 7 (p. 225).

and buy them things, and who weren't going to do anything for him but lie there. That's paraphrasing. He likes that I'm independent and have my own business. He's proud of me, and talks about me to a lot of people. He doesn't make me feel that it's not okay to be ambitious and successful, or feel threatened if I make more money than he does. I don't have the feeling I have to give up myself to be with him.

As Molly discovered, an equal relationship that provided support for her financial and personal goals also provided a new kind of chemistry:

We have an incredibly good sexual relationship. It's never even had a bad day, and this has been going on for two years. We have that!

Overcoming Moneyphobia: Creating the Climate for Positive Change

For most women, developing a healthy financial identity is a slow process of self-discovery, which demands recognition of problems and goals, a desire to change, and hard work and perseverence. Like those who suffer from *any* phobia, they reduce their fear by dealing directly with its source, and getting sympathetic help from supportive friends and trained professionals. Here are the steps that take a Moneyphobic woman to a healthy financial identity:

IDENTIFY MONEY PROBLEMS AND THE REASONS FOR THEM

A woman who wants to be non-Moneyphobic must admit that her financial behavior holds her back from realizing her goals. Instead of ignoring money issues, or lumping them together with other problems, like an unsatisfactory love life or job, she must open her eyes to money and get a clear view of her financial picture. She needs to look not only at the money she has at her disposal, how she uses it, and how much she wants to earn, but also at the way her financial identity has developed. To do this, she can examine the money messages she got from her parents and analyze her family money history.*

Defining the origins of financial problems can be a fascinating but threatening task. Many women have been avoiding money because they never expected to have to deal with it at all, and dismissing complicated problems with simplistic statements like, "I don't have any money" or "I'm terrible with money." The woman may not actually feel frightened when she thinks about money, however, but tired, bored, or even angry—emotions that conceal her anxiety from herself. The more Moneyphobic she is, the more she will resist this important first step.

WANT TO CHANGE AND BELIEVE IT IS POSSIBLE

Psychologically sophisticated women, who enjoy getting in touch with their inner lives, find it interesting to analyze money problems and investigate their emotional origins. Recognition of problems, however, should result in a desire to change and a belief that change is possible. Faced with the hard work such difficult changes call for, however, many women stop at this point. "There are so many other important things going on in my life," they say, "I obviously don't have time to deal with money," or, "I've inherited these problems, and there's nothing I can do about them now."

When women are unwilling to change the way they think about and act with money, their analysis of financial problems will remain an ineffective intellectual exercise. Those who don't want to change may still cherish rescue fantasies, or fear the results of true independence and economic self-determination.

* The Appendices provide tools that should help our readers define their financial identities and gauge their weaknesses and strengths in relation to money: Appendix 1, a modified version of the questionnaire we used to elicit subjective feelings for our money study; Appendix 2, The Family "Money Tree"; Appendix 3, The Financial Identity Checklist; and Appendix 4, The Six-Figure Fantasy Game.

WORK TO CHANGE AND PUT A
PLAN INTO ACTION

The third step in the direction of a healthy financial identity is to set specific goals and put a plan into action. If a woman has recognized her money problems, her goals should become apparent. The most effective method for accomplishing financial goals, we found, is to set small, specific tasks that are completed in a limited time frame. If a woman is moneyblind, for example, her first goal might be to balance her checkbook or learn to read a financial statement. If she suffers from moneyfolly, she may want to go on The Money Watch (Appendix 5) and keep a record of how much she spends. A moneyconfused woman may want to set a time to discuss financial issues with the man in her life. Broad, idealistic goals such as, "I want to make $50,000 next year," are too general to be effective. Modest goals should be set first to give her a positive feeling of accomplishment. A major goal can be broken down into "do-able" steps. A woman who wants to learn to invest, for example, might

(1) Make a list of her savings accounts, and if they are time deposits, when they come due.
(2) Read a book about investment strategies.
(3) Contact friends to get names of brokers.
(4) Make a list of questions to ask the broker.
(5) Call the brokers and interview them.
(6) Make one investment after researching it carefully.

This process might take a month or two, but she should give herself a deadline and complete it by then.

Sophisticated, intelligent women feel embarrassed and ashamed to admit how much they do not know about financial matters, or how anxious they feel about performing financial tasks they know are objectively simple, or insignificant. A resistant woman is likely to dwell on the reasons she feels incapable of changing her financial behavior, and to describe her anxiety in great detail. To overcome Moneyphobia, it is vital to choose an appropriate action and carry it out.

FIND "MONEY MENTORS"

Feminist psychologist Carol Gilligan has observed that women, more than men, define themselves in a context of important human relationships and see themselves as interdependent with other people. For this reason, it may be easier for a woman to change with the help of others than by herself. Conversely, if she is afraid of change, she will avoid those who could have a positive influence on her behavior. To vanquish Moneyphobia, women need sympathetic friends, acquaintances, and professionals who can give them information and support. Below are the types of relationships that can help a Moneyphobic woman become financially self-assured.

Money Buddies

Women often develop special friends with whom they discuss mutual problem areas, like career difficulties, traumas with men, and overweight. It is also possible to develop "Money Buddies" and discuss financial problems with them. These relationships may occur spontaneously. However, they can also be initiated by open questions and statements such as, "Do you have any savings? The interest rates are terrible now, and I want to invest in something else, but I haven't the slightest idea how to do it." Because finance is an area women seldom discuss frankly, those who share money confidences may feel they belong to a secret club; in these relationships, money can cement a friendship. The best "Money Buddies" are those who don't have negative attitudes toward financial goals and who sincerely want to change their behavior. Women who are smart about financial matters or sophisticated earners make excellent friends for the Moneyphobic. A woman and her money buddy might make a pact to accompany one another when a nervewracking financial task must be accomplished. They might also agree to rehearse negotiations or research appropriate investments together.

MONEY-AWARENESS GROUPS

The consciousness-raising groups of the seventies helped women air problems they thought were unique and private to a sympathetic support group whose concerns were the same. With these groups in mind, we formed our issue-oriented Money-Awareness Groups, which we have discussed in the Preface and referred to throughout the book. In Appendix 6, we give instructions for setting up and running a money group.

The group setting provides an excellent climate for change. When properly organized, a group can give the emotional support of a good family, and minimize its members' sense of isolation and shame about their lack of financial knowledge. To be effective, however, the group must encourage members not only to share fears and problems in relation to money, but also to perform specific financial tasks. When a task is assigned to a money group member (in our groups, most members decided on the task themselves, but in some cases, tasks were suggested), she feels a responsibility to others as well as to herself. Having to return to the group and report back is a good incentive to accomplish her goal. Said one of our New York money group members:

> The group provides an interior witness that I can't escape. I've said I'm going to do it; now I can't fool myself.

When a woman reports her accomplishment to the other members, their praise gives her emotional gratification she would not otherwise get. If she fails, the group's reactions may help her identify the underlying issues. The group also serves to question each member's convictions about financial behavior, and directly or indirectly, suggest alternative viewpoints. A group can provide a forum for exchanging financial information, too.

PROFESSIONAL MENTORS

Professional mentors can help a woman overcome earning barriers. Mentors may be men or women who work in the same field, or even in the same workplace. An on-the-job mentor can help make the marketplace feel more like a comfortable home. Whenever a woman finds a potential mentor, however, she must convince him or her that she is capable of filling the protégée role. Karen, who found a mentor in the large pharmaceutical firm where she soon became a rising star, described her role in creating the relationship:

> The medical director was fired and they were restructuring the department. I was being considered for a promotion. I walked right into the vice-president's office and thanked him for considering me. I told him I was interested and wanted to work hard. I asked him to recommend all the reading in the area that he could. He gave me some literature and I read it over the weekend. He asked me how much responsibility I could take, and I said, "I can take as much as you can give me."

The women in our study who had found professional mentors talked about relationships that in some ways resembled those they had had with lovers and family members, but were distinctly different. Karen described her mentor relationship like this.

> It's something you can't know unless you've had it. I think of myself as wanting to please him, like a daddy. Sometimes I think of him as being attractive and we can kind of flirt. There's friendship there, too. Together we are always very professional, but we talk about our feelings about business. He's a man who doesn't have to have total control. He leaves room for me to grow, and makes me feel that I'm special.

PROFESSIONALS IN THE FINANCIAL FIELD

Financial professionals—an important part of the non-Moneyphobic woman's supportive network—include financial planners, advisers, and brokers. Financial planners and advisers help their clients (a) analyze their current financial situation; (b) formulate goals; and (c) design a financial plan, which may include budgeting, tax planning, risk management strategies, investment management, and estate planning.

They also help implement, monitor, and adjust the plan once it is in process.

Planners and advisers are paid a straight fee for their counseling services, or earn their money on the basis of commissions, or a combination of both. Those listed in the *Registry of Financial Planning* * have met educational requirements, passed a written exam, and practiced for at least three years. Some give seminars on financial planning, which are widely available and relatively inexpensive. Brokers may also function as advisers, since they recommend investments known as financial products, but they make their money only on commissions, sometimes included in the product's price.

Moneyphobic women fear getting involved with financial professionals, or using their knowledge as a tool to help them make financial decisions. They see them as threatening unknowns who will take total power over their money. Instead of viewing these money mentors as helpful information sources and translators of financial jargon, they are afraid they will use what they don't know against them. At the same time, they see their professional knowledge as "magical," or the ultimate solution for their own financial ignorance and financial woes.

PERSONAL MENTORS: MONEY AND MEN

Women who are at ease with money and success are often found living with or close to men who don't inhibit their ambitions, or who make it possible for them to succeed. One of the best examples of personal mentorship is the relationship of the late painter Georgia O'Keeffe with the photographer Alfred Stieglitz. In 1916, O'Keeffe was an unknown, struggling painter who supported herself by heading the Art Department of the West Texas Normal College. A friend showed her work to Stieglitz, who proclaimed, "At last, a woman on paper!" and hung her work in his New York gallery. O'Keeffe traveled to New York to rebuke him for hanging her work without her permission. Stieglitz persuaded the artist to move to New York, give up teaching, and devote herself to her true vocation. After they married he continued to present

* This listing is available at no cost from the International Association for Financial Planning, Two Concourse Parkway, Suite 800, Atlanta, GA 30328.

annual one-woman shows of her work until he died. Having experienced the joys of life with a personal mentor, O'Keeffe found another supportive man even when she was well past middle age. Juan Hamilton, many decades younger than the artist, assisted her and managed her business affairs. Despite the difference in their ages, there were rumors of marriage.[2]

Like O'Keeffe, several of the successful women in our study had found men who played a supportive role in their professional lives. Myra, twenty-nine, decided to leave a low-paying teaching career and go to medical school.

> When I was twenty-four, I realized I would have to do something —fantasies aside—where I would be totally self-sufficient, so if I wanted kids on my own, or wanted to live alone, I could do it, and still have material things. I'm materialistic! I wanted to be in a financial position where I would never be nickel and diming it.

Her boyfriend, a doctor himself, "harassed" her to apply to medical school.

> He was the first man whom I felt wasn't going to compete with me, but who held values that I really wanted to hold in terms of his career and being successful. I said, "I need to figure out what I'm going to do for the rest of my life." He said, "Well, what are you going to do?" and I said, "I can't go to medical school." He said, "Yes, you can," and bugged me and pushed me.

When Myra's wealthy father, who had cherished unfulfilled ambitions to be a doctor himself, refused to give her any money, her boyfriend offered to provide financial support if she needed it. Both realized that his investment of support—both financial and personal—was a risk few men would be willing to take.

> He'd been married, and he didn't want to deal with another financially dependent woman. I'm not sure he knows what he's going to get.

It is hard to say which comes first: a woman's ambition to make money, or the personal relationship that makes it possible for her to feel free to express and act upon her goals. Women who are ambivalent about their goals, however, may unconsciously choose partners who are themselves unsuccessful or who are threatened by others' success.

Sometimes the personal mentor relationship works in reverse. A woman with a healthy financial identity may have a positive influence on a Moneyphobic man. One of the non-Moneyphobic women in our study, a Washington architect, married a high-earning moneyfolly victim who came from a large, poor family and relished the pleasures of spending. Slowly and systematically, she worked on restoring him to financial health.

> I thought, If it came between a spender and a miser, I'd rather he be a spender and try to teach him something.

When her husband, who had no savings, had to borrow heavily against his taxes by claiming more exemptions in order to convince the bank that his paycheck was large enough to warrant a mortgage, the non-Moneyphobic architect decided to act. She planned a budget and made sure her husband put his share of the mortgage in their joint account, instead of spending it (though he was wont to spend on extravagant gifts for her). She also began to tactfully suggest that he open a savings account.

> One day at breakfast I asked him if he planned to open a savings account, knowing it was probably the farthest thing from his mind. He said, "Not really," but I knew I'd planted the seed of an idea. I couldn't openly tell him he should begin to save, because it would have made him furious. You have to know how to handle people.

When her husband saw her filling out the questionnaire for our money study, he was horrified by her breach of financial confidence.

"You're going to answer those questions!" he exclaimed. I said, "Yes, and I want you to read them when I'm finished because they will tell you something more about me."

In this way, this non-Moneyphobic woman is slowly initiating the important dialogue about money all couples (especially those with differing financial styles) need to negotiate effectively, and becoming her husband's personal money mentor.

Change, of course, is a mysterious phenomenon, and how or why it happens cannot always be explained. Moneyphobic women may find only some of our suggestions useful and may want to adapt them to fit their individual goals. The results, however, provide inspiration no modern woman should deny herself: To "balance accounts" and achieve a healthy financial identity is to enjoy not only money, but a richer, more rewarding life.

Questionnaire

The following list of questions was selected from the questionnaire we used as a data base for our money study. We have edited it to include the questions that helped women initiate serious thinking about their financial situation and attitudes. We suggest that the reader either write down or record her answers.

FAMILY ATTITUDES

1. Classify the financial status of the family you grew up in: (a.) Lower class (b.) Working class (c.) Middle class (d.) Upper middle class (e.) Upper class
2. Briefly describe your father's attitude toward making and spending money.
3. Briefly describe your mother's attitude toward making and spending money.
4. Briefly describe sibling(s) attitude(s) toward making and spending money.
5. Who managed the money in your family?
6. Describe your parents' attitude toward your current occupation.

WORK HISTORY

1. When you were a teenager how did you think your financial needs would be taken care of when you reached adulthood?
2. Briefly describe your work history since childhood. (What was your first paying job? How old were you when you got it? How much were you paid? Second job? etc.)
3. How did you choose your present occupation? Did you receive help with this choice? If so, explain.

PRESENT FINANCIAL SITUATION AND GOALS

1. How much money do you need to live per year? Explain how you arrived at this figure.
2. Are you satisfied with your current income?
3. Would you like to make more money? Explain your answer, giving reasons.
4. What is your "ideal" income? How much of an increase does the "ideal" figure represent over your present income (percentage or dollars)?
5. How could you imagine earning your ideal income? Explain.
6. Can you imagine acquiring your ideal income in any way other than earning it yourself? Explain.
7. Are you currently engaged in any work or activity that might make it possible for you to acquire your ideal income? If yes, explain.
8. If you made more money, what would you do with it? Explain how your lifestyle would change, how you would invest the money, etc.
9. If you could have any job, title, or do any income-producing activity, what would it be?
10. If you could choose any type of work environment, what would it be?
11. Are you currently contemplating a career change?

12. If you don't earn money at the present time, under what circumstances would you begin to earn?
13. What are your individual annual earnings before taxes?
14. If your income varies by more than $5,000 annually, explain why.
15. Do you presently have (a.) Money market account (b.) stocks (c.) bonds (d.) other investments in financial products (e.) real estate (f.) IRA or another retirement account?
16. What is your net worth?
17. Who advises you how to spend or invest your money?

FUTURE FINANCIAL GOALS

1. Do you expect to continue income-producing activities? Until what age?
2. Where will the money you plan to live on when you are over sixty-five come from?
3. What do you imagine your financial situation will be like in ten years?

SUPPORT

1. At what age did your parents stop providing financial support?
2. Do you now support yourself?
3. Do you ever accept money from your parents? Explain.
4. Do you support, or partially support, anyone else (husband, child, relative, or other)?
5. If married, or living with someone, what percentage of household expenses do you supply?
6. Have you ever supported a man/men or helped a man/men financially? If yes, how and for how long? How did you feel about it? How did the man feel about it?
7. If you have been divorced or separated, how did the split affect your attitude toward making and spending money?
8. If you have a child/children, how has being a mother affected your attitude toward making and spending money?

9. Do you plan to have a child or more children? If yes, how do you see your money-making activities changing as a result?
10. Do you like the idea of being supported by someone else? Why or why not?

SPENDING

1. Do you classify yourself as a "saver" or a "spender"?
2. What do you spend most of your money on?
3. If you have "extra" money, what do you do with it?
4. Are you a compulsive or "binge" shopper? If yes, what do you shop for, and what moods or feelings induce you to shop?
5. Do you have debts (personal, bank loans, or credit card)? Explain. How do you feel about them?
6. If you have credit cards, how do you use them?
7. Do you have a weekly/monthly budget? If yes, do you stick to it?
8. Do others label you "cheap," "generous," or "extravagant"? How do you label yourself?

MONEY ISSUES IN RELATIONSHIPS

1. If you are married, living with or involved with a man, does he earn more or less than you do? How much more or less? Give percentage or dollars.
2. If there is a difference in your incomes, how do you feel about it? How does he feel about it?
3. How does your present partner feel about the money you make?
4. Is there career/financial competition between you and your present partner? Between you and the men you work with? Describe this competition and how you handle it. How does it make you feel?
5. Have you been married or lived with a man (men) in the past? If yes, for how long?
6. What did the man (men) do for a living? What did you do?
7. Did the man (men) earn more or less than you did? How much more or less (percentage or dollars)? Did the difference in your incomes change during the time you were together?

DREAMS, ANXIETIES, AND RISK

1. What role does money play in your daydreams and fantasies?
2. If you are, or have been, in psychotherapy or psychoanalysis, have money problems and anxieties been discussed or treated? If so, how?
3. Have you ever made an investment or taken a financial risk? Explain your feelings about doing it and the outcome.
4. Describe any anxieties or problems you now have or have had in the past in relationship to money. (Do you have saving/spending problems that make you uneasy? Do you have earning problems, negotiating or managing problems?)

The Family "Money Tree"

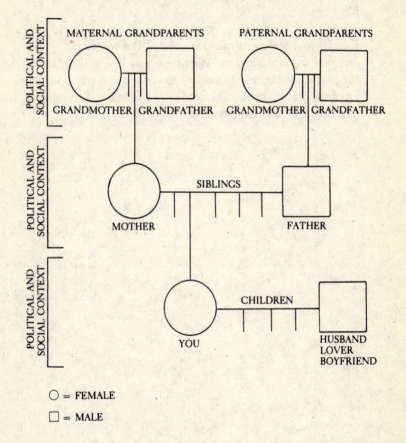

POLITICAL AND SOCIAL CONTEXT

MATERNAL GRANDPARENTS PATERNAL GRANDPARENTS

GRANDMOTHER GRANDFATHER GRANDMOTHER GRANDFATHER

POLITICAL AND SOCIAL CONTEXT

SIBLINGS

MOTHER FATHER

POLITICAL AND SOCIAL CONTEXT

CHILDREN

YOU HUSBAND
LOVER
BOYFRIEND

○ = FEMALE

□ = MALE

Tracing your family "Money Tree" will help you see which of your relatives' money attitudes you have inherited, and how they affect your financial behavior. Answer the ten following questions about each relative on the tree, then fill in the circles and squares with short phrases which capture that individual's attitude toward money.

1. What was the social and political climate in which he/she was living?
2. How much money did he/she earn?
3. What was his/her lifestyle like? Where and how did he/she live?
4. What role did he/she have in managing money?
5. What was his/her attitude toward planning, saving, and investing? Toward risk-taking?
6. How did he/she set financial goals?
7. What did he/she spend money on? Were his/her spending patterns consistent?
8. How did money fit into his/her life? Was money important to him or her?
9. What was his/her greatest success with money? Greatest failure?
10. In what ways are your financial attitudes and behavior similar to or different from this family member?

The Financial Identity Checklist

The following questions will help the reader evaluate her financial identity by defining financial tasks and asking her if she does them. The more financial tasks she accomplishes, the more highly developed her financial identity. Answer each question "yes" or "no." The "nos" indicate areas that need work or attention.

1. Are you able to talk about financial matters with friends and family members openly and comfortably?
2. Do you open, read, and understand all statements and information from financial institutions, like banks, brokerage houses, and insurance companies?
3. Do you participate in all financial decisions involving investments and major purposes instead of allowing someone else to make them for you?
4. Do you have a financial adviser or planner, or someone you turn to for help with financial decisions?
5. Is your name on all assets jointly owned with another person?
6. Do you have a will?
7. If your investments (including real estate and insurance plans) have been purchased by someone else in your family, do you understand the details and the terms?
8. Do you know how much you make and spend in a year?
9. Do you know what your net worth is?

10. Do you understand how your taxes are computed?

11. Have you taken advantage of all legal options for reducing your tax burden?

12. Do you have short-term financial goals? (That is, do you have plans that involve spending, saving, or earning money that you want to accomplish within the next year?)

13. Do you have long-term financial goals? (That is, do you have plans that involve spending, saving, or earning money that you hope to accomplish in the next five to twenty years, such as retiring from your job, reviewing the hours that you work, sending your children to college, or buying a country home?)

14. Have you formalized plans to meet both short- and long-term goals yourself, or through a cooperative effort with your partner?

15. If you are single or divorced, have you made plans to live on your own income, or on investments and savings made with your income, in the future?

16. If you are not happy with your present income, have you formulated specific plans about how to increase it yourself?

17. Do you see and investigate opportunities to increase your income, including making profitable investments?

18. Do you take advantage of opportunities to increase your income?

19. Have you formulated a network of people with whom you can discuss your professional interests and goals?

20. Do you save money on a regular basis?

21. Do you know what you are saving money for?

22. Is the money you have saved helping you fulfill your financial goals? (For example, if you are saving for retirement, is the saved money earning a maximum rate of interest?)

23. Do you always pay your "basic nut," or your regular monthly bills, on time?

24. If you use credit cards to make purchases, do you make monthly payments on time?

25. Do you avoid using a cash advance from one credit company to make a payment to another?

26. When you shop, do you buy only what you went shopping to purchase?

27. When you shop, do you pay the amount you had budgeted for the item, give or take a few dollars?
28. When you shop, do you feel satisfied with your purchases?
29. If you need a loan, do you shop around for the best available rates?
30. Have you shopped for the credit card that charges the lowest rate of interest and/or yearly fee?
31. If you have children, do you know what they do with the spending money you give them and approve of their purchases?
32. If you have children, are you giving them positive messages about earning, spending, and managing money?
33. When faced with a negotiation for pay, do you familiarize yourself with pay scales for your position in your field or for the job you are about to do before you negotiate?
34. Do you discuss the upcoming negotiation with a knowledgeable friend or mentor?
35. When you have to negotiate, do you go into the negotiation with a specific strategy?
36. Do you negotiate with people in your personal life, instead of ignoring money problems that arise? (For example, if you go out for dinner with a friend who asks you to split the check, and the friend's share is more than yours, do you discuss the matter if it bothers you?)
37. Have you devised a system for dividing expenses with your partner that is mutually satisfying?
38. If you are in the process of getting a divorce, are you familiar with the divorce laws in your state?
39. If you are married, are you aware of the value of the financial assets you have contributed to the marriage, and have you made your partner aware of them?

The Six-Figure Fantasy Game

The following game, which we discussed at length in Chapter 4, "Moneyeluding," helps women pinpoint the reservations and fears that are preventing them from making more money. It is best to play this game with a friend and tape-record it, so you can both listen back. Your friend should say the first words that come into her mind. Don't analyze or interpret until the game is over.

Step 1. Tell your friend she has been invited to a dinner party, and finds herself seated next to a very successful woman in her field. Use your imagination to make up the exact position the successful woman holds. Ask your friend to describe this woman's appearance and personality.

- If her description is generally positive, it means she can identify herself with a successful woman.
- If she sees the successful woman as masculine, hostile, or extremely withholding, she may not be able to identify success with femininity, or find it easy to accept the ambitious woman in herself.

Step 2. Ask your friend to tell you what she says to the successful woman, and what the successful woman says to her. If possible, get her to "act out" the conversation.

- A woman who is alert to "networking" strategies will be cognizant that her dinner party companion represents a golden opportunity, and her comments and questions will reflect that.
- If she treats the successful woman as a friend or mother, or assumes she will reject her, she is confusing her emotions or her low self-esteem with an income-producing opportunity.

Step 3. Have the successful career woman offer your friend the job and salary of her dreams—$100,000. Again, use your imagination to tailor the fantasy to your friend's individual fantasies and goals. Ask her if she accepts the offer. Why or why not?

- A woman who is not afraid of earning more money will approach the "golden opportunity" with a sense of realism and poise. She will want to know what the job description entails, and how the six-figure job will fit into the rest of her life.
- A woman who is afraid of success will reject the job for reasons of her own before she asks for a job description, or accept it too readily, without asking what is involved. She may express serious doubts that she "can do it," or attribute very high expectations to her future employer. She may also express moral reservations about earning too much money.

Step 4. If your friend has accepted the job, ask her what she plans to do with the money.

- If a woman can imagine herself as a high-earner her plans for increased income will be realistic. She will not blow the money, hoard it, or try to give it away.

Step 5. Ask your friend how her high income affects her relationship with (a) the man in her life, or men in general, (b) her parents and siblings and (c) her women friends.

- A woman who is not afraid of money will express realistic reservations about the effect of money on the people in her personal life. Unless she has partnered with a male "money mentor," and has successful parents and friends, she may reasonably expect some envy and resentment. She acknowledges this possibility and states her plans to handle envious feedback.

- If the game player is afraid of envy and competition, she will probably have already revealed this by expressing negative feelings about the female tycoon at the dinner table, or with deep reservations about her ability to do the job. Because this crucial step of the game is for her a total fantasy, she will anticipate no problems whatsoever, and imagine her friends and relatives will be "happy for her," or that they will fail to be affected by her huge success.

The Money Watch

The Money Watch is a money-awareness exercise that helps women detect their spending patterns and the anxieties and other emotions involved in them. Though it is especially useful to help overspenders curb their "appetites," it helps all women learn much about where and how they spend, and why. It is best to go on The Money Watch with a money buddy, or with members of a money-awareness group. Because this simple exercise is surprisingly traumatic, it is important to be able to discuss feelings about it, and desires to stop doing it, with an encouraging friend.

Step 1. Get a small notebook and make three columns labeled: (1) Amount Spent (2) On What and (3) Feelings.

Step 2. For an entire month write down on what every penny is spent, including rent, candy bars, and credit card charges. Emotions about the expenditure should be noted in the final column. If the feelings are complex, describe them in detail in the back of the notebook.

Step 3. At the end of the month, review all expenditures and the feelings they inspired. Moneywatchers often find their expenses have dropped in the course of the exercise, and that they have become more conscious of when and why they spend.

Forming a Money-Awareness Group

A money-awareness group is a consciousness-raising group devoted to money problems, in which each member formulates and accomplishes specific financial goals. The group should create a comfortable, accepting, uncritical atmosphere where each member can feel free to discuss her fears and failures, as well as her triumphs with money.

COMPOSITION

The group should include women who know each other, as well as some strangers. Choose women who are interested in developing money awareness—who are serious about wanting to change. Limit the size of the group to between seven and ten members.

CONTRACT

The group members should agree to commit themselves to a specific number of meetings (at least six to eight), and to decide how often the group should meet. Groups should meet at least once a month, until the agreed-upon cycle of meetings is completed. At this point, the group can negotiate to begin a new cycle of meetings and admit new members. A new member should not be admitted in the middle of a cycle. Each meeting lasts three hours, with a fifteen-minute coffee break.

GROUP RULES

Members should promise to keep group confidences. All members should participate equally. To make sure talking time is equally divided, the group may want to set time limits on how long any one person may speak at one time. Members should agree to support and share, and refrain from giving advice, unless the advice is asked for, or is about specific financial matters—for example, how to close on a real-estate purchase.

GROUP LEADER

Each session should have a leader and a timekeeper. These roles should be shared by group members. Because the subject of money is anxiety-producing, members may tend to stray off the subject. The leader's job is to bring the discussion back to the topic of money, and to encourage members to share their feelings of discomfort about discussing it. The timekeeper makes certain that the group sticks to its three-hour limit, and that no one member "hogs" the discussion. If the group has set limits on talking time, the timekeeper will be in charge of noting when the limit has been reached.

FORMAT

FIRST SESSION

1st hour
- Clarification and adoption of contract and rules
- Initial go-round (five to ten minutes), with each member introducing herself and describing the role money has played in her life—that is, the money messages she got from her parents, and how they affected her own concept of money in her career, lifestyle, and relationships with men and women. The Family "Money Tree" (Appendix 2) provides a good basis for this discussion.

2nd hour

Open discussion on a selected topic:

- How much money do you need?
- Shopping: the emotions that induce me to spend
- Money and men
- Negotiating in the workplace and at home
- Financial risk-taking
- Sharing financial information on investments, tax planning, etc.
- The Seven Symptoms of Moneyphobia, as we have defined them in this book, also provide good discussion topics. Members can be asked to relate to moneysqueamishness, moneydenial, etc.

For each topic members should attempt to relate their individual experiences to larger cultural and political issues. This helps remove inappropriate guilt for problems she cannot totally change.

Coffee Break

3rd hour

Formulating a personal goal and ways to implement it. Each member should describe her goal, how she has selected it, and the meaning it has for her. For example, if her goal is to balance her checkbook, she may discuss the feelings that have kept her from doing so in the past, and why she now wants to accomplish this task. The leader should write down each member's goal.

SUBSEQUENT SESSIONS

1st hour

Update on the goals. Each member describes her experience of accomplishing, or failing to accomplish, the goal she selected at the last session.

2nd hour
Open discussion

Break

3rd hour
Select new goals. If group help is needed to accomplish a goal, the member should ask for and describe it.

LAST SESSION
Evaluation of individual and group progress. What was helpful? What needs to be changed?

NOTES

Preface

1. John Kenneth Galbraith, *Money: Whence It Came, Where It Went* (New York: Bantam, 1976), p. 6.

Introduction: Why Women Are Afraid of Money

1. Robert Seidenberg, "The Trauma of Eventlessness," in *Psychoanalysis and Women*, ed. Jean Baker Miller, M.D. (Middlesex, England: Penguin Books, 1973).

2. William Serrin, "Experts Say Job Bias Against Women Persists," *The New York Times*, November 25, 1984.

3. William R. Greer, "Women Now Majority in Professions," *The New York Times*, March 8, 1986.

4. Jane Gross, "Against the Odds: A Woman's Ascent on Wall Street," *The New York Times Magazine*, January 6, 1985.

5. Serrin, *The New York Times.*

6. *Laurel Richardson, The New Other Woman: Contemporary Single Women in Affairs with Married Men* (New York: Free Press, 1985), p. 2.

7. "The Shower of Gold," in *The Complete Brothers Grimm Fairy Tales*, ed. Lily Owens (New York: Avenal, 1981).

Chapter 1: Moneyblindness

1. Diana Vreeland, *D.V.* (New York: Alfred A. Knopf, 1984).

2. The quotations and information in the Doris Day case history are from A. E. Hotchner, *Doris Day: Her Own Story* (New York: William Morrow, 1976).

Chapter 2: Moneysqueamishness

1. Sigmund Freud, "On Beginning Treatment (Further Recommendations on the Technique of Psychoanalysis)," in *Standard Edition of the Complete Psychological Works of Sigmund Freud*, Vol. 12, ed. and trans. James Strachey (London: Hogarth Press, 1958), p. 131.

2. Carol Hymowitz and Michaele Weissman, in cooperation with the Anti-Defamation League of B'nai B'rith, *A History of Women in America* (New York: Bantam, 1978), p. 64.

3. Nancy Woloch, *Women and the American Experience* (New York: Alfred A. Knopf, 1984), p. 101.

4. A. E. Hotchner, *Doris Day: Her Own Story* (New York: William Morrow, 1976).

5. The quotations in this section are from Terry Garrity with John Garrity, *The Story of "J": The Author of The Sensuous Woman Tells the Bitter Price of Her Crazy Success* (New York: William Morrow, 1984).

Chapter 3: Moneydenying

1. Jean Rhys, *Voyage in the Dark*, in *Jean Rhys: The Complete Novels* (New York: W. W. Norton, 1985), p. 16.

2. Jean Rhys, *Good Morning Midnight*, in *Jean Rhys: The Complete Novels* (New York: W. W. Norton, 1985), p. 369.

3. *Ibid.*, p. XXX.

Chapter 4: Moneyeluding

1. "What Baby Boomers Make," *Newsweek*, November 25, 1985.

2. For the discussion about the twenties and thirties we are indebted to Julie A. Matthaei, *An Economic History of Women in America* (New York:

Schocken, 1982) and Carol Hymowitz and Michaele Weissman, *A History of Women in America* (New York: Bantam, 1978).

3. Susan Ware, *Holding Their Own: American Women in the Thirties* (Boston: Twayne, 1982), p. 27.

4. Eleanor Roosevelt, *It's Up to the Women* (New York: Frederic A. Stokes, 1933), p. 148.

5. Betty Friedan, *The Feminine Mystique,* 2nd ed. (New York: W. W. Norton, 1983), p. 19.

6. *Ibid.*, p. 334.

7. "Reading Balance Sheets Instead of Poetry," *The New York Times,* January 26, 1986.

8. Jane Gross, "Against the Odds: A Woman's Ascent on Wall Street," *The New York Times Magazine,* January 6, 1985, p. 24.

9. Peter Davis, "The $100,000 a Year Woman," *Esquire,* June 1984, p. 72.

10. "$ucce$$ $torie$," *Playboy,* August 1984, p. 74.

11. Elizabeth Kolbert, "Judith Resnick," *The New York Times,* February 9, 1986.

Chapter 5: Moneyfolly

1. Jenny L. Herring, "Women's Financial Needs," *Financial Service Times,* April 1986.

2. Jane Gross, "Against the Odds: A Woman's Ascent on Wall Street," *The New York Times Magazine,* January 6, 1985.

3. "Savings Rate in U.S. Declines," *The New York Times,* October 29, 1985.

4. Barbara Ehrenreich, "Is the Middle Class Doomed?" *The New York Times Magazine,* September 7, 1986.

5. Our information about the life of Barbara Hutton comes from C. David Heymann, *Poor Little Rich Girl: The Life and Legend of Barbara Hutton* (New York: Random House, 1983).

6. *Ibid.*

7. Hans Christian Andersen, "The Little Match Girl," in *Andersen's Fairy Tales,* trans. Mrs. E. V. Lucas and Mrs. H. B. Paul (New York: Grosset & Dunlap, 1945).

Chapter 6: Moneyparanoia

1. Bonnie Siverd, "Love and Money in the 1980s," *Working Woman,* November 1985.

2. Our information about Hetty Green comes from Arthur H. Lewis, *The Day They Shook the Plum Tree* (New York: Harcourt, Brace & World, 1963).

Chapter 7: Moneyconfusion

1. Carolyn See, "Hers," *The New York Times,* June 5, 1986.

2. Joan Collins, *Past Imperfect* (New York: Simon & Schuster, 1984).

3. "The True Value of Women's Work," *Vogue,* May 1985.

4. "Pay Gap," *The Wall Street Journal,* June 3, 1986.

5. "The True Value of Women's Work," *Vogue,* May 1985.

6. Robert L. Simison and Cathy Trost, "Sexual Harassment at Work Is a Cause for Growing Concern," *The Wall Street Journal,* June 24, 1986.

7. Betty Lehan Harragan, *Games Mother Never Taught You: Corporate Gamesmanship for Women* (New York: Warner, 1977), pp. 378–79.

8. Philip Blumstein and Pepper Schwartz, *American Couples: Money, Work, Sex* (New York: William Morrow, 1983), p. 51.

9. Lenore J. Weitzman, *The Divorce Revolution* (New York: Free Press, 1985).

10. "Women's and Bar Groups Fault Divorce Law," *The New York Times,* August 5, 1985.

11. Katherine Bouton, "Women and Divorce: How the New Law Works Against Them," *New York,* October 8, 1984.

12. Deborah Rankin, "The New Economics of Custody Suits," *The New York Times,* April 6, 1986.

Chapter 8: Life Without Moneyphobia

1. Our information about Mae West comes from her autobiography, *Goodness Had Nothing to Do with It* (New York: Belvedere Publishers, 1959) and George Eells and Stanley Musgrove, *Mae West* (New York: William Morrow, 1982).

2. Edith Evans Asbury, "Georgia O'Keeffe Dead at 98: Shaper of Modern Art in U.S.," *The New York Times,* March 7, 1986.

BIBLIOGRAPHY OF
RECOMMENDED READING

Historical and Political Background

Friedan, Betty. *The Feminine Mystique* (New York: W. W. Norton, 1963; Revised edition, 1983). The book that helped launch the feminist revolution.

———. *The Second Stage* (New York: Summit, 1981). The author reexamines the woman's movement in light of women's more traditional needs and goals.

Gornick, Vivian, and Barbara K. Moran, eds., *Women in Sexist Society* (New York: Basic Books, 1971). A collection of feminist essays, including Doris B. Gold's "Women and Voluntarism."

Hymowitz, Carol, and Michaele Weissman, in cooperation with the Anti-Defamation League of B'nai B'rith. *A History of Women in America* (New York: Bantam, 1978). How women shaped American culture.

Matthaei, Julie A. *An Economic History of Women in America* (New York: Schocken, 1982). Examines women's role in labor within the framework of American economic history from Colonial times to the present.

Weitzman, Leonore J. *The Divorce Revolution* (New York: Free Press, 1985). An important discussion of what divorce means to modern women.

Woloch, Nancy. *Women and the American Experience* (New York: Alfred A. Knopf, 1984). History from the female viewpoint.

Women and Work

Gilman, Charlotte Perkins. *Women and Economics: A Study of the Economic Relations Between Men and Women as a Factor in Sexual Evolution,* ed. Carl N. Degler (New York: Harper Torchbooks, 1966). While other feminists were fighting for the vote, Perkins Gilman questioned the destiny of women in a modern industrial society. Originally published in 1898.

Harragan, Betty Lehan. *Games Mother Never Taught You: Corporate Gamesmanship for Women* (New York: Warner, 1977). Strategies that help women survive in the business world. Useful reading for all working women.

Hennig, Margaret, and Anne Jardim. *The Managerial Woman* (New York: Pocket Books, 1976). Discusses the way women managers adapted their personalities and goals to succeed in the marketplace.

Kessler-Harris, Alice. *Out to Work: A History of Wage-Earning Women in the United States* (New York: Oxford University Press, 1982). Explores the transformation of women's work into wage labor and the social repercussions.

Nieva, Veronica F., and Barbara A. Gutek. *Women and Work: A Psychological Perspective* (New York: Praeger, 1982). A review of all the psychological studies done on women and work.

Scott, Hilda. *The Feminization of Poverty* (Boston: Pandora Press/Routledge & Kegan Paul, 1985). Explains and discusses the growing presence of poor women.

Women's Psychological Development

Eichenbaum, Luise, and Susie Orbach. *Understanding Women: A Feminist Psychoanalytic Approach* (New York: Basic Books, 1983).

————. *What Do Women Want?: Exploding the Myth of Dependency* (New York: Berkley Books, 1985).

Both books provide major insights into women's psychological development from a clinical perspective.

Gilligan, Carol. *In a Different Voice: Psychological Theory and Women's Development* (Cambridge, Mass.: Harvard University Press, 1982). Examines theories of moral development and how they have distorted the psychological understanding of women.

Miller, Jean Baker, M.D. *Toward a New Psychology of Women* (Boston: Beacon Press, 1976). Examines the psychological consequences of sexual inequality.

————, ed. *Psychoanalysis and Women* (Middlesex, England: Penguin Books, 1973). A collection of papers by analysts appraising and defining the psychology of women, including Robert Seidenberg's "The Trauma of Eventlessness."

The Psychology and Sociology of Money

Borneman, Ernest. *The Psychoanalysis of Money* (New York: Urizen Books, 1976). Collection of the major works in the psychoanalytic literature on the origin and nature of money.

Brown, Norman O. *Life Against Death: The Psychoanalytic Meaning of History* (New York: Vintage Books, 1959). Chapter "Filthy Lucre" describes money as a manifestation of the death instinct.

Fenichel, Otto. "The Drive to Amass Wealth," in *PSA Quarterly*, Vol. 7, 1938. An orthodox Freudian analyst explores the influence of capitalism on the analytic understanding of money.

Simmel, Georg. *The Philosophy of Money* (Boston: Routledge & Kegan Paul, 1982). Provides a remarkably wide-ranging discussion of the social, psychological, and philosophical aspects of money.

Books That Demystify Money and Its Institutions

Connell, John R., Laverne L. Dotson, Robert E. Zobel, and W. Thomas Porter. *Touche Ross Guide to Personal Financial Management* (Englewood Cliffs, N.J.: Prentice-Hall, 1985). A step-by-step comprehensive guide with removable planning forms to help you create your personalized financial plan.

Galbraith, John Kenneth. *Money: Whence It Came, Where It Went* (New York: Bantam, 1976). Highly readable account of the evolution of banking.

Goodspeed, Bennett W. *The Tao Jones Averages: A Guide to Whole-Brained Investing* (New York: Penguin Books, 1984). A student of Oriental philosophy and an MBA demonstrates how you can anticipate changes on the stock market by using the logical and intuitive sides of your brain.

Gourgues, Harold W., Jr. *Financial Planning Handbook: A Portfolio of Strategies and Applications* (New York Institute of Finance, 1983). Geared to the professional financial planner but of interest to the more knowledgeable reader.

Hill, Napoleon. *Think and Grow Rich* (New York: Fawcett Crest, 1960). The granddaddy of how-to self-help books on achieving financial independence through the power of positive thinking and organized planning.

Lewin, Elizabeth, C.F.P. *Your Personal Financial Fitness Program* (New York: Facts on File, 1985). The author gives techniques and worksheets for achieving "financial fitness" in only a few minutes a day.

Smith, Adam. *Supermoney* (New York: Popular Library, 1972). Along with Smith's classic, *The Money Game,* a humorous, well-written, and informative work on the stock market.

Weinstein, Grace W. *Children and Money: A Parent's Guide,* rev. ed. (New York: Plume, 1985). How to give your children positive money messages.
————. *The Lifetime Book of Money Management* (New York: New American Library, 1985). A financial columnist for *Good Housekeeping* magazine explains the life cycles of financial planning.

Literary Works and Biographies with Financial Themes

Austen, Jane. *Sense and Sensibility* (New York: Bantam, 1983). A nineteenth-century writer shows her understanding of the role of money in structuring women's lives.

Brookner, Anita. *Hotel Du Lac* (New York: E. P. Dutton, 1986). "Earning is what you do when you're an adult," says Brookner's heroine, a romance novelist who refuses to marry for money.

Colette. *The Vagabond* (New York: Farrar, Straus & Giroux, 1955). One of the first feminist novels, recounting the adventures of a divorcée who supports herself as a music hall artist and rejects the comforts of love and marriage.

Heymann, C. David. *Poor Little Rich Girl: The Life and Legend of Barbara Hutton* (New York: Random House, 1983). The tragic life of the Woolworth heiress, one of the great female big-time spenders.

Hotchner, A. E. *Doris Day: Her Own Story* (New York: William Morrow, 1976). The trials and tribulations of moneyblindness.

Lewis, Arthur. *The Day They Shook the Plum Tree* (New York: Harcourt,

Brace & World, 1963). The story of Hetty Green, the "Witch of Wall Street," and her moneyholding habits.

Rose, Phyllis. *Parallel Lives: Five Victorian Marriages* (New York: Alfred A. Knopf, 1984). Famous Victorian marriages and the role money played in them. Includes money mentorship of George Eliot by George Henry Lewes.

West, Mae. *Goodness Had Nothing to Do with It* (New York: Belvedere Publishers, 1959). The flamboyant movie star's story reveals her adroitness with money and love.

Woolf, Virginia. *A Room of One's Own* (New York: Harcourt, Brace, 1929). A discussion of the importance of financial independence to creative women.

For a complete list of books available from Penguin in the United States, write to Dept. DG, Penguin Books, 299 Murray Hill Parkway, East Rutherford, New Jersey 07073.

For a complete list of books available from Penguin in Canada, write to Penguin Books Canada Limited, 2801 John Street, Markham, Ontario L3R 1B4.